CW01203779

Praise for
Buying at the Point of Maximum Pessimism

"Sir John's ability to comprehend complex concepts and distill these into money-making ideas for his investors was legendary. With this book, Scott Phillips extends Sir John Templeton's crystal clear vision to some of tomorrow's most interesting and powerful money-making opportunities. All readers should be prepared to learn—and profit!"

—**Jeffrey Everett**, Founding Partner, Everkey Global Partner

"The brilliant global investing strategy of Sir John Templeton finds new life in Scott Phillips' *Buying at the Point of Maximum Pessimism*. With the U.S. in trouble, savvy international investing is a must and this book shows you the best places to put your money for serious profits ahead."

—**Christopher Ruddy**, CEO, Newsmax Media, Inc.

"In *Buying at the Point of Maximum Pessimism*, Scott Phillips delivers a road map to investment success traveled by the very few but guaranteed to lead you to enormous profits. The book offers a delightful, common sense approach to investing that unfortunately is not so common."

—**Robert P. Miles**, author, *The Warren Buffett CEO*

"Many investment books are published every year. Unfortunately, many are me-too books spewing forth the same old self-help advice under the value or growth investment banner. This time readers have hit the jackpot with a new book by investment adviser and author Scott Phillips who has written a delightful, witty, and extraordinarily valuable book based on the wisdom of Sir John Templeton, one of the greatest investors of all time.

"While Templeton's wisdom inspired him, the truth is that Scott Phillips has abundant wisdom of his own to impart. Often investment tomes are produced by professional writers who research an aspect of investing but lack firsthand knowledge, or by investment pros whose writing skills are somewhat second-rate. In Phillips, the reader gets firsthand knowledge of a skilled value investor combined with wonderful, artistic writing skills. He has a fresh eye and wonderful humor to entertain and simultaneously teach both the novice and professional investor.

"The author deeply probes the current difficult investment landscape by examining six contemporary value investing trends. If you have had trouble understanding the subprime mortgage debacle that almost brought the world's economy to its knees, Phillips' first two chapters, 'The Fed Sentences the Consumer to Debtor's Prison' and 'The Biggest Gamblers Go All In on the Housing Bet' will clarify and edify you in a delightful, tongue-in-cheek manner.

"What more to say? Read this book. It is a 21st-century update on MacKay's *Extraordinary Popular Delusions and the Madness of Crowds*."

—**John W. Schott**, M.D, Principal and Director, Steinberg Global Asset Management, author of *Mind Over Money*, and Trustee of The John Templeton Foundation

Buying at the Point of Maximum Pessimism

BUYING AT THE POINT OF MAXIMUM PESSIMISM

Six Value Investing Trends from China to Oil to Agriculture

SCOTT PHILLIPS

Vice President, Publisher: Tim Moore
Associate Publisher and Director of Marketing: Amy Neidlinger
Acquisitions Editor: Jeanne Glasser
Editorial Assistant: Myesha Graham
Operations Manager: Gina Kanouse
Senior Marketing Manager: Julie Phifer
Publicity Manager: Laura Czaja
Assistant Marketing Manager: Megan Colvin
Cover Designer: Chuti Prasertsith
Managing Editor: Kristy Hart
Project Editor: Anne Goebel
Copy Editor: Gayle Johnson
Proofreader: Sheri Cain
Indexer: Lisa Stumpf
Senior Compositor: Gloria Schurick
Manufacturing Buyer: Dan Uhrig

© 2010 by Pearson Education, Inc.
Publishing as FT Press
Upper Saddle River, New Jersey 07458

This book is sold with the understanding that neither the author nor the publisher is engaged in rendering legal, accounting, or other professional services or advice by publishing this book. Each individual situation is unique. Thus, if legal or financial advice or other expert assistance is required in a specific situation, the services of a competent professional should be sought to ensure that the situation has been evaluated carefully and appropriately. The author and the publisher disclaim any liability, loss, or risk resulting directly or indirectly from the use or application of any of the contents of this book.

FT Press offers excellent discounts on this book when ordered in quantity for bulk purchases or special sales. For more information, please contact U.S. Corporate and Government Sales, 1-800-382-3419, corpsales@pearsontechgroup.com. For sales outside the U.S., please contact International Sales at international@pearson.com.

Company and product names mentioned herein are the trademarks or registered trademarks of their respective owners.

All rights reserved. No part of this book may be reproduced, in any form or by any means, without permission in writing from the publisher.

Printed in the United States of America

First Printing May 2010

ISBN-10: 0-13-703849-6
ISBN-13: 978-0-13-703849-7

Pearson Education LTD.
Pearson Education Australia PTY, Limited.
Pearson Education Singapore, Pte. Ltd.
Pearson Education North Asia, Ltd.
Pearson Education Canada, Ltd.
Pearson Educatión de Mexico, S.A. de C.V.
Pearson Education—Japan
Pearson Education Malaysia, Pte. Ltd.

Library of Congress Cataloging-in-Publication Data

Phillips, Scott, 1974-

  Buying at the point of maximum pessimism : six value investing trends from China to oil to agriculture / Scott Phillips.

     p. cm.

  ISBN 978-0-13-703849-7 (hbk. : alk. paper) 1. Investments. 2. Stocks—Prices—Forecasting. I. Title.

HG4521.P495 2010

  336.2—dc22

2009051970

To Mary Handly, asleep in her crib—Dream big.

Contents

Foreword xiii

Acknowledgments xv

About the Author xvi

Introduction 1

Chapter 1: The Fed Sentences the Consumer to Debtor's Prison 7
- An Economic Recovery Built on Borrowed Money 8
- The Fed's Potion of Low Rates and Rising Home Prices Becomes an Economic Elixir 14
- A Chicken in Every Pot? Try a Hummer in Every Garage 15
- The Three Cs of Credit Give Way to Financial Innovation 19

Chapter 2: The Biggest Gamblers Go "All In" on the Housing Bet 35
- Trouble in Paradise 37
- The Canary Died Unheard from the Boardrooms, Yachts, and Golf Courses 39
- The Credit Bubble Draws in Every Last Bull . . . 46

Chapter 3: Financial Chaos 53
- The Crisis Moves from Subprime to Prime Time 61

Chapter 4: Quis Custodiet Ipsos Custodes? 71
- An Alphabet Soup of Rescue Acronyms Will Save Us 72
- Strategy Number Two: Spend Our Way Out of a Spending Problem 75

	The Vestigial Effects of the Crisis Come into Focus 79
	The Visible Hand Is Coming into View, and It's All Thumbs 92
Chapter 5:	**A New Landscape for Investors** 101
	Entrepreneurialism Is Thriving in Many Key Emerging Markets. 105
	Crisis Is an Opportunity for Those in a Position to Seize the Opportunity. 111
	The New Landscape 113
Chapter 6:	**China: Ready for Prime Time** 117
	A Culture Well Suited for Capitalism. 119
	Putting Those Rainy-Day Savings to Work in the Worst Storm of the Past Century. 122
	Urbanization Is the Growth Engine. 126
	The Path Toward Consumerism and the Domestic Economy. 128
	Prime-Time Products 135
Chapter 7:	**Proteins and Agribusiness: Billions and Billions to Be Served** 141
	Where's the Beef (and Chicken and Pork, Too)? 142
	Eating Good in the Global Neighborhood. 146
	Brazil Has the Competitive Advantages in Agribusiness. 152
	Strong Fundamentals Across the Value Chain. . 161
Chapter 8:	**Formula for Success: Rise Early, Work Hard, Strike Oil** 165
	In the Long Term, Healthy Demand Meets Higher Cost Supply. 170
	Market Distortions from the Fed's Loose Credit and Easy Money 179
	Seeking Alternatives in the Hydrocarbon Space. 191

Chapter 9:	An All-Too-Common Tragedy 201
	Human Behavior Is Timeless 202
	Strong Demand Underscores the Overexploitation 206
	A Tragedy Leads to an Opportunity 210
Chapter 10:	What Happens When 700 Million Students Want Extra Help? 217
	Spending on Education Takes Precedence in Many Emerging-Market Households 220
	The Role of Technology and Innovation 223
	10 Million Students Applying for 6 Million Spots in College—No Pressure 225
	Continuing Education 227
	Financial Crisis Portends Continued Growth in the Emerging-Market Education Services. . . 230
	Education Plays and Their Fundamental Dynamics 234
Chapter 11:	A Rare Opportunity 241
	Demand for Global Technology Remains Strong 242
	It's Not Easy Being Green 245
	There Is Oil in the Middle East; There Are Rare Earths in China 249
	Index 257

Foreword

"Bull markets are born on pessimism, grow on skepticism, mature on optimism, and die on euphoria. The time of maximum pessimism is the best time to buy, and the time of maximum optimism is the best time to sell."
—Sir John Templeton, February 1994

My late great uncle, Sir John Templeton, kept a plaque on his desk that read, "Trouble is opportunity." He also coined the phrase "Investing at the point of maximum pessimism" to describe the optimal time to invest.

Buying at the point of maximum pessimism is more than a simple investment motto. It is a successful and time tested investment strategy that can significantly increase the odds of investment success in your favor. Accommodating the sellers, as my uncle always put it, is simple. But psychological inertia usually stands in the way of even the most rational investor during extreme market volatility. The most recent bear market is a prime example. Beginning with the collapse of two Bear Stearns hedge funds and ending with a bailout of the entire U.S. financial system, the recent crisis was no place for the faint of heart.

In the wake of these events, even the most seasoned investors proclaimed that the sky was indeed falling. It has always been interesting to me that during periods of market upheaval, perfectly rational individuals can and often do exhibit completely irrational behavior. Behavioral finance is a fascinating field of study. Regardless of the psychological or even biological reasons for the discomfort that many investors experience during a market correction, impediments to buying at the point of maximum pessimism exist.

In my opinion, the best prescription for the paralysis that often accompanies a stock market panic is advance preparation. We know that often the best opportunities present themselves during times of crisis. Most investors even recite the motto "Crisis equals opportunity," but few investors have the fortitude to take advantage of these precious occasions. Because crisis usually occurs when least expected, it is disturbing and usually induces our panic response. Investors must learn to look forward to these events and, more importantly, take advantage of them. For anyone who invested money throughout the bear market of 2007 through 2009, this represented a precious, if not once-in-a-generation, opportunity. Unfortunately for some, this opportunity may have been lost due to a lack of preparation for such intense volatility in stock prices and condensed selling in a short period of time. The most successful investors are prepared well in advance of market disruptions.

One technique that Uncle John always used to prepare himself for future market volatility was to maintain a list of stocks that he was interested in owning at a much lower price. This practice underscores the reality that the stock market is often too dynamic for anyone to predict with any accuracy. As investors, we should not spend all our time trying to predict or anticipate every move of the stock market. Instead, we should anticipate what actions we would take in order to capitalize on an opportunity should it present itself.

Following in the (albeit, very large) footsteps of my great uncle, my husband and I have made an investment career by continuously searching the world for bargain stocks on behalf of our investors. We believe that the long-term perspective on investing is not only applicable but also the best approach. In *Buying at the Point of Maximum Pessimism*, my husband Scott Phillips identifies several long-term investment opportunities in the stock market. Based on our research, we believe that these are long-term trends that should persist for many years to come. Investors might find it helpful to use the investment themes described in this book to refine their wish list of securities in order to capitalize on future market volatility. Moreover, the investment themes described in this book take into thoughtful consideration many of the abrupt changes that the global economy experienced in the wake of the financial crisis. In sum, this book should help investors prioritize investments as they seek to take advantage of points of maximum pessimism.

Happy bargain hunting!

Lauren C. Templeton
Principal and Founder
Lauren Templeton Capital Management, LLC

Acknowledgments

First and foremost, I offer a special thank you to my wife Lauren who was especially patient with the many nights and weekends I spent on this project. Her support and encouragement, all extended in the midst of caring for our newborn daughter, was critical to completing the project in a timely manner. In the same breath, I must thank my daughter, Mary Handly, who provided much needed inspiration to continue writing into the late hours of the night and maintaining the full-time schedule of a new dad and hedge fund manager, authoring a book in the little spare time left over to do so. Finally, I give abundant thanks to Jeanne Glasser and the entire team at FT Press, including Anne Goebel and Gayle Johnson, for their guidance, suggestions, and patience throughout this project.

About the Author

Scott Phillips is a portfolio manager and principal with Lauren Templeton Capital Management, LLC, an alternative and traditional asset management firm. Prior to joining Lauren Templeton Capital Management, LLC, in 2007, he spent four years as a research analyst and consultant to Green Cay Asset Management, located in Nassau, Bahamas. While at Green Cay, he was the lead research analyst on the Siebels Hard Asset Fund, a long/short equity hedge fund focused on hard assets and commodities. Prior to joining Green Cay, he was a research associate analyst with SunTrust Robinson Humphrey and its predecessor companies. During his five years at Robinson Humphrey, he provided equity research on consumer durable goods companies to institutional clients and portfolio managers. Phillips is the coauthor of *Investing the Templeton Way* (McGraw-Hill, 2008) with Lauren C. Templeton. He is also the author of a quarterly newsletter on investing called "The Maximum Pessimism Report," distributed to readers worldwide.

Introduction

In March 2009, the world stock markets unveiled a tremendous opportunity for bargain hunters. March 9, 2009 represented a new low in the 2007 through 2009 bear markets. To be more precise, the March 9 low represented a 57% decline in the S&P 500 from its previous high in October 2007. On a personal note, March 9, 2009 was a particularly exciting time for me. On that day, I sat in a hospital delivery room, simultaneously entering buy orders on my laptop and awaiting the birth of my daughter. To be sure, buying cheap stocks falls far short of becoming a father among life's precious moments. There is no comparison. Still, the gravitational pull of a bargain hunter to inexpensive stocks can overcome many obstacles, including a less than enthused delivery nurse. The response to buy during periods of sharp market turmoil is not totally unique; there are other stories of investors doing the same. However, the total amount of buyers in the stock market during March 2009 were clearly a minority. Otherwise, the market could not have reached such a low. Sir John Templeton always said, "The only way a stock can become a bargain is from other people's selling. There is no other way." That being said, nearly all investors can appreciate in hindsight the large number of bargain stocks created by the heavy selling in early 2009. The ability to recognize the opportunity in real-time, or possess the conviction to act on it, is a whole different matter. Clearly, there are psychological impediments to becoming a buyer in the stock market when it reaches a point of maximum pessimism. Overcoming these obstacles, however, is important because the minority of investors who were buying in March 2009 were likely rewarded for doing so. *Buying at the Point of Maximum Pessimism* is intended to help investors overcome these impediments when the market presents future buying opportunities.

Many investors view themselves as value investors or mention that they admire successful investors such as Sir John Templeton or Warren Buffett. Unfortunately, though, many investors find that they lack the conviction to buy when the market presents the greatest opportunities. Investors are commonly betrayed by their own short-sighted behavior when the greatest discounts appear in the market. The reason for this is clear; experiencing losses introduces uncertainty and a loss of confidence in one's own investments. Until investors can counteract this routine behavioral reaction to market selling, they may be prone to selling at the wrong time. More specifically, I am referring to investors' time-honored mistake of selling rather than buying at the bottom of a market. One significant step toward correcting this behavior is to prepare for these buying opportunities before they appear. Through this preparation, the investor learns not only to expect market sell-offs but also to look forward to these events. Ultimately, the goal of this preparation is to safeguard against the likely loss of confidence that every investor is susceptible to when the entire market falls in price. Once properly prepared for these events, an investor should be armed with the psychological fortitude to become a buyer during moments when most others in the market are sellers. The investor who wants to capitalize on points of maximum pessimism must be willing and prepared to replace the market's perspective with his own. When the market is pessimistic, the challenge to the bargain hunter is to be optimistic, and vice versa. During his long and famous career on Wall Street, Sir John Templeton developed numerous methods and strategies that were designed to overcome the psychological inertia presented by the market. He often kept standing limit orders on stocks at prices well below the market that would force buying activity at the right time. Likewise, he also maintained a wish list of stocks that he had researched in advance in his desk drawer that he could use to make purchases as the market presented opportunities. This book follows a similar thread of investment strategy in that it provides a group of investment themes that could be used in a wish-list manner, or to make purchases during market corrections or future points of maximum pessimism. Naturally, all these investment themes represented bargain opportunities in late 2008 and early 2009 as the market descended toward its lows. Many of these stock ideas remain attractive bargains as 2009 comes to a close. Going forward, however, the attractiveness of the stock valuations tied to these themes may require some discretion. For this reason, the ideas may be most useful when applied during market corrections.

Buying at the Point of Maximum Pessimism introduces a half dozen investment themes that should maintain their fundamental appeal over the next five to ten years. The purpose of this book is to answer the question of what to buy during future bouts of market volatility. In sum, these themes could be thought of as CliffsNotes to be used in preparation for future tests in the stock market. These themes should help investors, at a minimum, inventory a list of investment ideas that may be applied over the years to come. The six investment themes described in this book are far from exhaustive. However, these themes have been targeted for their long-term nature. In addition to their longer time horizons, they also consider the growing risks created by policy makers around the globe, from their shortsighted responses to the financial crisis.

One substantial risk that is identified is the growing probability of a loss in the purchasing power of the U.S. dollar. We can all appreciate the large sums of money printed by governments in response to the financial crisis, but some investors may still be searching for ways to protect their hard-earned savings in the event that inflation rises. Inflation risk should be considered a staple risk to investment returns, irrespective of economic conditions. Inflation has been present for many decades in the markets, and the U.S. market has been no exception. For investors familiar with Sir John Templeton's methods, it is no surprise that among his "16 rules" for successful investing, targeting a real return after inflation and taxes is the number one rule on the list. Most relevant in the current environment, though, is that recent policy responses by the U.S. government to the financial crisis have increased this risk for future inflation. Many investors have become attuned to this risk, but the advice seems to largely be the same in most corners: Buy gold. Rather than offering the recommendation to purchase gold as a response, *Buying at the Point of Maximum Pessimism* highlights other areas for investment, such as oil and energy, as well as agribusiness. These investments have historically offered protection against a loss of purchasing power in the U.S. dollar and also possess attractive long-term growth drivers. In this respect, the investment themes in this book illustrate the compelling fundamental growth drivers as a backdrop to investment in these spaces. The reason for this emphasis is that we cannot know with much certainty the future outcome of inflation, but we can become comfortable with the long-term dynamics of energy and agribusiness, including proteins. In the event that inflation appears, the investor still receives some protection, as indicated by historical relationships between commodities and the U.S. dollar. Conversely, the arguments for purchasing gold rest mostly on speculative outcomes as opposed to long-term growth drivers. In sum, the book presents investment themes that hold merit beyond attempting to protect against a loss of purchasing power.

Other risks that the book considers relate to the large amounts of both public and private indebtedness, as well as the increased scope for regulation that has resulted from policy makers' responses to the financial crisis. The discussion of these risks, as well as the aforementioned specter of inflation, requires some context. For that reason, the book begins with the events leading into, culminating with, and lingering from, the financial crisis of 2008 and early 2009. These discussions are not meant to provide a thorough history of the events, but instead help explain how the investment themes have developed. The basic idea is that investors have been left with a new landscape that they must contend with and seek opportunity within over the coming years. These chapters help provide a picture of this landscape.

In the chapters that follow this discussion, I arrive at the previously mentioned investment themes. These chapters describe in detail six investment themes that investors may find an opportunity to deploy over the years to come. From a top-level view, some of these investment themes will sound familiar. For instance, many investors understand that China offers long-term opportunity for continued growth. In this case, however, the book fleshes out the most salient aspects of this growth. It also offers better insights into more specific fundamental drivers, as well as areas to target for investment in the country's transition from a prototypical Asian exporter to a domestic economy. Still other investment themes, such as the state of the world's fisheries, or the rare earths discussed in Chapter 11, "A Rare Opportunity," may be less familiar to investors. They offer an opportunity to invest in areas with growth potential that have been neglected by investors.

- INTRODUCTION

In any event, the purpose of this book is to provide solutions to investors who are searching for long-term investments—in particular, what investments should be prioritized when the market presents future opportunities during a sell-off. Given the significant volatility in the stock market relative to these long-term investment themes, investors may find them most useful during future points of maximum pessimism, which is the best time to buy.

1

The Fed Sentences the Consumer to Debtor's Prison

If you approached someone on the street and he was old enough to recall where he was on November 22, 1963, he probably could tell you what he was doing at the moment he heard that John F. Kennedy had been shot. The same could be said for people of many different generations of their ability to recall profound historic events ranging from the fall of the Berlin Wall on November 9, 1989 to the terrorist attacks of September 11, 2001. On the other hand, if you asked someone what he was doing on June 25, 2003, you would likely get a blank stare. That is because unless you were employed in some finance-related business, or were a regular observer of the financial markets, the day the Federal Reserve lowered its Fed Funds rate to 1.0% was just another day. Far from it. This event played a discernible role in sparking a chain of events that would come to affect hundreds of millions of people's lives the world over, a little more than five years later.

June 25, 2003 was symbolic of an effort that the Federal Reserve and its leaders had undertaken to cushion the blow from the March 2000 unraveling of a stock market bubble that had in its own right reached historic proportions. Fearing the pangs of excess economic capacities, rising unemployment, and deflation, the Fed was then in the final steps of its assault on the fallout from the burst stock market bubble. In fact, beginning with the 6.0% Fed Funds target rate in March 2000, the June 25 rate cut represented a 500 basis point reduction in this key rate from which all other financial contracts take their cue. At the time this move represented the most aggressive accommodative interest rate policy since the 1950s and was the economic equivalent of slamming a sputtering automobile's gas pedal firmly into the floorboard. As it were, the world's largest economy proved up to the challenge and responded in kind. In a relatively short time, Americans were accepting the Fed-induced economic incentives to borrow at low interest rates and forgo saving in favor of consumption. In sum, the interest rate policy worked according to plan, and the U.S. economy began to accelerate in the third quarter of 2003 on the back of higher consumer spending.

An Economic Recovery Built on Borrowed Money

The battle-tested U.S. consumers who had performed so well in the wake of the 2000 stock market bust and September 11 attacks were once again stirred by the Fed's call to arms. They grabbed their wallets, ready to *charge* ahead. They did not disappoint. Third quarter 2003 gross domestic product (GDP) growth of 8.2% represented the fastest growth in twenty years for the U.S. economy. The policy makers were quick to take credit for what on the surface appeared to be a virtuous recovery in U.S. economic growth. In what seemed trivial rather than prophetic at the time, consumer spending was led by a surge in home and car sales.

So although many financial observers took comfort in the resumption of economic growth during late 2003, a longer-term perspective suggested that the latest economic activity instead represented a resumption in the long-running story of ever-higher household debt and lower personal savings rates for the American consumer. In fact, the personal savings rate in the United States had been in a steep multidecade decline beginning in the early 1980s, as shown in Figure 1.1.

As mentioned, the decline in savings was accompanied by a steady rise in household debt since the early 1980s. To bring the rising debt level into focus, Figure 1.2 presents it as a percentage of GDP as it stood in 2003.

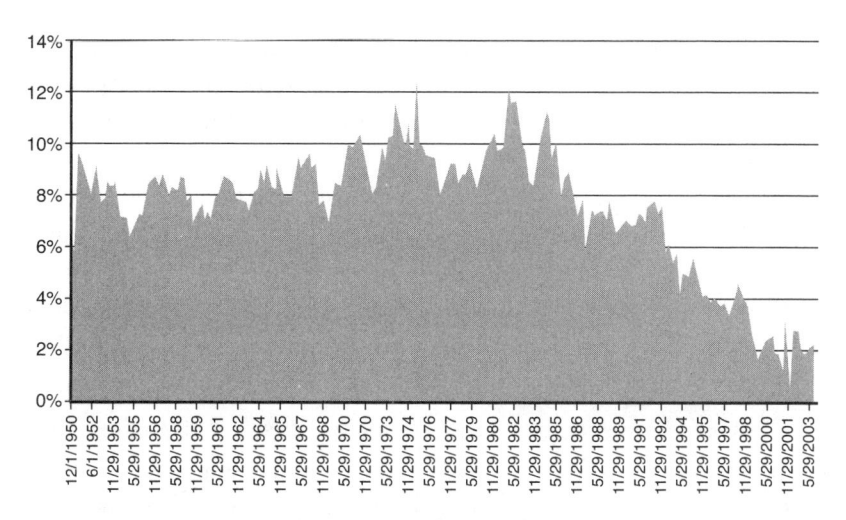

Figure 1.1   U.S. personal savings rate as a percentage of disposable personal income

Source: Bureau of Economic Analysis

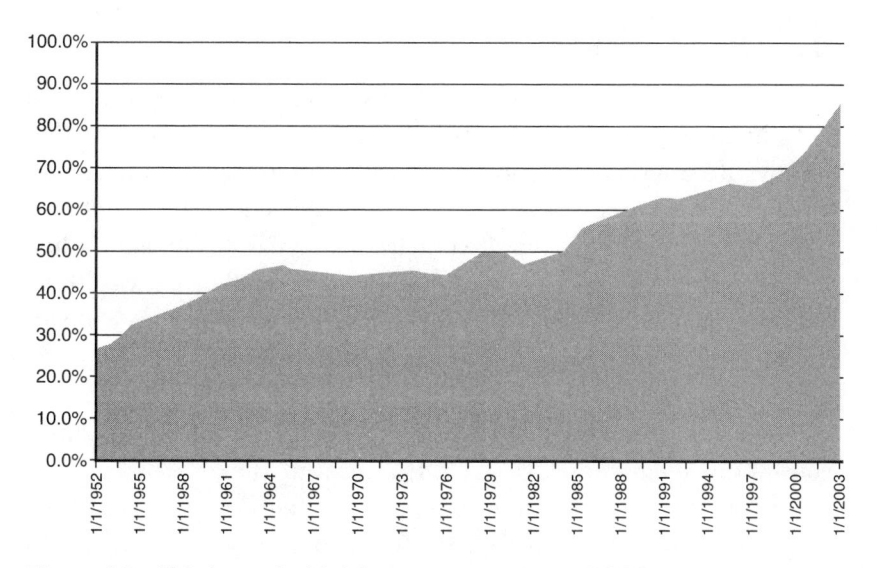

Figure 1.2   U.S. household debt as a percentage of GDP

Source: Federal Reserve

Despite the flimsy nature of this lower-saving, higher-borrowing economic paradigm, policy makers soon grabbed their pom-poms and joined in a self-congratulatory pep rally of economic sentiment. By the end of 2003, consumer sentiment had rebounded in the United States, and a new feeling of optimism was taking hold. Based on the University of Michigan's Consumer Sentiment Index, which showed a reading above 90 by year-end, Americans had turned nearly giddy when compared to the dark mood back in March 2003 surrounding the U.S. invasion of Iraq. Still, in spite of the good news on consumer sentiment, something was amiss in this economic rebound.

Upon closer inspection, an observer could see that as the economy accelerated in late 2003, it was not supported by the usual accompaniment of increased payrolls or higher personal income. The absence of an improvement in these variables represented a puzzling departure from the previous six recessions and subsequent recoveries. Instead of being propelled by a more wholesome expansion in the fundamental drivers of the economy, this recovery was being driven by an expansion in consumer spending backed by increasing levels of household debt.

As it turns out, the low interest rates provided by the Fed created a strong incentive for Americans to buy homes, because the low Fed Funds rate translated into low mortgage rates as well. As this home-buying activity accelerated due to the persistence of low interest rates, home prices began to rise due to the increasing demand. When Americans saw the prices of their homes increase, they felt wealthier, which was a natural reaction. As Americans felt wealthier, they sought ways to utilize their wealth to consume more. In order to consume more, they began to borrow against the higher value of their home and, in turn, meet their goal of spending a little of that new wealth. As consumers spent more, U.S. GDP improved (nearly 70% of U.S. GDP was consumer spending), and, voila, the economy was again growing. As U.S. GDP picked up from consumer spending, world GDP growth also accelerated, because Americans were avidly buying goods imported from many different countries. All was right, and everyone felt good, because it was an economic miracle. Policy makers again marveled that the U.S. economy was so resilient and that growth had rebounded so soon after the economic shocks of the 2000 dotcom bust and the September 11, 2001 attacks. On the other hand, a closer look at the data suggested that Americans were now attempting and at least temporarily succeeding at borrowing their way into economic prosperity. From a commonsense perspective, this prompts the following question: Why did Americans believe they could borrow their way to better times and continuously higher standards of living? The answer lies in one of the most expensive financial myths ever floated off a tongue:

House prices do not fall in value.

Obviously, as we turn to the present day, and the world economy has been bludgeoned by years of falling home prices, this myth has taken its place alongside the Easter Bunny and Tooth Fairy. Better still, though, *plenty* of people back in the early 2000s correctly predicted the oncoming housing bubble and the shortsightedness of the housing bulls. One man in particular, Sir John Templeton, described the formation of the housing bubble as early as 2001. He recalled that during the Depression of the 1930s, housing prices in some areas of the United States had declined 90%. Sir John and several other wise observers' opinions did not matter, though, because in any financial bubble, inconvenient Cassandras are shoved aside until they later become vindicated by history.

Irrespective of the prescience of some observers, there was heavy financial incentive for Americans and their developed-market friends to buy into the hype. Incentive number one was the creation of sudden wealth from a dramatic rise in home prices. Historically, the wealth effect from rising asset values often proves ethereal to those who mishandle its psychological by-products. Nonetheless, the paper wealth that could be monetized from newly opened home equity lines of credit felt like real wealth to those involved. For that matter, all the flat-screen televisions, new cars, and around-the-world vacations purchased with the extracted equity had most Americans feeling like Donald Trump. As you can see in Figure 1.3, which shows house price data compiled by Yale University professor Robert Shiller, the sudden rise in house prices due to low interest rates, and a few other financial "innovations" that we will discuss shortly, demonstrate the magnitude of what transpired in three short years. Figure 1.3 shows the professor's calculation of an index of home prices in the United States that is adjusted for inflation, or presented in real terms. In real terms, house prices in the 113 years leading up to 2003 had only appreciated at an annualized rate of 0.4%. However, in the three short years from 2003 to 2006, the index appreciated 32.5%. Jerry-rigging an entire economy with easy money and loose lending will do that.

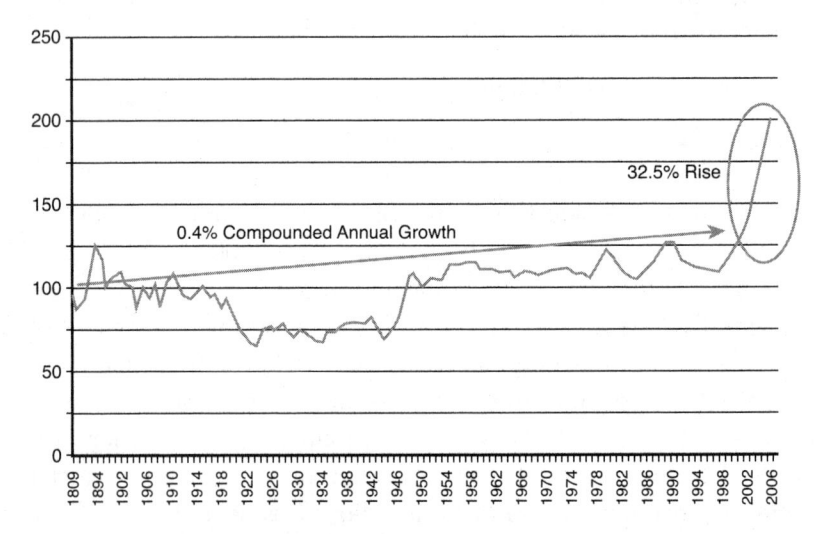

Figure 1.3 Robert Shiller's real home price index

Source: Robert Shiller, *Irrational Exuberance*, 2nd Edition, 2005, Princeton University Press

In light of what was transpiring in the U.S. housing market (and others), it is easy for us to armchair-quarterback the Fed and second-guess its interest rate policies. On the other hand, the Fed's established conventions for managing the economy meant that by and large, it tended to ignore asset prices and any developing asset bubbles in favor of simply mopping up the subsequent mess with yet another round of loose monetary policy (as it did after the dotcom bubble). The Federal Reserve had made it relatively clear in its rhetoric that it would address inflation as it arose in its traditional Consumer Price Index (CPI) measure of goods and services in regard to setting interest policy. House prices made for a hearty academic discussion, or maybe a lunchtime speech to a club, but they would not figure into policy-making decisions.

Some consider the housing bubble an obvious form of runaway inflation resulting from aggressive interest rate policy. For those people, the distinctions between the price actions in the thoroughly massaged components of the CPI compared to what is often the most important purchase a person can make in his or her lifetime ring hollow. With that said, the alternatives would be having the Fed inflating and pricking asset bubbles as it sees fit in any of the various markets—equities, real estate, commodities—or simply having no Fed and allowing the market system of banks and lenders to determine interest rates. The first alternative implies that the Fed can "time" asset markets with its policies, no differently than speculative market timers attempt to do in the stock market. Chances are the government would prove to be a terrible market timer, alongside all the other pundits who try it in the stock market. The second alternative was actually in place for some time in the United States and occasionally led to various liquidity and solvency panics, such as the Panic of 1907. Of course, it goes without saying that the current Fed managed to steer us into a liquidity and solvency panic also. So perhaps no one-size-fits-all banking system can please everyone or avert occasional disaster.

Returning from that brief digression, if we consider that the Federal Reserve was primarily focused on the CPI at the time, we can appreciate that from its perspective it saw mostly sunny skies on the horizon and had little reason to adjust interest rate policy. So during the course of late 2003 and the first half of 2004, the Federal Reserve saw more possible risk in economic growth stalling and producing some possible deflation, as opposed to a risk of acceleration in economic activity creating upward pressure on prices. To some extent, this was true in the traditional economy of goods and services at the time, where there was still apparent slack in the productive resources regarding employment and capacity utilization. However, this perspective ignored what was occurring in asset prices, such as residential and commercial real estate. In turn, this phenomenon of steadily growing GDP and low inflation measured in the CPI rekindled the often-used term "Goldilocks" economy.

The Fed's Potion of Low Rates and Rising Home Prices Becomes an Economic Elixir

The term "Goldilocks" when used in reference to an economy alludes to low inflation and modest economic growth. In other words, it's not too hot and not too cold, just like the young girl's favored bowl of porridge. This economic environment is clearly ideal for a number of activities, but the Goldilocks economy of the early 2000s was far from ideal. The problem was that the Fed held rates too low for too long, waiting until mid-2004 to edge up the Fed Funds rate to 1.25%. By holding rates in this aggressive range—for instance, below 2% from late 2001 through late 2004—the Fed provided a multiyear period of economic incentive to consume rather than save. Consumers typically see little reason to sock money away at such painfully low rates of interest. Put another way, people do not feel like they are giving up much in the future by consuming in the present when interest rates are exceedingly low. When interest rates are high, people recognize the potential income to be gained from saving, and typically they respond to this market signal. Because policy makers want GDP to grow, and U.S. GDP is heavily tilted toward consumer spending, they viewed low interest rates to spur consumption as a natural solution. As we alluded to earlier, consumers began to view their homes as an economic panacea to nearly all their financial problems. For instance, we know from our earlier discussion that wage growth in the United States did not rebound in its typical fashion coming out of the 2001 recession. This was of little consequence in the Goldilocks economy, because as house prices increased in value, homeowners awarded themselves with a raise by extracting the increased home value out of the house through a home equity line of credit. This meant in effect that homeowners could treat their house like an ATM (as long as prices continued rising). So, economic problem number one, which was stagnating income levels, was solved by the low interest rates that spurned home purchases, which in turn continued to drive home prices higher. Problem number two with the U.S. consumer also draws back on our earlier discussion regarding the ever-diminishing personal savings rate. Given that homeowners were tying up increasing amounts of financial resources in their homes, and these same homes were steadily increasing in value, these consistent capital gains were thought to be doing all the saving on behalf of the homeowner. Extending this linear reasoning into time meant that when retirement came, homeowners could simply sell their house to downsize into a smaller home and thereby save the capital gains from the transaction to provide funds for future income. To be fair, a home can be an adequate store of value over time and provide some protection from inflation, but it rarely makes sense from a risk standpoint to place all your financial resources into a single asset, whether a house or a single stock. It also goes without saying that you should not use too much leverage to obtain an asset, whether a mortgage or a stock, unless you can handle the downside. In this case, though, any conception of risk management was ignored in favor of getting in on the game. Homeownership had left the sphere of utility and had become a key driver of the U.S. economy. Rising home prices were leading to increased wealth and higher standards of living. Figure 1.4 shows the net worth of U.S. households. It is easy to see that Americans had every reason, based on the supposed value of their balance sheets, to feel wealthier with each year that passed in the housing boom. With every passing year, Americans were getting wealthier and wealthier without lifting a finger—or so it seemed.

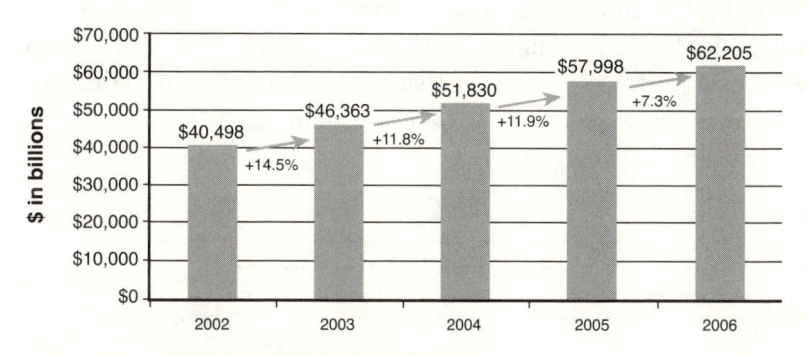

Figure 1.4 Net worth of U.S. households

Source: Federal Reserve

A Chicken in Every Pot? Try a Hummer in Every Garage

Every time period or era has a set of images or symbols from popular culture that stick in people's minds. The 1970s gave us sideburns and endless shades of orange and brown. The 1980s offered neon colors and white suits with rolled-up sleeves. The 1990s provided the drab Seattle grunge look. In the 2000s, American culture shamelessly flaunted the height of its self-indulgence with an array of gluttonous icons, including a Hummer parked in front of a McMansion (or crib, if you prefer). Fair or not to the owners of these beasts, the Hummer became emblematic of a culture that was embarking into a bold new frontier of wasteful excess. Originally it was adapted from the U.S. military vehicle called a Humvee, which rumbled into living rooms around the world during the live broadcasts of the U.S. military's Operation Desert Storm in Iraq. This vehicle was famously enthused among suburban warriors through its endorsement and ownership by Arnold Schwarzenegger. The imposing, heavy SUV eventually became reviled among environmentalists due to its significant thirst for gasoline and brash presence on the road (the originals were basically too wide for most standard lanes and parking spaces). Mr. Schwarzenegger, demonstrating his political skills, sufficiently sniffed out the green backlash against his favorite toy and retrofitted one of his half dozen or so Hummers to accept biofuels. As if wasting corn instead of oil makes it better. Turning to the data, we can see how quickly the Hummer became popularized as a key accessory to the red-hot McMansions selling around the country. In Figure 1.5, data from General Motors illustrates that in 2001, a mere 768 Hummer vehicles were sold, but by 2006, GM was selling 82,000 of these vehicles per year.

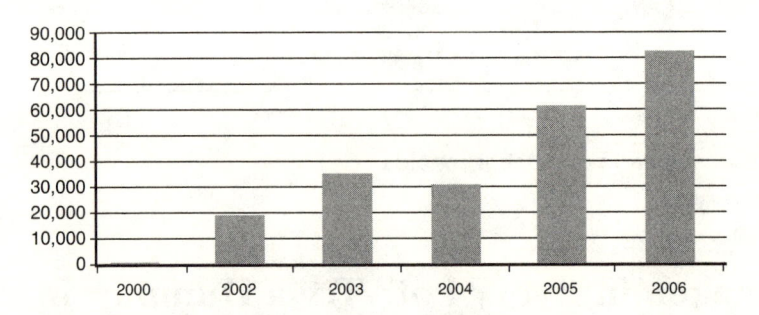

Figure 1.5 Annual sales by unit of the GM Hummer

Source: General Motors

One of the more puzzling sidebars to the explosive growth in sales of Hummers relates to their notoriously bad gas mileage and how this rise in sales coincided with substantial increases in the cost of oil. The gas mileage data for the larger Hummer H2 and H1 models (the H1 was discontinued in 2006) is not published, but it is anecdotally pegged at around 10 miles per gallon in the city and 14 on the highway. Needless to say, the same loose monetary policy propelling house prices had also infiltrated automobile financing, since these cars cost upwards of $50,000. But with the teaser "zero-percent" financing carrot dangled, many consumers chased the bait. If it was a stretch to afford one, no matter; the house could be sold for a large profit sometime in the future and would pay for everything. So although oil prices rose from approximately $18 per barrel in 2001 to $77 per barrel in 2006, a mere 328%, sales of Hummers gurgled ahead every step of the way. Under normal conditions these types of increases in the price of oil help put the brakes on an economy and conspire to bring on a recession. Although it is difficult to conclude that oil price shocks are the cause of postwar recessions, they always seem to be hanging around the scene of the crime. For evidence, consider the coinciding oil shocks and global recessions of 1973 to 1974, 1979 to 1980, and 1989 to 1990. The underlying factors of geopolitical-induced supply disruptions underscored those prior supply shocks (think Iran hostages, Gulf War) and spurred rapid price increases in the preceding periods. However, the 2001 to 2006 run-up was more likely due to surging demand in the emerging markets, coupled with an utter stagnation of production in the Organization for Economic Cooperation and Development (OECD) countries. Nevertheless, a quadrupling of oil prices over six years is a serious matter for a group of consumers who witnessed little growth in their income over the corresponding time horizon. This should have presented a major problem for the economy, but U.S. consumers had a trick up their sleeve: borrow more money. The answer was to offset these rising expenses by obtaining a raise in income—negotiated not with an employer, but with a banker who extended more credit as needed. Figure 1.6 shows that the amount of debt households were taking out to maintain a supersized lifestyle grew at a steady double-digit rate from 2000 to 2006.

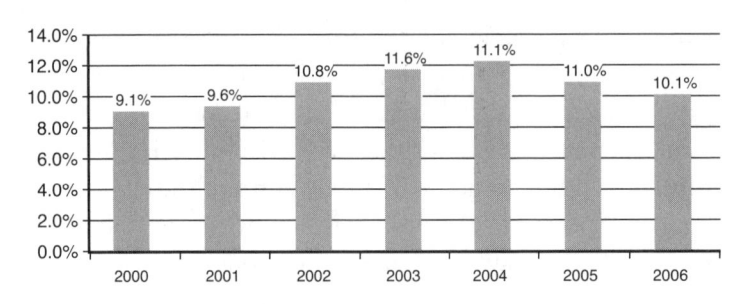

Figure 1.6 Year-over-year growth in total household debt
Source: Federal Reserve

Year	Growth
2000	9.1%
2001	9.6%
2002	10.8%
2003	11.6%
2004	11.1%
2005	11.0%
2006	10.1%

In the wake of this behavior, a new pattern of financial success came into acceptance: maximizing the amount of money you could invest in residential real estate. The old models of working harder or advancing through self-improvement were tossed aside in favor of the game of continuously taking out loans, buying homes, and selling them at a profit. This easy path to wealth creation has been tried and has failed so many times in the history of the world's financial markets that the events have gained notoriety, ranging from tulips in the seventeenth century to technology shares in 2000. The reality is that these financial events occur frequently over time and are just a function of human nature. The time and location change, but this script, like others before it, was followed with precision. What began as an easily discernable bull market in real estate soon transformed into near hysteria. Any stock day traders who were bold enough to get off the mat following the dotcom meltdown were the perfect candidates to jump aboard the Fed's latest amusement park ride—flipping homes in a housing bubble. For anyone who was unknowledgeable on the subject, this was of little consequence, because a seemingly endless number of self-help real estate seminars, infomercials, and cable TV shows were dedicated to showing you how to cash in on the real estate bonanza. The numerous TV shows were surprisingly entertaining. Most often they documented a novice flipper of some variety, a person or couple, purchasing a somewhat rundown or neglected property (for what appeared to be way too much money). The show then followed their progress as they attempted to install granite countertops, stainless-steel appliances, huge spa-like master bathrooms, or whatever superficial high-end touches would distract the buyer from the smell of mold or the sagging foundation and help them flip the house for a quick buck. Invariably, the show's subjects always discovered that not just anyone can knock out walls, install cabinetry, hang drywall, rewire a room, or replace rotted window frames, all while staying on budget and completing the job in a few weeks. Usually some outside help (such as a brother-in-law or cousin who was a contractor) had to be called in to help get the job done as its complexity, cost, or scale predictably spiraled out of control for the greenhorns. Still, the flippers would manage to complete the job, stage the house, and make the sale, usually at a much smaller profit than anticipated, but nonetheless at a profit. When asked about their experience at the show's conclusion, they always replied, "I can't wait to do it again!" Interest-only mortgage: $12,000. Appliances: $20,000. Paint: $300. Confusing a bull market with genius: priceless!

The Three Cs of Credit Give Way to Financial Innovation

If American consumers were addicted to easy credit and all the assorted highs that resulted from buying more stuff, surely some dubious counterparties were supplying this stream of never-ending credit. Time to meet their drug dealers.

In 1912, the famous American financier J. Pierpont Morgan was called in front of Congress to offer testimony during some variety of Congressional investigation into Wall Street practices. The senators questioned Mr. Morgan on his practice of extending credit. Mr. Morgan famously discussed, to the senators' dismay, the role of integrity and character in the lending process. The senators were digging for a response that uncloaked "good ol' boy, make the rich richer" types of lending criteria. To their surprise, the senators received a far different answer regarding the profile of people to whom Pierpont Morgan sought to lend money. He answered, "He might not have anything. I have known a man to come into my office, and I have given him a check for a million dollars when I knew that he had not a cent in the world." His point was, know your customers, and know their character. This practice in banking, knowing your customers and lending on character alongside collateral, was followed as a best practice in banking for many decades.

Unfortunately for the few austere bankers left in the world, several financial "innovations" that occurred in the latter part of the twentieth century gashed a deep void where the role of character once stood. The opening salvo of financial innovation was first heard in 1970 as the capital markets were introduced to the securitization of mortgage loans. Simply put, this meant that loans that had normally been held on the bank's books were packaged alongside a group of similar loans that the bank then sold to an outside investor in the form of a tradeable security. That same year, the song "We've Only Just Begun" by the brother-sister singing duo The Carpenters raced up the charts. However apropos, the song was probably not directed at the burgeoning market of structured finance, but it may as well have been. The game of packaging home loans and nearly every other type of credit into a tradeable security was set to ascend from financial novelty to global infamy over the course of the next thirty-plus years.

The supposed virtues of the securitization market relied on the fact that loans of all varieties could be marketed to a considerably larger investor base, beyond the traditional balance sheets of a lending institution. These securities were effectively assimilated into the bond market, so from that point on nearly any type of investing entity from almost anywhere in the world could hypothetically become a creditor in these asset markets. These could range from a bond mutual fund in the United States, to a pension fund in Europe, to a hedge fund in Asia. The result was that there was much greater demand for these loans than likely imagined and, in time, the market grew to be large. Forever opportunists, U.S. government institutions such as Congress quickly grasped the social benefits of these investments. They recognized the ease with which more and more Americans could attain the goal of home ownership through this innovative financing process. To the U.S. government, this looked like a no-brainer. The rapid proliferation of the American dream created happy voters, so the U.S. government had plenty of incentive to grease the wheels of this financial machine. One way the U.S. government greased the wheels of the securitization market was to implicitly backstop the loans securitized and sold by Fannie Mae and Freddie

Mac. For instance, banks around the United States were able to sell their loans to Fannie and Freddie, who then for an extra fee would guarantee that the securities they created were protected against default from the respective homeowners. Obviously, investors liked this aspect. Although Fannie and Freddie were privately held by shareholders, the U.S. government—and therefore the U.S. taxpayers—were understood to ultimately back the two firms against financial catastrophe. This mix of privately held profits and publicly held risk for loss between the firm's shareholders and U.S. taxpayers created a situation that was ripe for disaster. Before we get ahead of ourselves, though, Congress first began its formal meddling in this structured finance scheme by passing the Federal Housing Enterprises Financial Safety and Soundness Act of 1992. It sought to replicate the effects of the Community Reinvestment Act of 1977 through Fannie and Freddie in the securitization market. The Community Reinvestment Act was legislation that mandated that banks must make a certain percentage of their loans to low-income or blighted communities. The Act was a policy tool that could be used to penalize lenders who did not make what Congress, through its banking regulators acting as its policemen, deemed the appropriate number of low-income demographic loans. In the end, it was just a law that literally forced banks to make risky loans to borrowers in low-income areas. If a bank did not comply, the penalties included disallowing the violating bank from opening new branches. When this policy was extended to cover Fannie and Freddie in 1992, it created the regulatory necessity for a considerable amount of suspect credit to flow into the world's capital markets, on an exponentially larger scale—all guaranteed against default by the U.S. taxpayer, no less.

Naturally, though, if money can be made by issuing securities, this is a job better left to the pros, such as Wall Street and its assortment of investment banks. So although the U.S. government facilitated a great deal of this lower-income securitization activity through Fannie and Freddie, and the Fed provided aggressive interest rate policies, they both eventually had to share a crowded stage with the investment banks in this financial tragedy. In 2003 government-sponsored entities controlled 76% of the mortgage-backed securities market, but by 2006 their share had fallen to 43%. This rapid shift in market share coincided with Wall Street's share of the mortgage-backed securities market jumping from 24% to 57% over the same time period. Wall Street had figured out the new game in town.

The acceleration in the issuance of mortgage-backed securities over this time horizon is unmistakable in the data. From the beginning stages of the low-interest policy following the dotcom fallout in 2000 and through the en masse involvement of the investment banks in mortgage securitization in 2003, mortgage-related securitization grew at a compound annual growth rate of 15.4% (see Figure 1.7).

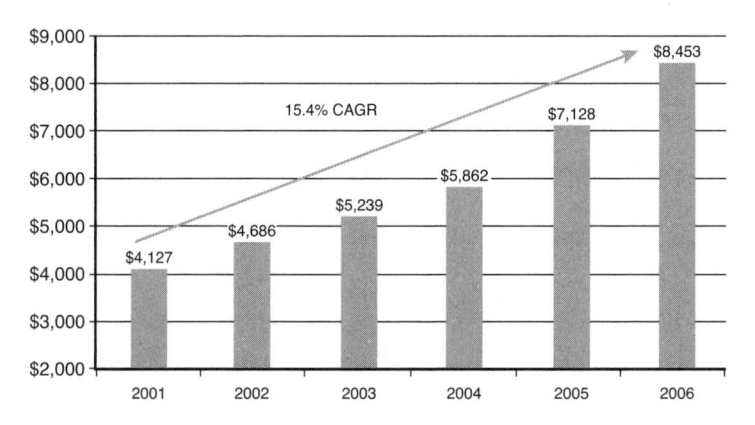

Figure 1.7 The mortgage-related securities market

Source: SIFMA

At the same time, this market was not relegated to mortgage activity alone. The asset-backed securities market, shown in Figure 1.8, covered loans and credits of multiple varieties, including automobiles, credit cards, and student loans, to name a few.

In contrast to the mortgage-backed securities market, the broader category of asset-backed securities was "only" growing at just under 11% per year. Figure 1.8 sheds some light and relevance on our earlier discussion about how so many consumers could readily afford those $50,000 Hummers. The answer ostensibly rests in the fact that it was easy to get a loan to buy one. Particularly since the lender was some random investor, sitting behind a Bloomberg screen, possibly on the other side of the world.

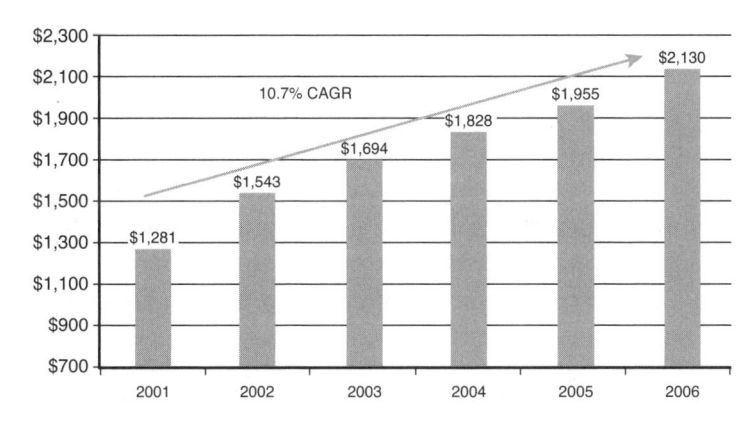

1 • THE FED SENTENCES THE CONSUMER TO DEBTOR'S PRISON 23

Figure 1.8 The asset-backed securities market
Source: SIFMA

[Chart data: 2001: $1,281; 2002: $1,543; 2003: $1,694; 2004: $1,828; 2005: $1,955; 2006: $2,130; 10.7% CAGR]

As we examine what for all intents and purposes appears to be the profile of a growth market erupting in the fundamental backdrop of the world's largest mature developed-market economy, the essential question arises: Who was buying all these securities?

The term "hedge fund" has become a catchall for a wide range of similarly legally structured financial vehicles, as well as assorted images of financial risk taking, wealth, greed, and, unfortunately, scams. No matter what your impression is of a hedge fund, it is a matter of empiricism that one segment of the hedge fund industry that was focused on fixed income and its derivatives played a heavy role in the consumption of mortgage and asset-backed securities issued into the market. The allure of these securities for launching an asset-backed hedge fund strategy was the simple employment of borrowing money at one low rate and investing in these asset-backed securities to earn a higher rate. The major emphasis in this equation was indeed accessing the low interest rates available from the prime broker in order to borrow and employ, on average, $10 for every $1 that an investor gave the manager. Thanks again to the Fed, whose low interest rates paved the way for rampant speculation on borrowed money. The Fed cannot take all the blame, though. Now we must also acknowledge that the leverage was provided by the prime brokerage department of the investment bank, which in some way probably facilitated the creation of the securities itself. Put more simply, the investment banks in many cases had subsidiaries originate the loans for the securities. Then they packaged the securities and lent money to their clients to buy them. The investment banks were making money coming and going in these cases. Still, as long as interest rates were low, everyone in this picture got what they wanted. The home purchaser got more house than he or she could otherwise afford. The lending institution or mortgage broker got a fee for consummating the loan. The investment bank got a fee for creating the security. The rating agency collected a fee for its stamp of approval on the credit. The hedge fund got a security it would borrow large sums of money to buy, in the hopes that it would collect 20% or more of the investment returns for itself (and it often did). Finally, the fund investor received a stable supply of investment returns with low volatility and low risk of default—or so the investor thought. In predictable fashion, once financiers find something that works, it is replicated, piled into, and exploited until every last penny is wrung out of the opportunity. The credit markets in 2003 to 2007 are a sparkling example of how finance truly is a commodity business. One good example comes from a 2007 survey performed by Greenwich Associates, a hedge fund consultancy. It found that asset-backed strategy hedge funds had come to represent 30% of all fixed-income trading volume, which was double the 15% recorded at the same time a year ago. Given the tandem of low interest rates and a powerfully efficient machine of financial securitization, the volume of mortgage-backed securities and their derivatives proliferated across the globe. As late as 2005, though, public officials such as Alan Greenspan were extolling the virtues of this creation, and how financial risk was now being spread into the larger system, versus remaining on the books of the lending institutions.

In April 2005, Greenspan delivered the following rhetoric in a speech on consumer credit:[1]

> "The development of a broad-based secondary market for mortgage loans also greatly expanded consumer access to credit. By reducing the risk of making long-term, fixed-rate loans and ensuring liquidity for mortgage lenders, the secondary market helped stimulate widespread competition in the mortgage business. The mortgage-backed security helped create a national and even an international market for mortgages, and market support for a wider variety of home mortgage loan

products became commonplace. This led to securitization of a variety of other consumer loan products, such as auto and credit card loans.

"With these advances in technology, lenders have taken advantage of credit-scoring models and other techniques for efficiently extending credit to a broader spectrum of consumers. The widespread adoption of these models has reduced the costs of evaluating the creditworthiness of borrowers, and in competitive markets cost reductions tend to be passed through to borrowers. Where once more-marginal applicants would simply have been denied credit, lenders are now able to quite efficiently judge the risk posed by individual applicants and to price that risk appropriately. These improvements have led to rapid growth in subprime mortgage lending; indeed, today subprime mortgages account for roughly 10 percent of the number of all mortgages outstanding, up from just 1 or 2 percent in the early 1990s."

Effectively, the policymakers were generally sanguine on the role of securitization in the capital markets. They actually praised its virtue of opening the mortgage market and homeownership to less creditworthy borrowers. Had they understood better what was occurring on a more granular level in the market, they might have been less glib on the double whammy of low interest rates and rapid securitization.

The problem at hand returns us to our earlier comments on the role of character in lending and Mr. Morgan. The act of securitization changed the process of originating loans in this easy credit environment so profoundly that it nearly toppled the global financial system in a matter of five years. In the past, a lender simply had to know its customer in order to ensure that a safe loan had been extended and that the bank was likely to be repaid its principal and interest. In the early 2000s, however, advances in technology and financial engineering capsized the role of character in lending. Because the financial institutions were unlikely to hold the mortgage on their books due to the ease with which securitization could be transacted, this paved the way for a number of nonlending, sales-driven financial players to enter the game. Mortgage brokers were primarily in the business of originating mortgages and then selling them to a larger distributor such as a commercial or investment bank, which could then securitize the loan and sell it into the capital markets. Mortgage brokers had tremendous financial incentive to make a sale but very little financial incentive to make sure it was a wise sale. Put another way, the majority of transactions that initiated the creation of these securities were based on a mere ability to complete some paperwork rather than a more thorough examination of a borrower's character or creditworthiness. This shift in the market created a lending backdrop that was dominated by hitting sales targets at the expense of creating a safe loan portfolio. At the outset, the process of mortgage brokering and securitization in the early 2000s was as innocent as just another way of sourcing mortgages and mortgage-backed securities. Financially responsible homeowners or purchasers tapped into the market to refinance or realize their goal of becoming a homeowner. As interest rates remained enticingly low for several years, though, more and more players were drawn into the mortgage finance industry. All were competing for a dwindling number of financially conservative, creditworthy borrowers. Once the supply of these conservative borrowers was exhausted though, they began targeting a new set of borrowers in order to maintain the growth in sales and originations.

The mortgage finance industry and the securities that resulted operated no differently than the local butcher making hamburger meat. At first the butcher uses only the best ingredients to run through the grinder and place on the shelves. The butcher starts with the finest ground chuck, which he calls his "prime" selection. As demand continues to surge for these delicious burgers, he eventually realizes that with only a limited supply of chuck roast, he must start to fill the package with some still quality but less demanded cuts such as sirloin. With customer demand still surging for ground chuck, as well as ground sirloin, the butcher realizes that he has no more of these cuts. But he can process some other cuts. Even though they aren't part of his prime selection, he can still legitimately label the package "hamburger meat." His customers, still coming back for more of the ground chuck and sirloin, buy the lesser "hamburger meat" on his good reputation and the great results from his prior packages, as well as the fact that his product was inspected and U.S. Department of Agriculture (USDA)–approved. Not ready to consume this meat right away, his customers store it in the freezer for later. All the while, customers continue to pile into the shop and the butcher had nearly exhausted his supply of cuts, but feels that he must take advantage of this boom in business either way—he knows it will not last forever. He begins to scrape up whatever he can find from his trimmings, off the floor and counters. He runs it through the grinder and packages it for sale as less than prime, or "subprime," hamburger meat. He thinks it is possible that this meat is not fit to sell, or may go bad, but he makes the sale nonetheless. Some customers begin to question this latest product, saying it does not look the same as their earlier purchases and smells funny. The butcher explains that if the customers are concerned, they can simply take their other packages of ground chuck, ground sirloin, and hamburger meat, and combine them with this new meat. He says that by combining these various cuts and packages of meat, you can produce an outstanding burger, and you will not be bothered by the poorer quality of the subprime meat. Taking him at his word, and unwilling to ask exactly what was ground up in this latest offering of subprime meat, his customers continue to buy and mix together the various forms of meat into one of the butcher's "structured" burgers. In the beginning, the butcher proves somewhat right, in that his customers do not notice much of a difference when just a bit of the subprime meat is mixed into the patty. In time, though, the customers begin to run out of the prime meat and start mixing the so-called "hamburger meat" with the subprime meat. This concoction, although still approved by the USDA, not surprisingly results in food poisoning, E. coli, trips to the hospital, and even some deaths. If this metaphor seems ridiculous, we can agree that the world of structured finance transgressed into practices that were somewhat ridiculous. Nevertheless, some bright financial minds fell into this trap and willingly gobbled up this garbage, applying similar threads of logic. Much of what was believed in "high finance" about the investment attributes of collateralized debt obligations (CDOs) rested on a line of reasoning that said combining a magic formula of good and bad credits into an investment, in a certain manner, somehow negates the downside. Common sense, on the other hand, says not to expect magical results when buying bonds containing cash flows tied to bad credits. In particular, packaging bad credits as good credits mixed in with bad credits amounts to a pool of bad credits—common sense. Diversification works only if a pool of assets is actually diversified.

When you look at what happened in the real world of mortgage finance and the types of loans that the mortgage brokers contracted and sold to the investment banks and other parties for securitization, it was no less disgusting than the hamburger metaphor. Mortgage brokers were scraping up whatever types of borrowers they could find to siphon loans into these securities, and the situation only got worse over time.

It may seem incredulous that the agents for lenders would behave so aggressively in the pursuit of brokering mortgages. But the steady deterioration in the rate of default for later loan vintages over the time span of the credit mania reveals the truth. Figure 1.9 shows default rates by the vintage of the subprime loan. It is easy to see that loans extended in 2006 and 2007 performed exponentially worse than loans made just a few years prior, in 2004 and 2005.

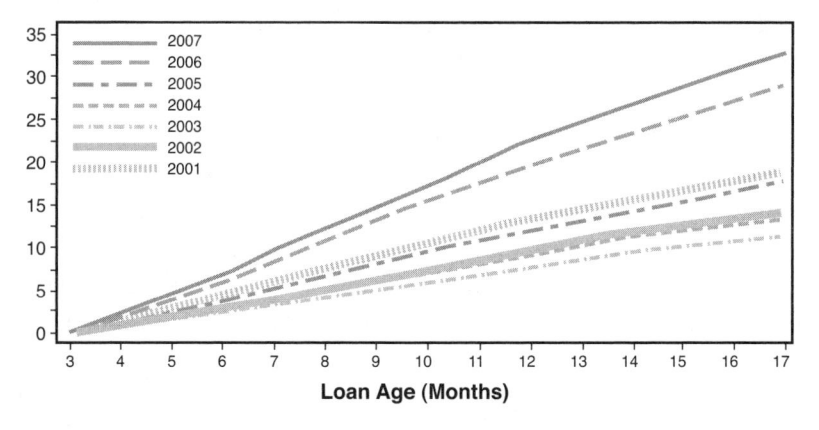

Figure 1.9 Actual delinquency rate (as a percentage)

Source: Federal Reserve Bank of Cleveland, NYU, from "Understanding the subprime mortgage crisis" by Yuliya Demyanyk and Otto Van Hemert, *The Review of Financial Studies* (May 4, 2009). Reprinted by permission of Oxford University Press, Oxford Journals.

Aside from simply pushing the envelope on the borrower's profile, mortgage originators were equipped with an arsenal of financial gimmicks that played right into the hands of would-be speculators and spendthrift consumers looking to maximize the amount of leverage they could employ in the transaction. For most of the twentieth century the basic premise of a mortgage loan was to put down 20% of the purchase price and borrow the remaining the 80% at a fixed rate, usually over a 30-year period. However, this convention would never suit the sales quota culture of the credit bubble. When you think about it, borrowers addicted to consumption or home price speculation would be either unqualified or tapped out rather quickly with this loan product. Instead, the mortgage originators had a stable full of innovative ways to extend more credit within the established confines of the structured finance framework. These products were shamelessly meant to entice the borrower, not unlike those carts of gluttonous sugar-coma-inducing desserts that occasionally get wheeled through a restaurant in search of an undisciplined sweet tooth. In this menagerie of financial products, many types of loans appealed to all the mortgage vices. "Oh, you want to purchase this as a second home? You're right—people have made good money in the real estate market. I think the interest-only loan is the one for you." Far from simple interest-only loans, though, you also had adjustable-rate mortgages (ARMs), where the loan structure had a predetermined period of one fixed rate that would later reset based on the level of a certain index, such as London InterBank Offered Rate (LIBOR) plus a fixed spread over the index. Among the ARM products, the 5/1 hybrid was one of the more popular. It represents the majority of the ARMs outstanding in the market still waiting to reset after the credit bubble. Again, the idea behind the ARM hybrid loan was to entice the buyer into a contract, this time with a low teaser rate for five years that would, in all probability, reset to a higher rate. The attractiveness of this plan rested on selling the house for a profit prior to the reset date. Once the witching hour struck, it was likely that higher payments would be necessary. This was based on the interest rate index chosen as the benchmark, either LIBOR or T-bills, and whether the contract had been interest-only before its reset versus interest plus amortization of principal. In addition to the gimmicks of interest-only loans and ARMs, there was also a healthy exploitation of Alt-A mortgages, which require little documentation of a borrower's income. Originally they were intended to reduce an onerous amount of paperwork for self-employed individuals who might have multiple income streams. But this kind of loan became a conduit to securitizing mortgages from borrowers who tended to fit between the prime and subprime categories. These borrowers usually had some previous credit issues, but not enough to put them in the subprime category. However, armed with a valid excuse to provide little documentation of the borrower's background, it is easy to see how these loans came to be abused and nicknamed "liar loans." In addition to the Alt-A mortgage, there was also the balloon mortgage, which postponed the majority of the loan's amortization payment until its end, thereby creating a lump-sum "balloon" payment. It was designed to minimize cash outlays for as long as possible, making it conducive to speculative purchases. For borrowers who needed the hard stuff, the real street drugs of mortgage finance, there was the negative amortization loan. The negative amortization loan allowed borrowers to pay less than their sticker rate of interest, but any forgone interest payments became a part of the loan balance. Therefore, at some point, after their grace period of skipping the full interest payment had expired, the borrower had to pay interest and principal on the loan's original amount, plus the sum of all those previously skipped interest payments. In many cases the borrower taking full advantage of the negative amortization loan was gambling that she could sell the property before her monthly payments increased threefold. If all these loans seem familiar, you certainly get the picture. Keep the payments low at first, until they become nearly usurious at some predetermined, fixed point in time. The mortgage market had been jerry-rigged for speculation and was in plain view for all to see. The local mortgage office now resembled a casino full of financial games where unwitting gamblers were playing with stakes beyond their cognition. For evidence, let us turn once again to the data. As shown in Figure 1.10, in 2001, the percentage share of purchase mortgage originations derived through interest-only and negative amortization loans was just 1% of the total, probably what you would expect. By 2005, though, these types of risky loans comprised 29% of the total, representing an exponential increase in the amount of risk that borrowers were willing to take in order to make low monthly payments in hopes of unloading their house at a higher price within the next several years.

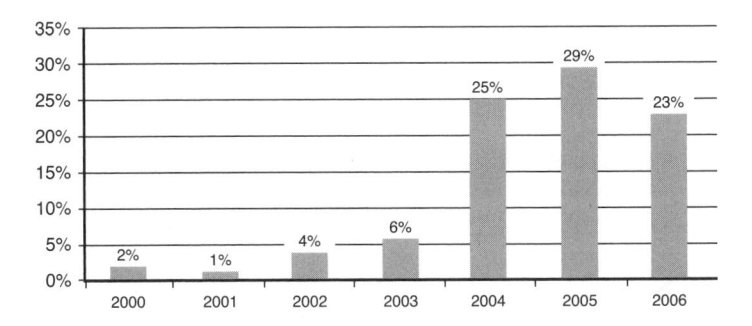

1 • THE FED SENTENCES THE CONSUMER TO DEBTOR'S PRISON   31

```
35%
30%                                          29%
25%                                 25%
                                                    23%
20%
15%
10%
                            6%
 5%   2%            4%
            1%
 0%
     2000  2001   2002   2003   2004   2005   2006
```

Figure 1.10 Interest-only and negative amortization share of mortgage originations
Source: Brookings Institute, Credit Suisse, LoanPerformance

Figure 1.11 illustrates the explosion in subprime loans, Alt-A loans, and home equity loans in comparison to the sharp decline in conforming, conventional mortgages. From this data, it is relatively clear that the steady growth in mortgage securitization we described earlier was being fueled by a growing number of financial gimmick loans. In sum, the growth in these types of risky loans, coupled with the decline in the bread-and-butter 30-year conforming fixed-rate mortgage, suggested a powder keg of default risk. The risk lay in the likelihood that across the mortgage industry and the securities it spawned, borrowers were by design not planning on seeing the contracts through. Instead, they were paying a carry in order to obtain short-term profits. Another perspective worth considering on the financial risk that borrowers were assuming in these transactions is the two sides of their balance sheet post transaction. On the left side, the asset side, the speculator was placing a traditionally long-term asset designed to be held for many years, or even forever. On the right side, the liabilities side, the home speculator was placing a debt that financed the asset. With a conventional 30-year fixed-rate mortgage, the contract on the debt matches the asset's time horizon. However, the ARM financing structure in effect has two sets of financing contracts. One provides a low rate of interest set to expire. A second contract takes over after the first expires. This contract contains a high probability of attaching a higher rate of interest. Most of the speculators were chasing higher prices, or already-high prices, and

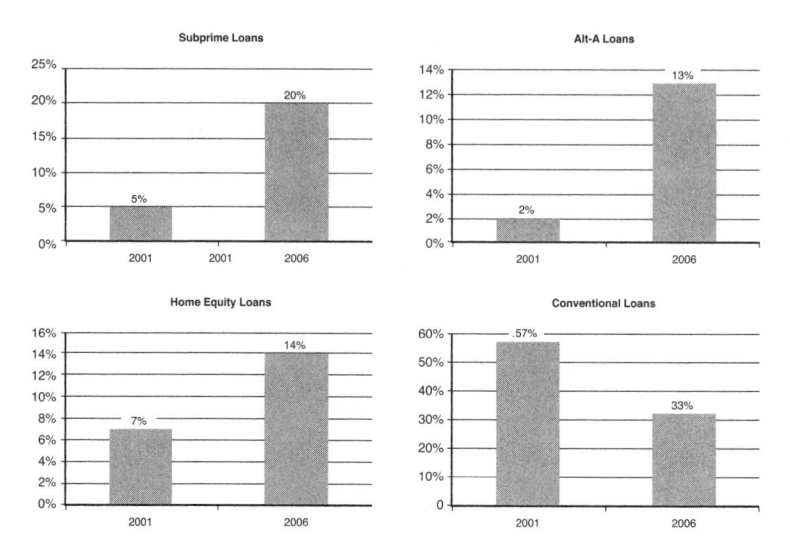

Figure 1.11 Subprime, Alt-A, home equity, and conventional loans as a percentage of mortgage originations

Source: Brookings Institute, Inside Mortgage Finance

likely could not afford to service the debt once it reset at a new interest rate. Therefore, we can call this game what it really was: using short-term debt to purchase long-term illiquid assets. This risky financing game has a history of toppling entire countries and famous hedge funds, as we saw with the Asian Financial Crisis of the late 1990s and the Long Term Capital Management episode. If the borrower is too leveraged, and the composition of its assets are too illiquid to raise cash quickly to meet the debt payment, and it cannot obtain new short-term funds from new borrowing, it is often game over. The ARM contracts that were so popular among borrowers were *designed* to cancel out and give way to more onerous long-term contracts. In this case, if the rate reset at a higher level that forced payment demands exceeding a combination of the borrower's cash reserves, incoming cash flows, or ability to access short-term financing from credit cards, their game would be over. At its core, everyone in the housing speculation game needed two conditions to stay in place—*rising* house prices and a *liquid* market through which they could sell the house and extinguish the debt. If house prices fell, or the speculator could not sell the property in a timely manner, severe consequences might result. These potential risks were ignored, though, as homebuyers and speculators used these loans to chase prices higher with short-term bets on the housing market.

In addition to assuming the risk of an interest rate reset and higher payments, the borrowers in these products were also pushing the envelope on the loan to value, or the amount of equity they would place in their purchase. As suggested by the sharp decline in the percentage of conventional loans taken as a percentage of originations, as well as the surge in home equity lines of credit, the amount of equity that homeowners had in their asset was falling precipitously (see Figure 1.12.) This implied that these borrowers were becoming more and more vulnerable to a decline in housing prices and the possibility of owing more than the house was worth in that scenario.

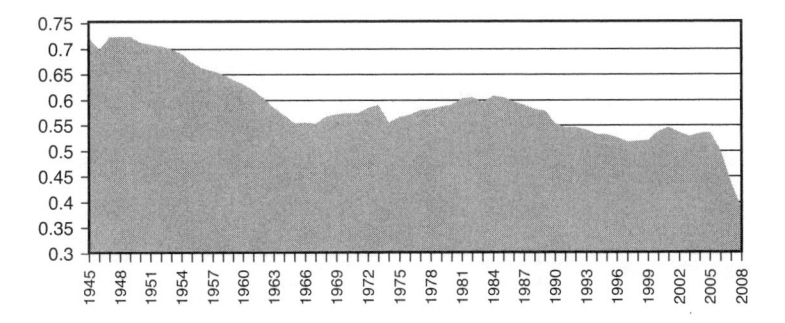

Figure 1.12 Household owners' equity as a percentage of real estate assets

Source: Federal Reserve

Of course, this behavior could be seen as risky only if housing prices declined in value. Because most speculators "knew" prices had never declined on a nationwide basis, there was little cause for concern.

Endnote

[1] U.S. Senate, Committee on Banking, Housing and Urban Affairs. Federal Reserve Chairman Alan Greenspan. "Regulatory Reform of the Government-Sponsored Enterprises," April 6, 2005, http://www.federalreserve.gov/boarddocs/testimony/2005/20050406/default.htm.

2

The Biggest Gamblers Go "All In" on the Housing Bet

By now, we have reasonably illustrated the deterioration in the mortgage market from responsible borrowers refinancing their homes in early 2001 to 2003 to the runaway speculators betting on higher home prices in 2006. We have described many of the key actors in this comedy of errors, from the spendthrift consumer looking to monetize his house's appreciating value, to the house price speculator buying up second and third properties, as well as the mortgage brokers, policy makers, and hedge funds that all helped make it happen. Conspicuously absent from our roll call have been the real players in the mortgage securitization charade, the big fishes in the pond, the *real* borrowers, the *real* house price speculators, the *real* hedge fund operators—the investment banks. Everyone else in on the game until now was small potatoes. As we noted earlier in our discussion, the investment banks picked up on the securitization game in 2003 and doubled their share of the securitization market in just three years. Without question, Wall Street was designed for this game, and it played it like a master. Problems took root when the investment banks transitioned from merely shuffling these securities out the door to their customers to consuming them in house too. Wall Street's transgression from seller to consumer in this market can find any number of sad analogies—the bookie turned gambler, the bartender turned drunk, the drug dealer turned addict. Obviously, those analogies have negative connotations. The outcome of the investment banks placing these securities, or exposure to them, on their balance sheets provides no less of a bad outcome.

At the beginning of the credit boom, the investment banks were content to generate steadily increasing profits from the basic securitization process. But the relentless pursuit of higher bonuses and compensation was inseparable from the culture of these firms. With that said, it is no surprise that these firms sought and eventually discovered new ways to monetize the credit bubble. In the stand-alone securitization model of the business, the investment banks simply brought new issues of collateralized debt obligations (CDOs) and various other credit vehicles to the market for purchase by institutional-size investors. The profit came from charging a fee, not unlike their classic business of delivering an initial public offering (IPO) to the equity market. Once the deal was done, the search was on for the next one. This model generated few potential risks, with the exception of a potential loss of income from prior levels once the new business slowed in growth. However, another major component of the investment banking revenue stream comes from trading on both an agent and principal basis. The allure of trading these asset-backed securities for profits on behalf of the firm, and supposedly its shareholders, provided the impetus for an unmatched level of financial risk taking. The most terrific and easily visible of the investment banks' adventures into direct investing in asset-backed securities lay in the creation of two hedge funds by the 85-year-old firm Bear Stearns. In 2003, Bear Stearns established the High Grade Structured Credit Fund as a hedge fund that invested primarily in investment-grade CDOs backed by mortgages. It was also a vehicle that borrowed money in the short-term repo markets to invest in tranches of CDOs. The idea was simple: borrow at one low rate, and invest in asset-backed securities to earn a higher rate. The returns the hedge fund would generate could scale with the amount of leverage that the fund employed, all other things being equal. This game plan worked like a charm from its inception in late 2003 through 2006 as the fund recorded 40 months of returns without a loss. The fund was so successful, and the managers were so confident in this mortgage- and asset-backed market, as well as their own abilities, that they launched a second fund in August 2006. It was called the Enhanced Fund, which in financial parlance means more leverage. More leverage, indeed. The Enhanced Fund was borrowing on the order of $20 for every $1 that an investor had contributed.

Trouble in Paradise

By the time spring 2007 arrived, these funds had been heavily feasting on the aforementioned subprime meat of the fixed-income market—and they had been using a great deal of borrowed money to do so. Perhaps blinded by their success, as often happens to investors, the fund managers did not feel the tremors that signaled that the ground was about move beneath them and swallow them whole. Incidentally, some of the rancid inventory of subprime credits that had been scraped up by the sales-driven mortgage originators was spoiling on the shelves of these hedge funds (and countless others). As early as February 2007 the funds began to show their vulnerability to the subprime market defaults as the Enhanced Fund lost money that month. Conditions continued to slip in March 2007 as the High Grade Fund lost 3.71% and the Enhanced Fund lost 5.41%. This was the same month that the fund's manager, Ralph Cioffi, removed $2 million of his money from the Enhanced Fund and simultaneously reassured investors that everything was OK. This suspicious behavior eventually landed him a date with Federal investigators. At the end of April, the Enhanced Fund's managers had just reported to its investors that it was down 10%—or so they thought. The fund had the great misfortune to return to its investors weeks later and issue a reappraisal of its April valuation due to quotations received from one of its trading partners, Goldman Sachs. As it turned out, Goldman was already beginning to aggressively mark down market prices for subprime-related CDOs. Goldman's desk was not receiving offers in the market in line with what many others thought to be the prices at the end of April. Goldman reportedly believed that prices for these asset-backed instruments—that other brokers reported to be closer to 90 cents on the dollar or more—were actually nearer to 50 *cents* on the dollar. This may seem drastic at first blush, but this is the nature of illiquid assets, and the CDOs that the Bear funds held were thinly traded. The fund managers had little choice but to recognize this updated valuation and incorporate it into their existing fund valuation. When investors received a new letter telling them that their investment was down 23%, rather than 10%, they had seen enough. Investors sought to flee the funds through redemptions, but the fund quickly suspended redemptions because it could not meet them due to the illiquid nature of its investments. Likewise, the fund's creditors began responding to the declining valuations of asset-backed securities and forced margin calls on the fund. The fund's creditors had supplied the fund with short-term borrowing contracts, while the fund had invested in long-term, illiquid assets. Sound familiar? Incidentally, these sophisticated hedge funds were taking the same ill-advised risks that the multitudes of home speculators were assuming through their gimmicky mortgage products. By June, one of the fund's creditors, Merrill Lynch, put little faith in Mr. Cioffi's assurances or request for a 30-day stay on margin calls. It promptly seized over $800 million in collateral, with the intent to auction the securities. By July the High Grade Fund had lost 91% of its value, and the Enhanced Fund was wiped out. That fast. Moreover, if this looks like a swift demise, just wait. In what was perhaps one of the more foreboding episodes of these funds' total meltdown, Bear Stearns attempted to rescue them by committing over $1.6 billion of its own capital. Not only did this rescue fail, but it also plainly illustrated that the top brass of the investment banks were deeply out of touch with reality. In addition, it showed just how quickly these securities could annihilate capital.

What transpired in the Bear Stearns episode was a microcosm of what would take place across the world's capital markets in a little over a year's time. In sum, many of those reckless borrowers who had been taking out home equity loans to buy Hummers, or second and third mortgages to speculate on future housing price increases, were beginning to demonstrate that they were unable or unlikely to continue sending in payments on their mountain of debt. In fact, subprime defaults were accelerating in early 2007, and housing prices had already started to fall from their lofty highs. The problem among the borrowing base was twofold: Interest rates were beginning to reset at higher levels on the ARM contracts, and housing prices had started to fall. As rates reset, the cost of servicing the loans spiked, and the borrowers faced a stark realization—they could not afford the homes under the new financing terms on their base of income. In fact, the speculators had pushed housing prices so high in proportion to income levels that the relationship was almost hopeless for anyone caught in these loans as their rates reset. Figure 2.1 shows the ratio of national median home prices to median income levels based on data compiled by the National Association of Homebuilders. The data demonstrates that housing prices in relation to income had risen to a level far above the norm, which had traditionally been approximately 3x.

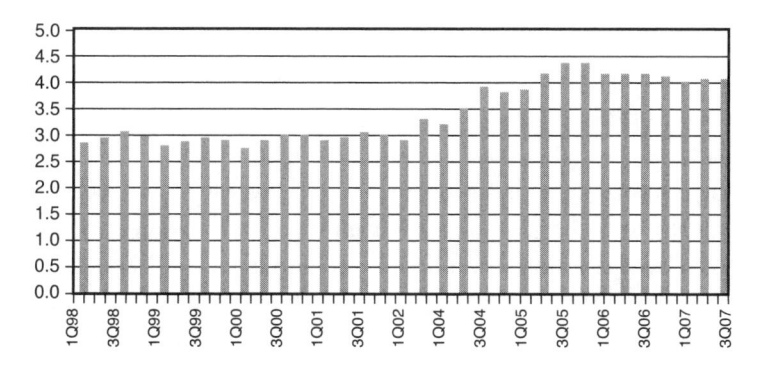

Figure 2.1 National median house price to median income
Source: National Association of Homebuilders

As rates began to reset on borrowers who were already too stretched, the writing was on the wall.

If the Bear Stearns hedge fund managers had the audacity to take $1.5 billion of capital and leverage it into well over $20 billion in investments, what can we say about an entire firm that was leveraged 30:1?

The Canary Died Unheard from the Boardrooms, Yachts, and Golf Courses

Lehman Brothers had enjoyed a longstanding place in Wall Street's colorful history since its inception 158 years prior to the second week of September 2008. The firm had enjoyed playing a role in cultivating many capitalistic icons from America's past and present. These included the financing of railroads, as well as storied companies such as Sears Roebuck and RCA, among countless other business feats. Despite its tradition and ability to escape the worst financial disasters on record up until 2008, 2001 and the Fed's ushering in of the low-interest-rate environment pulled Lehman into the mortgage-backed securitization craze like no other. By the time 2006 and 2007 arrived, Lehman was the top U.S. underwriter of mortgage-backed securities, with 10% of the market. Keep in mind that 2006 and 2007 were probably the worst possible years to be leading the market in securitizing these loans, as our earlier illustration of loan vintages demonstrated. The loans from these years were being extended to the least creditworthy or, put another way, the hardcore junkies of the credit bubble. More problematic for Lehman, though, was its steady consumption of its own cooking, so to speak, or the inventorying of mortgage-related securities and leveraged loans on its own books. Owning a large exposure of mortgage-related securities, CDOs backed by various other credits, leveraged loans, and so on was a problem in and of itself, but borrowing in short-term debt to own them was a cyanide pill waiting to dissolve. One of the more remarkable sidebars to the investment banks' strategy of using short-term debt to buy long-term securities was that they all had a front-row seat to the Asian Financial Crisis. There, a similar combination of financial mismatches eventually shook the world. From a practical standpoint, the firm's 30:1 leverage was more than just a gutsy data point. It also meant that every $100 of borrowing was supported by $3.30 of equity, so if the value of the assets declined 3.3%, equity would be wiped out. This was a rigid balance sheet that would simply break rather than bend if put under even the smallest amount of stress. If the rapid markdown of the CDOs in the Bear Stearns hedge funds meant anything, it should have demonstrated that if the defaults occurring in subprime began to spread into what were assumed to be conforming loans, the firms using leverage to own these products should have been deeply concerned. Lehman and other investment banks that were similarly leveraged fell complacent on what was occurring in the subprime market. They viewed the subprime defaults as a problem that would remain in the confines of securities labeled as subprime. This is logical enough, and it was indeed the conventional wisdom spreading from the head policy makers and pundits around Wall Street. What this belief system overlooked, though, was the degradation of the loan originator model that we discussed earlier, where mortgage brokers effectively extended loans to anyone with a pulse and a signature. What the banks missed was that prime was just as infected as subprime—or, better yet, that the packages had been mislabeled.

Up to this point, we have directed much criticism at the abusers of the securitization system inhabiting the point of sale, but they needed assistance too, even if it was somewhat inadvertent. The labelers of the securities, such as Standard & Poor's and Moody's (the USDA of the hamburger analogy in the preceding chapter), provided no less of a letdown to investors than the other players in the securitization markets. The role of the credit rating agencies was at best disappointing and at worst involved some malfeasance. Without question, their role involved bouts of incompetence. Any way you look at it, the ratings agencies were on the securitization dole as they collected handsome fees for providing their ratings, just as they would on any normal bond issue (such as AAA or AA). For instance, one of the largest agencies, Moody's, saw its revenues from structured finance products jump from under $300 million in 2001 to nearly $900 million for two years running at the height of the market in 2006 and 2007. Even if the agencies had also become too complacent to simply charge a fee for services rendered—services in this case being simply running some numbers through one of their prebuilt quantitative models—we can be relatively sure that mistakes were made. In May 2008 the *Financial Times* reported that Moody's had erroneously awarded AAA ratings to billions of dollars of a structured finance product during 2006.[1] For $900,000,000 per year, you might think Moody's could hire someone to actually go through the model and double-check it! What takes this story in a painful direction is that nearly all investors in structured products had placed their faith in the due diligence and credibility of the ratings agencies. To worsen matters, their ineptitude for rating these investment vehicles extended beyond simple oversight or sloppy work and into the more theoretical basis they used to rate the instruments. One example came from a March 2007 conference call between the credit ratings agency Fitch and managers and analysts from a mutual fund manager called First Pacific Advisors. The CEO of First Pacific, Robert Rodriguez, recalled later[2] that on the call, one of his analysts asked the Fitch analysts to describe their rating process for subprime asset-backed securities, which the Fitch analyst said was based on FICO scores (credit scores) and projected price appreciations of 1% to 2% in the housing market. When the First Pacific analyst asked what would happen if prices in the housing market declined on the order of 10% to 20%

over the next ten years, the Fitch representative said the model would "break down" and that AA and AAA securities would have serious problems. The revelation was that at the core, at least one of the major ratings agencies was applying a model as the basis for its ratings that accounted for only one outcome: housing prices that continue to rise. Was anyone not drinking this Kool-Aid? Basically, all the asset-backed investors had outsourced their homework to a group of researchers whose work was, to put it kindly, lacking. The problem was not only that ratings agencies were not performing the thoughtful work that investors had counted on, but additionally that the work itself would be very difficult to perform without solid institutional-level research capabilities. Put succinctly, the securities are difficult to analyze in real detail. The structures of these credits were complex, and the credits themselves could be a hodgepodge of loans coming from different geographies, industries, and originating sources. So if the price started to fall in one of these investments, and the research analyst or portfolio manager wanted to take a closer look at what was going on, this could be a Herculean research task. Then take into account that an entire portfolio could be constructed from these investments, and you get the picture.

So while Lehman Brothers had been piling mortgage-backed securities onto its balance sheet, and was now up to its eyeballs in exposure ($65 billion in 2008), the other investments banks like Merrill Lynch, Morgan Stanley, and Goldman Sachs were at least up to their waists (if not further) in the same morass of securities. More important, all these firms were leveraged to the hilt by the end of 2007. If we take a look at gross leverage (assets divided by equity) across the major investment banks, we can see that Lehman was in pretty good company, as shown in Table 2.1.

TABLE 2.1 Gross Leverage Multiples (2007)

Goldman Sachs	26.2x
Lehman Brothers	30.7x
Merrill Lynch	31.9x
Morgan Stanley	33.4x
Group average	**30.6x**

Source: Company reports

One good question following Table 2.1 might be, "Why run up so much debt?" This question can be answered in a few ways. The first comes from comments made by an ex-SEC (Securities and Exchange Commission) official named Lee Pickard. In a 2008 article in *American Banker*,[3] he described changes made by the SEC in 2004 that allowed five investment banks (the four mentioned in Table 2.1 plus Bear Stearns) to no longer be constrained to leverage of 12x net capital. The SEC gave exemptions to investment banks with over $5 billion in capital that allowed them to monitor their risk based on an assortment of complex mathematical models, instead of a good old-fashioned cap on the amount of debt they could assume. Why the SEC chose to meddle with a regulation that had worked for decades is puzzling. Nevertheless, shortly thereafter the amount of debt these banks employed mushroomed. Still another answer to the question about using so much debt on their balance sheets lies in their ultimate incentive to assume this financial risk. That incentive was the enormous sums of money that were being made at these firms during the credit boom. Understanding the bulge bracket investment banking culture and their motivation is simple: aggressive, profit-driven, and Darwinian. If we take a quick jaunt back to 2001, when the Fed was embarking on its adventures in interest rate experiments, these firms, for all and intents and purposes, were still reeling from the fallout of the dotcom mania. Massive layoffs, corporate governance scandals, weak profits, and an easily foreseeable witch hunt by anyone who had lost big in the tech bust. Let's face it—times were terrible in the early 2000s for the investment banks. Then, along came those low interest rates. As soon as they were combined with a growing securitization market, these people knew how to turn a buck, and it was off to the races. This phenomenon is easy to see in the historical revenues and compensation levels of the aforementioned investment banks, shown in Table 2.2.

TABLE 2.2 Let the Good Times Roll: Revenues and Compensation Expenses for the Major Independent Investment Banks

Net Revenues	2001	2002	2003	2004	2005	2006	2001-2006 CAGR
Goldman Sachs	$15,811	$13,986	$15,965	$20,811	$24,782	$37,302	19%
Lehman Brothers	$6,736	$6,155	$8,647	$11,576	$14,630	$17,583	21%
Merrill Lynch	$21,684	$18,436	$19,838	$22,059	$25,911	$32,666	9%
Morgan Stanley	$18,991	$15,574	$17,441	$20,175	$23,332	$29,839	9%
Group	**$63,222**	**$54,151**	**$61,891**	**$74,360**	**$88,655**	**$117,390**	**13%**
Compensation Expense							
Goldman Sachs	$7,700	$6,744	$7,393	$3,606	$11,688	$16,415	16%
Lehman Brothers	$3,427	$3,139	$4,318	$5,730	$7,213	$8,669	20%
Merrill Lynch	$12,685	$10,677	$9,810	$10,663	$12,441	$16,860	6%
Morgan Stanley	$8,625	$7,170	$7,726	$9,853	$11,313	$13,986	10%
Group	**$32,447**	**$27,730**	**$29,247**	**$35,852**	**$42,655**	**$55,930**	**12%**

Source: Company reports

As is evident from Table 2.2, all the major independent investment banks enjoyed a sharp acceleration in their revenues and, not surprisingly, in their compensation expense. Even with the rush of wealth flooding the halls of these banks, Lehman stood out as exceptional with its 21% compound annual growth in revenues from 2001 to 2006. Equally exceptional was the compensation at the firm. Richard Fuld, Lehman's CEO, earned over $80 million during 2006 and 2007. The other bank chiefs also made out well. Lloyd Blankfein, the CEO of Goldman, pulled in $54 million in 2006, and John Mack, the CEO of Morgan Stanley, made just under $47 million in the same year. The investment banks quickly learned in the credit boom that using cheap money to increasingly expand their operations into the securitization boom was profitable to everyone involved, especially at the top of the organization. Without surprise, we have once again identified players in the credit boom who were borrowing vast sums in short-term funding to tie up in assets with less-than-ideal liquidity. Far from being alone in their exposure to real estate credits, mortgage-backed securities, and CDOs, the investment banks were not the only ones to figure out how to make this system of low interest rates and growth in credit issuance work to their advantage. In fact, the commercial banks were just as eager to play the credit boom. This was despite the fact that commercial banks were more apt and designed to hold loans on their own balance sheets and assume more credit risk (but within the confines of lower allowed leverage than the investment banks due to regulation). Based on available data from the Federal Reserve, U.S. chartered commercial banks grew their mortgage portfolios at a 12.0% compounded annual growth rate from 2002 to 2007, as shown in Figure 2.2. Clearly, this growth was exceptionally high for a mature low-single-digit growth economy and implied that the industry was pushing the envelope on who could receive financing.

Even more ominous than the strong growth in mortgage issuance that occurred in the credit boom was the increasing concentration of real estate loans held on the books of the U.S. chartered commercial banks. Based on data from the Federal Deposit Insurance Corporation (FDIC) dating all the way back to 1934, Figure 2.3 shows that as 2006 came to a close, real estate loans comprised 57.4% of the total loan portfolios in the banking system, an all-time high. Again we can surmise that 2006 was probably the worst possible year to have an all-time high exposure of loans to real-estate-related ventures. But then again, March 2000 would have been the worst possible time to hold a portfolio dedicated to technology shares. The simple fact that all the banks were so heavily concentrated in real estate is deeply foreboding from a contrarian perspective.

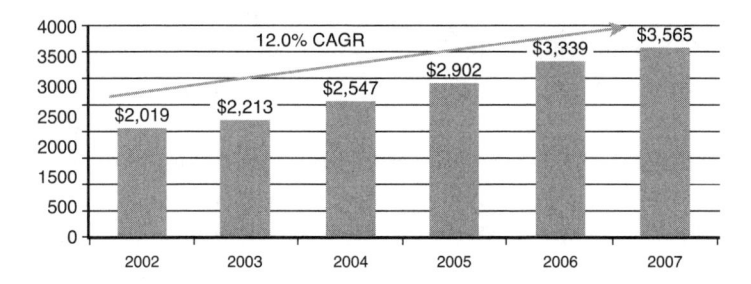

Figure 2.2 U.S. chartered commercial banks' total mortgages
Source: Federal Reserve

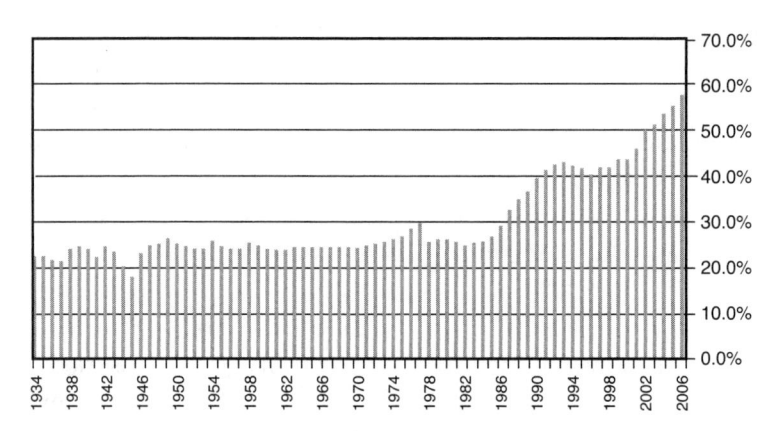

Figure 2.3 Real estate loans as a percentage of total loans
Source: FDIC

The Credit Bubble Draws in Every Last Bull

So the stodgy old bankers proved to be risk takers after all. As we said earlier, finance is a commoditized business. If someone is making extra normal returns in an area, it will not be long before the whole industry converges on the scene and pushes down returns on capital to nil. One after another, nearly every financial business in the United States (and beyond, for that matter) was exploiting the credit boom and real estate bubble, through whatever means relevant to their raison d'etre.

Actually, getting hooked into this mess did not always require being a financial business. As the credit boom stumbled along toward its inevitable letdown, many run-of-the-mill commercial producers and retailers of goods tried their hand at the game as well by opening or heavily expanding preexisting financing arms. From a business manager's standpoint, why not? These finance businesses can carry nice returns on equity through the application of leverage, which can boost profits in an otherwise-mature business. Formally known as Industrial Loan Companies (ILCs), during the credit boom many otherwise-nonbanking enterprises took advantage of an old state chartered banking classification from 1910 that allowed commercial businesses to set up internal financing arms. The idea back in 1910 was to provide unsecured credit for workers at industrial companies because this was a lending business that traditional banks did not engage in at the time. Originally barred from accepting deposits, the ILCs created "thrift certificates" that were de facto deposits under a different name in order to be legal. Because ILCs were barred from taking deposits, they were also disallowed from having FDIC insurance. In 1982, however, the passage of the Garn–St. Germain Depository Institution Act provided for FDIC insurance on thrift certificates. This regulatory change precipitated stronger growth in the category. By the credit boom of the early 2000s, many well-known nonbanking enterprises had become big players in the banking space. For instance, General Electric, General Motors, Target, Harley-Davidson, BMW, Pitney Bowes, and Toyota all had sizable banking businesses, subject to less supervision than what would otherwise apply to a run-of-the-mill chartered banking institution. An example gives you an idea of the type of growth these ILC banks experienced. In 1987 the ILCs had $4.2 billion in assets, and by 2006, as the credit boom was cresting, the ILCs possessed *$212 billion* in assets. In other words, these businesses posted annualized growth in their various loan books of 22.9% per year from 1987 to 2006. These businesses were doubling in size every three years. This is an irresistible growth rate if you are the largest automobile maker in the world (GM) that is operating primarily in mature-growth economies. To put this in perspective, before GM moved to sell off a stake in GMAC during 2006, GMAC was chipping in approximately 80% of GM's profits. For all intents and purposes, by the peak of the credit boom GM was a finance company that sold cars on the side.

As the credit boom persisted from its humble beginnings in 2001 to its juggernaut status in 2006, it sucked in as many parties as existed for the taking. Even the most boring, plain-vanilla financial vehicles fell prey to this environment as money market funds, the pooled funds that try to invest cash in near-term instruments for a small yield, gobbled up CDOs. In hindsight, we can reasonably ask what money market funds, charged with safekeeping cash and eking out a small yield, were doing in CDOs. For this, we can again partly thank the credit rating agencies for their AAA seals of approval. The AAA CDOs often produced higher yields than similar AAA-rated instruments that the money market funds were required to hold. Therefore, the fund managers were more than happy to toss these investments into their funds alongside all those sleepy T-bills and certificates of deposit. In short, these holdings made their yields more competitive and still met their "high quality" investment restrictions. In bubbles past, housewives hit the streets of London to trade stock in the South Sea Bubble of the early eighteenth century, and octogenarians traded tech stocks in 2000. Now even the most conservative and unlikely of candidates, the money market funds, had become creditors to the subprime bonanza. In sum, once the last bulls on a bubble get drawn into the mix, no bulls are left in the market to drive the assets higher. And as the market exhausts its supply of bulls, it is set to turn. As this activity fed on itself from that fateful day of June 25, 2003, two major components of the U.S. economy, the consumer and the financial institutions, moving in sync with each other guided their balance sheets into increasingly uncharted territory.

If one clear conclusion can be drawn from Figure 2.4, it is that the U.S. consumer and U.S. financial sector had taken on aggressive debt levels. We can appreciate the large rise in the early 2000s as compared to the preceding 50 years shown in the figure. But based on an even longer-term perspective, U.S. households were taking on debt levels not seen since the Great Depression. That was the last time household debt was in the range of 100% of gross domestic product (GDP).

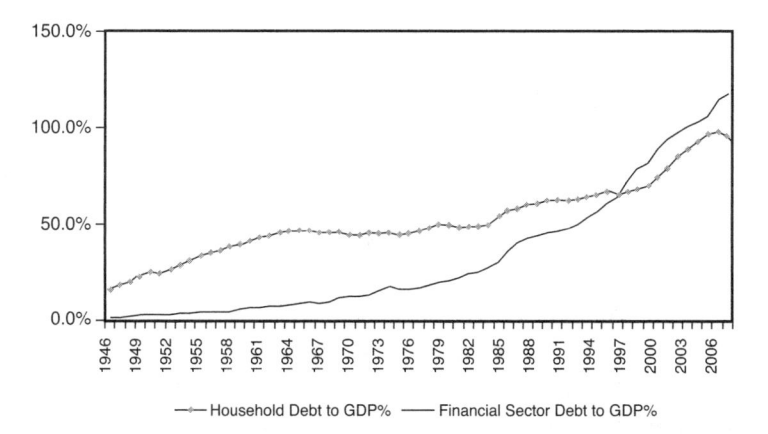

Figure 2.4 U.S. debt to GDP ratios for household and financial sectors

Source: Federal Reserve

This was an ominous sign. Just as the liabilities side of the consumer's balance sheet was hitting its highest level since the 1930s, the assets on the other side of the balance sheet were beginning to show signs of weakness. This nascent dynamic in the housing market signaled potentially grave financial circumstances for any borrowers who were overextended. If housing-related assets fell in value, any debt backing them would stay the same in the absence of being paid down ahead of schedule. If we use the Case-Shiller home price index as our market proxy, as shown in Figure 2.5, housing prices across the 20 MSAs included in the most comprehensive version of the index had risen over 85% since the beginning of 2001. They hit an all-time high in July 2006.

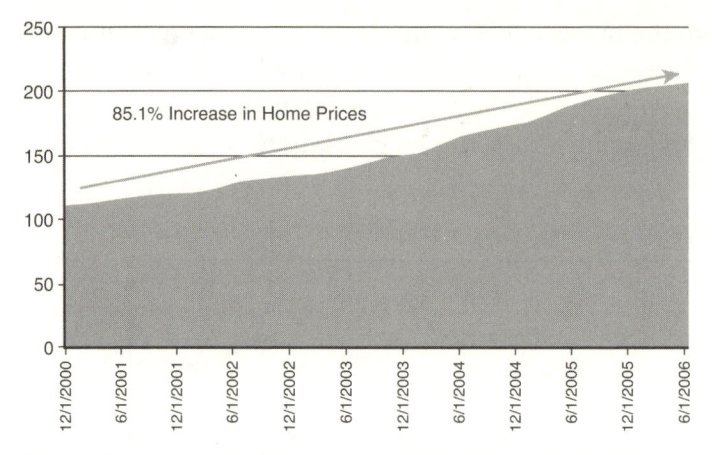

Figure 2.5 Case-Shiller composite 20 home price index
Source: Bloomberg

In 2005, three years before the crisis erupted and while the world's economies were still riding high on the wave of optimism resulting from unchecked spending and easy access to credit, one of the world's greatest investors penned a memo to his friends, associates, and managers. Rather than displaying optimism, as was customary for Sir John Templeton, he compiled the following thoughts and comments into a piece he titled "Financial Chaos":

MEMORANDUM

Financial Chaos—probably in many nations in the next five years. The word chaos is chosen to express likelihood of reduced profit margin at the same time as acceleration in cost of living.

By John M. Templeton

June 15, 2005

Increasingly often, people ask my opinion on what is likely to happen financially. I am now thinking that the dangers are more numerous and larger than ever before in my lifetime. Quite likely, in the early months of 2005, the peak of prosperity is behind us.

In the past century, protection could be obtained by keeping your net worth in cash or government bonds. Now, the surplus capacities are so great that most currencies and bonds are likely to continue losing their purchasing power.

Mortgages and other forms of debt are over tenfold greater now than ever before 1970, which can cause manifold increases in bankruptcy auctions.

Surplus capacity, which leads to intense competition, has already shown devastating effects on companies that operate airlines and is now beginning to show in companies in ocean shipping and other activities. Also, the present surpluses of cash and liquid assets have pushed yields on bonds and mortgages almost to zero when adjusted for higher cost of living. Clearly, major corrections are likely in the next few years.

Most of the methods of universities and other schools that require residence have become hopelessly obsolete. Probably over half of the universities in the world will disappear as quickly as the next thirty years.

Obsolescence is likely to have a devastating effect in a wide variety of human activities, especially in those where advancement is hindered by labor unions or other bureaucracies or by government regulations.

Increasing freedom of competition is likely to cause most established institutions to disappear within the next fifty years, especially in nations where there are limits on free competition.

Accelerating competition is likely to cause profit margins to continue to decrease and even become negative in various industries. Over tenfold more persons hopelessly indebted leads to multiplying bankruptcies not only for them but for many businesses that extend credit without collateral. Voters are likely to enact rescue subsidies, which transfer the debts to governments, such as Fannie Mae and Freddie Mac.

Research and discoveries and efficiency are likely to continue to accelerate. Probably, as quickly as fifty years, as much as ninety percent of education will be done by electronics.

Now, with almost one hundred independent nations on earth and rapid advancements in communication, the top one percent of people are likely to progress more rapidly than others. Such top one percent may consist of those who are multimillionaires and also, those who are innovators and also, those with top intellectual abilities. Comparisons show that prosperity flows toward those nations having most freedom of competition.

Especially, electronic computers are likely to become helpful in all human activities including even persons who have not yet learned to read.

Hopefully, many of you can help us to find published journals and websites and electronic search engines to help us benefit from accelerating research and discoveries.

Not yet have I found any better method to prosper during the future financial chaos, which is likely to last many years, than to keep your net worth in shares of those corporations that have proven to have the widest profit margins and the most rapidly increasing profits. Earning power is likely to continue to be valuable, especially if diversified among many nations.

In 2005, these words represented a dark forecast of events to come. By 2008, they proved eerily prophetic.

Endnotes

[1] Sam Jones, Gillian Tett, and Paul J. Davies. "Moody's error gave top ratings to debt products." *Financial Times*, May 20, 2008.

[2] Richard Rodriguez. "Absence of Fear." A speech given at the CFA Society of Chicago, June 28, 2007, http://www.fpafunds.com/news_070703_absense_of_fear.asp.

[3] Lee A. Pickard. "Viewpoint: SEC's Old Capital Approach Was Tried—and True." *American Banker*, August 8, 2008.

3

Financial Chaos

As the second half of 2006 progressed, all the reckless financial behavior that had underpinned the constant buying and selling of properties up to that point during the credit boom was starting to collapse under its own weight. In our earlier discussion of gimmicky loans and their explosive penetration into housing finance, we detailed how the majority of those loans were adjustable-rate mortgages (ARMs) whose low interest rates were set to expire after a given period of time. Because this form of financing was most preferred among speculators whose only intention was to play the rising prices, it actually created what amounted to a ticking time bomb of selling activity. In other words, as the ARMs on these waves of speculative purchases approached their reset dates, more and more houses were placed on the market, which increased supply. Likewise, as the rates began to reset in 2006 on the 2/28 ARMs (two years fixed, 28 years floating), the payments that these stretched purchasers had to make in order to carry their inventory of listings began to spike. This created a greater sense of urgency among the sellers. Still other sellers, the bottom-of-the-barrel subprime borrowers who were piling into the market toward the end thanks to aggressive mortgage brokers, were now going belly-up on their loans in as little as a month or two into their purchase. The net effect of these fundamental drivers was that by the end of 2006, the supply of vacant homes for sale on the entire U.S. market had jumped 34% from the beginning of the year (see Figure 3.1). Although eye-catching, this data does not even do justice to more specific geographic areas such as the Northeast that had been more deeply affected by the credit boom. There, vacant homes for sale had increased nearly 100% from a year earlier. Suddenly, many forces in the market were beginning to conspire against the tired bull, and, not surprisingly, its legs began to slow.

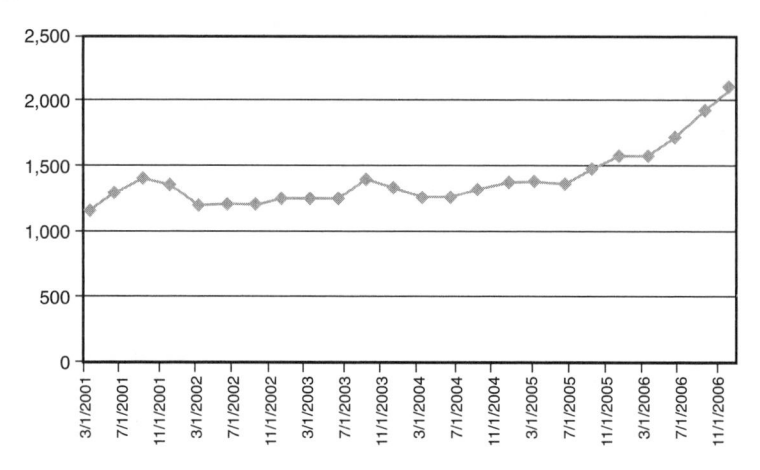

Figure 3.1 Vacant housing units for sale (in thousands)
Source: U.S. Census Bureau

Prices in the housing market began to give way under the pressure of increasingly desperate sellers and rising defaults. Sometimes there is no better way to capture a moment than to go back and examine what was being said at the time. A July 30, 2006 article in the *New York Times*, "Taking the Measure of the Market,"[1] featured an interview with a real estate agent in Long Beach, New York. She described a recent experience with a couple who had just listed their home: "A couple in their late 30s came in to price their three-bedroom ranch. The interest rate on their mortgage had risen to 9.5 percent, from 3.5 percent three years ago. They didn't have the equity or good credit to qualify for refinancing at a lower rate. To make matters worse, on July 1 the City of Long Beach raised property taxes 25 percent. They needed to get out because they were so overwhelmed.'" As more and more sellers attempted to unload on the market because their ARM was resetting, due to a simple inability to keep up with so many payments, or because of the race to get out, prices in the market continued to decline as 2006 moved into 2007. As the "not possible" reality of falling home prices firmly set in during 2007 (see Figure 3.2), it was clear that the rush to get out of real estate was trending toward a stampede.

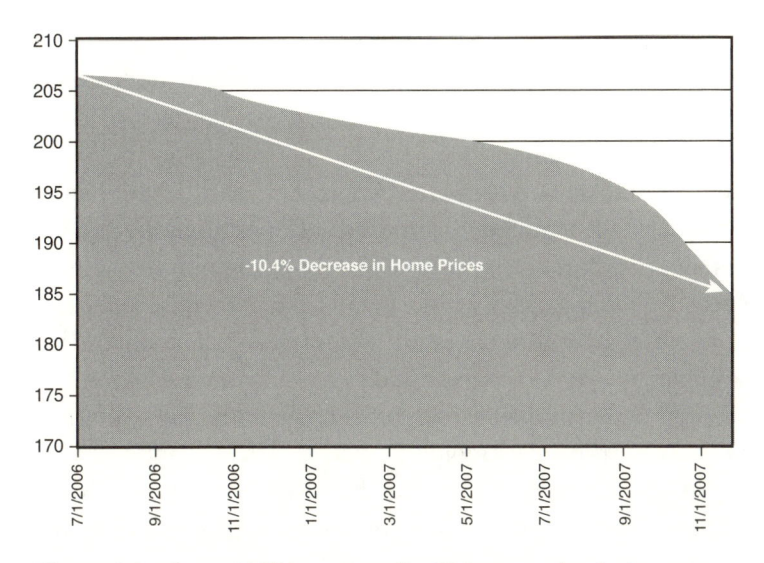

Figure 3.2 Case-Shiller composite 20 home price index
Source: Bloomberg

As prices in the housing market continued to decline during 2007, defaults on subprime mortgages continued to surge. Based on data from Bloomberg, the number of subprime mortgages that had gone 90 days without payment (that were in default) taken as a percentage of the total was 6.6% at the beginning of 2006. By the end of 2007, this number had climbed to a staggering 15.8% of the total in only 12 months. The jump in defaults during 2007 started to produce more visible effects on the financial system as a multitude of mortgage lenders started to drop like flies due to the carnage. In 2007, about 200 mortgage lenders failed—and this was only what was reported. The problems facing mortgage lenders in 2007 were numerous. For one thing, the existing inventory of loans in the system was going south through default. Second, lenders' sources of funding relied on cash flows from sales or near-term borrowings, because many of these largest mortgage originators were not deposit-based institutions. Among these types of large nondeposit institutions that came to dominate mortgage origination, Countrywide Financial was the poster child for rapid growth, corporate excesses, and eventually a total meltdown. Countrywide, much like the consumers it lent to and the creditors it borrowed from, was heavily reliant on being able to continuously borrow in short-term loans to fund its operations. In August 2007, Countrywide got an up-close preview of what happens when suddenly a lending institution cannot access sources of near-term debt as its own lenders turn to it and say, "No more for you." The firm had to quickly borrow $11.5 billion from 40 different banks. Countrywide was accustomed to funding its operations by issuing commercial paper (short-term debt paid back in nine months or less). In the weeks preceding August, the firm claimed to have had easy access to over $50 billion of the stuff. By mid-August, though, that access had changed, and changed quickly. As Countrywide went to the commercial paper market to borrow money, no lenders could be found. As it were, the investments tied to subprime lending were unraveling so quickly that the market for loans shut down almost instantly. This ostensibly spelled game over for mortgage lenders that relied on obtaining short-term borrowings to fund their operations. Figure 3.3 shows a brief timeline of some key events tied to this phenomenon in 2007. It includes the Bear Stearns hedge funds implosions, Countrywide's liquidity crunch, and the massive write-downs of subprime-related securities held on the books of the investment banks in October 2007.

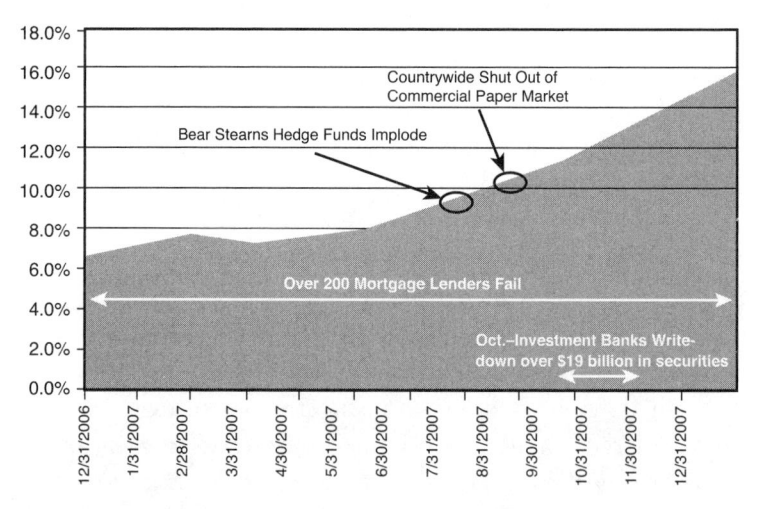

Figure 3.3 Subprime mortgage delinquency rates 90+ days as a percentage of the total

Source: Bloomberg, ml-implode.com

As defaults on subprime loans surged during 2007, consequences arose across the financial system. Entities that had invested in the collateralized debt obligation (CDO) products that were tied to these loans also started to default, causing large losses among hedge funds and the investment banks that held the securities. Likewise, the market for issuing new CDOs on which the investment banks had become so reliant as a part of their earnings stream also evaporated beginning in the third quarter of 2007 (see Figure 3.4). As investors were being stung by rapid losses in their portfolios, their appetite for more of the securities went from rabid to practically nonexistent in a little over a year.

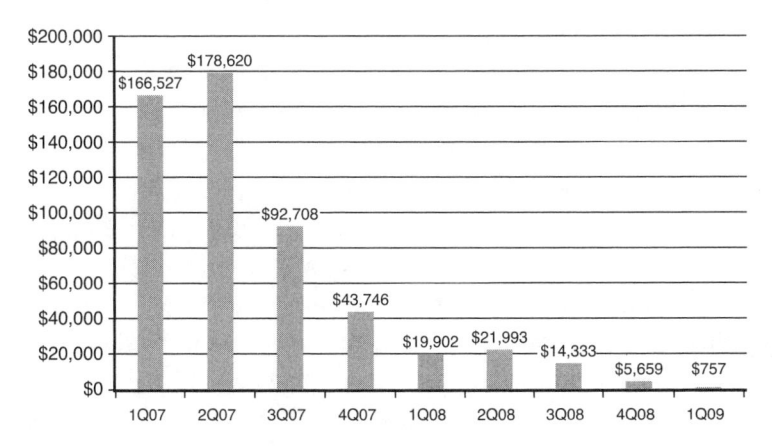

Quarter	CDO Issuance ($ millions)
1Q07	$166,527
2Q07	$178,620
3Q07	$92,708
4Q07	$43,746
1Q08	$19,902
2Q08	$21,993
3Q08	$14,333
4Q08	$5,659
1Q09	$757

Figure 3.4 CDO issuance in millions of dollars

Source: SIFMA

The closing of the CDO market should have meant the quick dismantling of a ridiculous investing paradigm in which investment banks were facilitating reckless lending to consumers and selling their institutional clients overpriced slop. But that was wishful thinking. The game had persisted long enough to present substantial problems on a broader scale. As the investment banks found that the market for their CDO issues was drying up, the inventory that they were constructing for sale began to back up onto their shelves. Instead of being a mere conduit from the borrowers to the creditors, the investment banks had become de facto creditors during late 2007 and into

2008. In the meantime, in the stock market the subprime debacle had certainly grabbed headlines and was on investors' minds, but by and large it remained somewhat of a novelty. Stock investors on average continued to see the subprime mess as a problem contained to reckless borrowers and the fixed-income investors who had become their creditors. On October 2, 2007, a *New York Times* article titled "Stocks Soar on Hopes Credit Crisis Is Over"[2] captured the mood. One commentator's quote in particular summarized the feeling: "Whatever problems emerged last quarter are last quarter's problems. They're over; that's it; they're done. So let's move on to the next thing." Although the worsening credit environment, defaults, and tremors created by liquidity problems at Countrywide had not gone unnoticed, there was a general feeling that the worst was over. In fact, on October 9, 2007 the S&P 500 climbed to an all-time high. If October 2007 presented a moment of stock market complacency, the months afterward were marked with deepening worry.

If Bear Stearns was the first investment bank to signal problems cropping up through its various exploitations of the subprime lending market, perhaps it was apropos that it was the first investment banking firm to be shown the door from the public market. By March 2008, the firm had already been through the ringer for its losses in the subprime market. Along with several other investment banks, Bear had reported its first-ever loss on its quarterly income in the prior quarter. Bear's chairman, James Cayne, had ceded his CEO title in January to the firm's widely respected top investment banker, Alan Schwartz. Mr. Schwartz had the unfortunate job of trying to extinguish a growing firestorm of distrust. People doubted that Bear Stearns could continue to exist under the weight of its losses and exposure to mortgage-backed securities given its number two position as a mortgage-backed securities issuer behind Lehman Brothers. One of the unique qualities of financial firms is that prophecies can become instantaneously self-fulfilling. In mid March 2008, Bear's creditors were beginning to pull back on the money they extended to the firm in short-term loans. Even worse, Bear's clients began to withdraw their assets from their accounts. This was an old-fashioned Depression-style run on the bank, in an updated 2.0 version. Incidentally, the short-term loans and client assets provided much-needed liquidity that cushioned Bear against the write-downs in mortgage-related securities. On March 12, 2008, Mr. Schwartz appeared on CNBC. "The reluctant CEO," as he came to be known due to his rather ad hoc appointment, talked down the growing skepticism of Bear's financial condition. Despite his best efforts to channel Jimmy Stewart in a reprise of George Bailey, confidence in Bear had already been too destroyed to stave off the ensuing run. In just a matter of days, Bear Stearns' cash position had fallen nearly 70%, from $18.3 billion to $5.9 billion. Hedge fund clients, trading partners, creditors, and bond funds almost simultaneously broke their ties with the firm and pulled their money. Recognizing that drastic times call for drastic measures, Mr. Schwartz phoned James Dimon, the CEO of J.P. Morgan, at a family gathering for his 52nd birthday. He suggested urgently that something needed to be done before Bear went under. Using the Federal Reserve as the backstop to guarantee the credit, J.P. Morgan announced that it would provide Bear Stearns with as much credit as needed over the coming 28 days. Although the stock traded down 47% on Friday, March 14 following the news, Schwartz felt as if he had bought the necessary time to find a suitor to buy the firm. Not so fast. According to later reports from the *Wall Street Journal*, Mr. Schwartz did not even make it home that Friday before Treasury Secretary Henry Paulson and New York Federal Reserve President Timothy Geithner phoned him. They told him he needed to have a deal worked out to sell Bear by Sunday night. As it turned out, and in the face of much employee and investor dissent, Bear Stearns announced that it would be sold to J.P. Morgan at $2 a share on Sunday, March 16. In what amounted to a costly oversight based on reports from the *Wall Street Journal*, the terms of the contract allowed for the guaranteed backing of financing Bear's trading activity for a year. As Mr. Dimon discovered this detail, he contacted Mr. Schwartz, informing him that "we" have a problem. But the beleaguered banker had finally caught a break, and he simply responded "What do you mean 'we'?" Realizing that Bear shareholders could vote down the deal and still keep Bear running for a year thanks to the financing guarantee, J.P. Morgan raised its offer to $10 a share, and the deal was done. The deal allowed Bear to survive in the corporate nest of J.P. Morgan. The firm's shareholders received a lesson in how swiftly these firms could unravel thanks to their massive leverage and just how vulnerable they were to losses in the mortgage-related securities held on the books of the investment banks. In just a week's time, prior to the revamped $10 deal, Bear shareholders had lost 92% of their money in the stock.

As the summer of 2008 began to move toward fall, the situation in the mortgage default arena was transitioning from calamity to meltdown. By July 2008 nearly one quarter of the loans made in the subprime category of the mortgage market were defaulting. This deterioration produced more casualties. They were becoming larger and even more headline-grabbing as the seventh-largest mortgage lender, IndyMac Corp., failed and was seized by regulators. We pick up in the action by extending our earlier subprime default timeline, as shown in Figure 3.5.

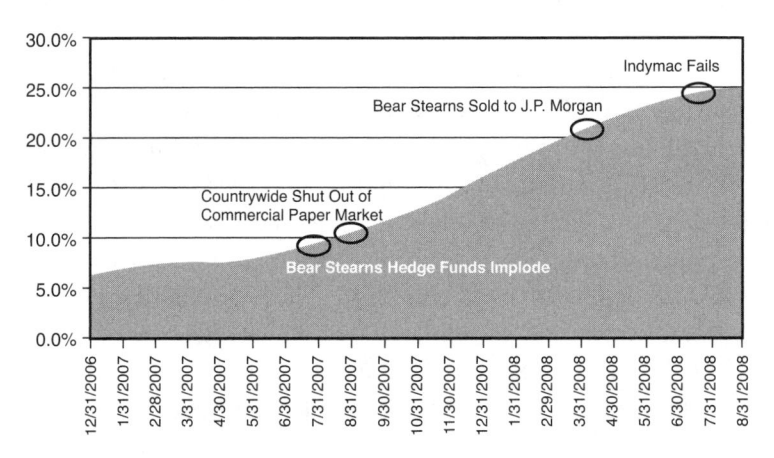

Figure 3.5 Subprime mortgage delinquency rates 90+ days as a percentage of the total

Source: Bloomberg

During the summer of 2008, the foreclosure crisis was reaching such a fever pitch that there was rampant news of borrowers who simply walked away from their homes. They had decided that they were too far underwater on their home loans (market value less than loan outstanding) due to a combination of aggressive financing and a continued decline in house prices. Based on data from Moody's,[3] by the summer of 2008 approximately 9 million households, or 10.3% of all single-family homes, were underwater on their loans. Most notable were reports of relatively high-profile celebrities who had been sucked into the credit craze. To start, there were reports that the retired Major Leaguer and American League MVP Jose Canseco had walked away from his $2.5 million home near Los Angeles. Likewise, there were reports that Ed McMahon, Johnny Carson's longtime sidekick, was facing foreclosure after becoming $644,000 in arrears on payments tied to his plush Beverly Hills abode. While engaging, and capturing the public's attention, these events were merely sideshows to the main event that was about to unfold in September 2008.

The Crisis Moves from Subprime to Prime Time

In the second week of August 2008, the *New York Times* ran an article titled "Mortgage Giants to Buy Fewer Risky Home Loans."[4] It described the staggering losses that were now unfolding in the financial statements of Fannie Mae and Freddie Mac. The headline was responding to comments from Fannie Mae executives who were now attempting to push back from the trough after reporting losses that were three times greater than analysts' estimates for the recent quarter ended. The executives at Fannie Mae unveiled their plans to cease purchasing Alt-A mortgages by year end and said that generally they would slow their overall purchase of mortgages. Although they were a little late in the game, these moves were probably essential for the government-sponsored entity if it were to have any hope of not failing as losses continued to mount. At the same time, these decisions could spell disaster for the already-reeling mortgage market as ARMs were resetting. Any pushback in demand from the only clowns still buying these mortgages would send mortgage rates skyrocketing and break the backs of borrowers who were still vulnerable to higher rates. Also in August, Freddie Mac had announced in its earnings filings that there was "a significant possibility that continued adverse developments" could cause the firm to fall below its government-mandated capital levels. This may have well been code that the end was near, because there was no sign of relief in the housing market. Incidentally, Treasury Secretary Paulson had already received approval from

Congress to deploy funds to rescue the firms should that become necessary. In early September, the necessary occurred, and Fannie Mae and Freddie Mac were placed into conservatorship by the U.S. government. In one day of trading, shortly after the government's announcement, shares in Fannie Mae fell 90% to close at $0.73.

Financial chaos had arrived. Next the focus shifted to the mortgage-backed mavericks at Lehman Brothers, who were scrambling for alternative courses of action as they too faced a loss of confidence in the market in almost identical fashion to Bear Stearns six months earlier. One idea that Mr. Fuld, the CEO of Lehman, was considering was jettisoning the rotting subprime assets from the firm's balance sheet in a spin-off move following the "good bank/bad bank" model from historical banking crises. In any event, in the week leading up to Fannie and Freddie's takeover, Lehman was still seen as a viable going concern in a rough patch. Even *Mad Money*'s Jim Cramer saw the stock as a "screaming buy." As the Fannie and Freddie news hit and trading opened on Monday, September 8, the picture for Lehman as it was portrayed in the stock market was set to unravel. Many investors and financial pundits had likened Lehman's situation to that of Bear Stearns and figured that another version of a U.S. government-brokered transaction would emerge. This widely held consensus was primed to take a major hit on Tuesday, though, as three pieces of information were about to enter the market. To begin with, Lehman had been in talks to raise funds through an equity stake purchased by the Korea Development Bank. As these talks reportedly fell through on Tuesday, Lehman shares dropped 45%. Then, on Wednesday, the firm reported a $3.9 billion loss for its most recent quarter. As is often the case, the credit rating agencies came in belatedly and pointed out the obvious—that the firm needed capital, or even a partner, to get on stronger financial footing. Nevertheless, on Thursday the stock fell another 42%. With the stock now down to just $4.22, from $16.22 on the previous Friday, some white knights had started to reveal themselves. As reported in the *Wall Street Journal*, Bank of America and Barclays were showing interest in a possible purchase of some kind. At the same time, in comments that might not have been taken at their full value, the U.S. government was posturing that Lehman would need to take care of itself. Also, Federal funds would likely be unavailable, as they were in the Bear Stearns transaction. In an outspoken version of this message, William Poole, the former president of the Federal Reserve of St. Louis, gave an interview[5] that Thursday. He stated, "Absolutely, I would say we cannot provide assistance in this case... This case is different, and we're not going to provide that assistance, and you've got to make your own decision. We'll help you work through it, but we're not going to give you any cash... Lehman needs to resolve this situation quickly, and the more quickly, the better." This advice proved prescient, but as Friday's trading concluded, Lehman shares had fallen a modest 14% in comparison to sessions earlier in the week. Many believed that, like Bear Stearns before it, Lehman would hash out a deal over the weekend, since Bank of America and Barclays were clearly kicking the tires. That Friday afternoon, though, Treasury Secretary Paulson and New York Fed President Geithner called in the heads of the largest investment banks in New York for a meeting. According to reports in the *New York Times*, Geithner stressed to the investment banking heads that the U.S. government would not put taxpayer money on the line for this rescue, and that the ball was in the court of these bank chiefs. What Paulson and Geithner hoped for was a replay of the events in 1998, when the investment banks pooled resources to stave off the collapse of Long Term Capital Management. Ultimately, though, no agreement could be reached, and Bank of America, lacking the form of U.S. government guarantee that was in place for the Bear Stearns deal, also backed out. The last hope was Barclays, which was still interested but that simply could not arrange the necessary shareholder vote by Monday morning in accord with London Stock Exchange rules in order to approve a transaction. Lehman had reached the end of the line. In what proved to be a busy weekend for Wall Street bankers and the government officials from the Fed and Treasury who were charged with overseeing the chaos, Treasury Secretary Paulson received additional word that the world's largest insurance company, AIG, was on the verge of collapse. AIG was not an obvious casualty of the subprime fiasco until the late innings of the game. The firm was well known for its size, strong balance sheet, and reach into the global insurance markets. But like many other financial firms in the credit bonanza, it had spotted and successfully exploited its own role in the credit mania. It would write insurance against the potential default of CDOs by selling an instrument called a credit default swap (CDS). AIG Financial Products (AIGFP), which was the small division of the insurance giant responsible for underwriting the business, was incredibly buoyant and confident in the fast-growing earnings stream it had produced over the years. In what can only now be seen as a fit of hubris reserved for instances of "pride goeth before a fall," in 2007, the head of AIGFP made the following comment to an audience during a presentation: "It is hard for us, without being flippant, to even see a scenario within any kind of realm of reason that would see us losing one dollar in any of those transactions."[6] A little over a year later, AIG's small financial products division, with only 377 employees compared to the 116,000 employed throughout the company, was on the verge of taking down the entire conglomerate, and perhaps more. Sophisticated financial risk engineers apparently overlooked the simple arithmetic of what could happen if you suddenly owe too many people too much money all at once by trying to guarantee these CDOs. In financial parlance, these risks are often called "fat tailed" risk in reference to their probabilities lying so many standard deviations from the mean, or in the "fat tails" of the risk curve. The financial markets and the world itself have shown us too many times that the occurrence of events does not conform to this risk curve paradigm, yet academics and practitioners alike cling to this idea with unwavering resolve. In any event, the message Mr. Paulson received that weekend in September as Lehman was headed toward a bankruptcy filing was that AIG needed at least $30 billion to $40 billion immediately—or else. The Federal Reserve and Treasury were sufficiently spooked by the potential fallout from AIG's counterparties, which included the investment banks, as well as a global spider web of financial firms. As the weekend concluded, Lehman was thrown out into the cold, and it faced a bankruptcy filing the next day. AIG was a matter that had been heavily resisted by U.S. government officials, and it remained unresolved. On Monday, September 15, 2008, Lehman filed for bankruptcy, and its stock collapsed in a 94% decline. In just a little over a week, more than $11 billion of shareholder wealth had been vaporized.

As all eyes turned to AIG, and U.S. government officials had not intervened, its stock too entered free fall. On Wednesday of the same week, sufficiently concerned with how many businesses would be deeply affected by AIG's failure, the U.S. government surprised nearly everyone with an offer of a two-year loan of $85 billion and the issue of warrants that could be exercised to control 80% of AIG's shares. While the lifeline meant that AIG would continue as a going concern, shareholders had been whipsawed by a 91% decline in a mere week and a half. Shareholders also had taken a backseat to the U.S. government, which had, for all intents and purposes, just nationalized the country's largest insurer. The financial markets were tenuous, and these were unmistakably uncharted waters for investors accustomed to comparatively laissez faire markets. Far from being over, though, the week had already provided additional fireworks. Merrill Lynch, sensing its own mortality during the Lehman powwow, had sneaked off with Bank of America in what amounted to a corporate makeout session to see if the two could get along as partners. Incidentally, the CEO of Bank of America, Ken Lewis, and the CEO of Merrill, John Thain, thought the firms made a good pair. So a deal for B of A to buy Merrill through a stock transaction was announced. Despite Merrill's status as a Wall Street icon with its famous bull, it too had been deeply mired in the mortgage security debacle. It had already taken $45 billion in write-downs and ousted its CEO, Stanley O'Neal. Far from being complacent over the subprime crisis, Thain had already been raising money in a total of seven transactions. These included selling assets such as the firm's stake in the Bloomberg empire, completing an equity offering for $9.8 billion, and unloading mortgage-related assets at deep discounts. Although this was a disappointing end for many who cherished the firm's independent culture, at least it could now live for another day. Its chances of doing so without a deal were slim. Needless to say, the broader equity markets did not digest this information with ease. Measures of volatility for the stock market such as the volatility index (VIX) rose sharply, as what was once seen as a subprime problem was now looking like a *prime time* problem. In a matter of weeks in September 2008, the markets for financial instruments of all varieties were being called into question. Bankers who would have lent to anyone just a year ago with no proof of income suddenly would not even lend to their thrifty grandmother. Lending institutions around the world almost instantly and all at once realized the severity of the situation and cut off lending in nearly all forms, launching into a state of self-preservation. Anyone and everyone who attempted to borrow under these conditions was presumed guilty before being proven innocent. GMAC, the industrial loan company (ILC) of GM, found this out when it borrowed one-week commercial paper at an interest rate of 5.25%. U.S. Treasuries rallied so sharply in a flight to safety from all other assets that yields shot to zero on near-term issues. The entire stock market continued to seesaw in wild gyrations and fits of anxiety. On September 25, just a week or so after the initial shock and awe began, the largest bank failure in U.S. history was announced. The Fed seized Washington Mutual, and the firm was promptly sold to J.P. Morgan. As the panic heightened surrounding nearly all financial instruments, one of the more unimaginable events that unfolded was when the money market mutual funds "broke the buck." Breaking the buck means that investors who had stored their cash savings in a money market fund with the expectation that every dollar invested would still equal at least a dollar when they went to withdraw their funds suddenly heard otherwise. As we said earlier, money market funds had been enticed by the fool's gold of AAA ratings on CDOs and had bought these instruments for their funds. As the crisis increased in intensity, one dollar invested was suddenly worth $0.97, and the fund managers halted redemptions, thereby locking up investors' cash. The anxiety this created among the innocents of the world, with little hands-on knowledge of the turmoil ravaging the financial markets, was now palpable. In an article from Bloomberg titled "Reserve Fund Investors Wonder When They Will Get Access to Their Cash" from September 29, an investor in the famous and well-reputed originator of the money market funds had this to say: "When I ask TD Ameritrade when I can get my hands on my money, they refuse to give me an answer. I have insomnia, heart palpitations—my entire life seems to be in disarray."[7]

If the 8.9% decline in the S&P 500 during September was not enough for investors, the 16.8% decline in October surely would be. With the crisis still rampaging through the credit markets in October, Wachovia, whose stock had plummeted on the news of the Washington Mutual seizure, began to experience increasingly heavy customer withdrawals in the following days. Over the weekend that followed WaMu's seizure, Wachovia was bleeding deposits at an alarming rate, according to interviews after the fact, and larger clients were lowering their deposits to under the $100,000 threshold for FDIC insurance. It was clear that confidence in the bank was failing and action was needed. Over the weekend Wachovia mobilized to sell itself and struck a deal with Citigroup, only to later sell itself in another offer from Wells Fargo a few days later instead. Also in the first week of October, AIG was back in line with its hat in hand. It received an additional $37.8 billion on top of its original $85 billion from just a couple of weeks earlier. This was a remarkable event, because the company had already blown through $61 billion in a just a week or so after having the money. In effect, we can see how the bailout of AIG was just as likely a de facto bailout of the investment banks and others who sat on the counterparty side of the contracts that AIG could not honor in absence of additional funds from the government. So, in the end, there was the taxpayer, getting hammered by house price declines and stock market declines, helping siphon money into AIG, which in turn could honor its reckless insurance contracts, made with reckless investment banks that had leveraged themselves to speculate in the credit mania. Elsewhere in the stock market, many hedge funds that had grown used to applying large amounts of leverage in their portfolios were receiving margin calls to sell and take down their borrowing. In some cases, this was because they were sustaining losses. In other cases it was because their prime broker, a division of an investment bank, was crying uncle and trying to deleverage its own books, raise cash, and eliminate financial risk. The massive deleveraging in the stock market forced the selling into overdrive. As prime brokers instructed funds to raise cash, this forced selling, and the selling forced down share prices, which in turn led to a new round of margin calls. Anyone using too much leverage in this market sell-off would have been wiped out in short order. This market was evolving into a brutal bear that spared no one, from Warren Buffett all the way down to a teenager opening her first stock account.

In the meantime, the political scene in Washington was also in a volatile state. The presidential election race between Barack Obama and John McCain was drawing toward its November 6 conclusion. In Congress, debates were heated over a bailout package in the banking system. By this time it was becoming evident that without the flow of credit through the U.S. financial system (and beyond), the wheels were coming off the economy. In fact, by late October, there was ample evidence that the entire global economy had been stopped in its tracks. Because banks had become too skittish to even transact with one another, ships transporting cargo around the world were stopped before entering port, because the bank had not secured a letter of credit. The exporter would not deliver the goods in absence of a guarantee that it would be paid by the importer, and the banks would not back the purchaser with credit. At the most fundamental level, global commerce had stopped.

The world economy was in a bad spot, and the U.S. consumer who had become so accustomed to the easy flow of credit during the past five years suddenly was experiencing life with little or no access to credit. On top of the sudden withdrawal of credit in the financial system, which was sharply affecting consumers and businesses that relied on access to near-term credit, the U.S. household was now witnessing a reversal in the large amount of wealth it had presumably built since the early 2000s. In short, wealth thought to have been stored in houses and stocks was being destroyed at record speed. In one year, during 2008, Americans saw over $2 trillion of their wealth stored in real estate vanish. As if that were not enough, this same group had lost an additional $3.7 trillion in the stock market. All told, across U.S. households' balance sheet, $11 trillion in net worth was gone by the end of 2008. This meant that despite all the wild spending, house speculation, and general feeling of prosperity that occurred over the past several years, they were actually no better off than they were in 2004 from a net worth perspective. All the supposed wealth that had accumulated had been hitched to a growing mountain of debt, but the wealth was gone and the debt remained (see Figure 3.6). Taken on a historic basis, we can see the effects of what happened and just how much the U.S. consumer's balance sheet expanded its use of debt—debt that in time needs to be paid down.

Feeling whipsawed and disillusioned in the fourth quarter of 2008, Americans sought change and elected it by making Barack Obama their 44th president. In a worsening economic landscape, Americans looked to their government, of all places, for answers despite the thinly veiled reality that the government had facilitated several aspects of the current predicament. In any event, the alarm was sounded, and the cavalry prepared to rush to the scene: bailout mania, spendthrift policy makers, feuding regulators, political favoritism, and all things Washington.

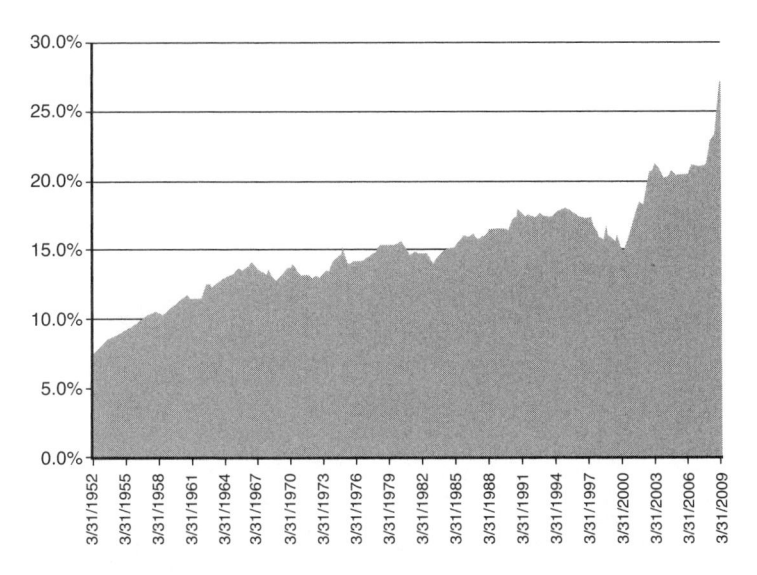

Figure 3.6 Household debt divided by household net worth
Source: Federal Reserve

The free markets are dead; long live the free markets!

Endnotes

[1] Valerie Cotsalas. "Taking the Measure of the Market." *New York Times*, July 30, 2006.

[2] Michael M. Grynbaum. "Stocks Soar on Hopes Credit Crisis Is Over." *New York Times*, October 2, 2007.

[3] Edmund L. Andrews and Louis Uchitelle. "Rescue for Homeowners in Debt Weighed." *New York Times*, February 22, 2008.

[4] Charles Duhigg. "Mortgage Giants to Buy Fewer Risky Home Loans." *New York Times*, August 8, 2008.

[5] William Poole. "Poole Says Fed Shouldn't Give Funding to Any Lehman Agreement." Bloomberg Television, September 12, 2008.

[6] Anna Schecter, Brian Ross, and Justin Rood. "The Executive Who Brought Down AIG." www.abcnews.go.com, March 30, 2009.

[7] Alexis Leondis. "Reserve Fund Investors Wonder When They Will Get Access to Their Cash." Bloomberg, September 29, 2008.

4

Quis Custodiet Ipsos Custodes?

The title of this chapter is a question in Latin: Who will watch the watchers? Many observers of the U.S. government during late 2008 and much of 2009 posed the same question as budget deficits, loose money, and financial rescues with taxpayer money cascaded into a waterfall of financial irresponsibility. The lighthearted corollary of this chapter title may come from Ronald Reagan's famous quote that the nine most terrifying words in the English language are "I'm from the government, and I'm here to help." By no means intended to alienate people along political lines, this quote is only given in reference to the unprecedented levels of government intervention that have occurred in the United States in the wake of the worst financial crisis in a century. Irrespective of political party, the stock market pays attention to spiraling private and public debt balances, runaway monetary policy, double-digit deficits as a percentage of gross domestic product (GDP), and how much of GDP is controlled by the government. If these risks are carried too far, they become everyone's problem. This chapter introduces these developments and shows how they might contribute to risk.

To begin, let's resume our storyline from late 2008. As October 2008 indiscriminately gored investors across the capital markets, the American people looked increasingly to their government for answers. Truth be told, in the fourth quarter of 2008, the gears of the world's markets were grinding to a near halt. The engine was not stalling; it was failing. An entire commercial system based on trust was riddled with distrust, suspicion, and anxiety. The problems that underscored these emotions were very real—many people and banks were sliding toward bankruptcy. People felt that they could not really tell if a business or counterparty on the other side of a transaction could back their side of the deal. Still, this is the nature of the U.S. financial system. The entire economy functions on the back of one word: trust. There is no better way to describe what was occurring in the economy of late 2008 than a total meltdown in trust: "Is my bank safe?" "My sister-in-law said the bank downtown is in trouble." "Should I remove my money?" These words were not whispered among finance-minded people; they were spoken anxiously by cleaning crews in the hallways of office buildings. The fear had become pervasive.

An Alphabet Soup of Rescue Acronyms Will Save Us

The U.S. government, and really the majority of governments around the world, recognized this on some level, at least, and mobilized their efforts to restore trust in the financial system. The situation was perhaps most dire in the United States and the other developed markets, because many of their citizens were dependent on a regular extension of credit. With the banks and credit institutions frozen, and these same lenders afraid to extend overnight loans to one another as they normally do on any given day, the velocity of money in the economy was plummeting. Money became tight and scarce. This economic environment was summoning a ghost that haunts all policy makers and officials in Washington, DC. A white whale was swimming in the Potomac, and its name was deflation. Incidentally, Federal Reserve Chairman Ben Bernanke had dedicated much of his scholarly pursuits to studying the Great Depression. He understood the blunders of the Fed during the Depression. Because he saw it as his raison d'etre, he would not repeat the mistakes of the Captain Ahabs who came generations before him, and he sought to flay this white whale in plain view for all to see. Given that Mr. Bernanke's nickname had for years been "Helicopter Ben," in reference to a Milton Friedman metaphor regarding a helicopter drop of money, no one questioned what was coming—only how far he might be willing to go. We can be sure that Mr. Bernanke's strategy at a minimum was to fight off deflation with whatever requisite political will was necessary. Bernanke was not alone in this call to arms, flanked by long-time Wall Streeter Hank Paulson as the Secretary of the Treasury. Given his background as the former head of Goldman Sachs, Paulson bridged the gap between Washington and Wall Street, for better or worse. At the same time, Paulson's proximity to Wall Street would keep him under ample scrutiny and suspicion of favoring his former firm and others.

Reviewing the record, both Bernanke and Paulson had already begun to respond to the environment prior to the credit freeze and economic meltdown in late 2008. Bernanke, in his role as Fed chief, had already been guiding the Fed Funds rate downward in the first part of 2008; he paused at 2% in April 2008. By the end of October, he had taken off another full percentage point, moving the rate down to 1%. Paulson had already been involved in all the aforementioned bailouts and interventions up until late 2008, including Bear Stearns, Fannie Mae, Freddie Mac, and AIG. Now, with the crisis increasing in severity, this dynamic duo redoubled their efforts and initiated a broader bailout plan in September 2008 for the banking system. The program Paulson devised, called the Troubled Asset Relief Program, or TARP, was met with widespread public criticism at its outset. On September 29, it failed in the House of the Representatives. However, as September rolled into October and the crisis deepened, Congress relented in a second go. It made some modifications and passed the Emergency Economic Stabilization Act, which provided the Treasury with a $700 billion kitty for its TARP. The idea behind TARP was to use funds to buy the heavily depressed collateralized debt obligations (CDOs) off the books of the investment banks and commercial banks. This would hypothetically rid the banks of their bad assets, provide them with cash to lend, and potentially make money for the taxpayer as the bad assets increased in value after the crisis settled. This simple plan quickly morphed into a complicated mess. Six weeks after the bill was passed, Paulson changed the plans. He decided to take the funds and make direct cash infusions into banks through the purchase of preferred stock. Stop the presses! The U.S. government was now wrangling for stakes in commercial banks? The Gipper's team was getting routed before halftime. Not to mention, far from building confidence in policy makers and their ability to restore the financial system to working condition, the public and the stock market became even more anxious because of these developments. Irrespective of criticism, and the overtones of nationalization notwithstanding, this was the course chosen by policy makers. Aside from the banks, and hopefully to no one's surprise, other beggars suddenly came out of the woodwork for these public funds. They included auto manufacturers, state governments with deteriorating fiscal conditions, and insurance companies. As long as Paulson was shifting on the fly, other leaders hopped along for the ride. President Bush decidedly wiggled into the mix and redirected a $17.4 billion slug of the TARP money to the automakers in December. This $700 billion in overall TARP money provided by the taxpayers looked like a chicken leg dropped into a fish tank of piranhas.

Far from sitting on his hands, Mr. Bernanke released another form of rescue plan in November that he had devised for the financial system through his Term Asset-Backed Securities Loan Facility, or TALF. TALF, as it was designed by the Fed, was established to offer one-year financing to firms from the Fed to fund the purchase of asset-backed securities. Because the total dismantling of the securitization market took much-needed liquidity out of the financing markets for consumers, the Fed reasoned that coaxing back investors with sweetheart interest rates and a guarantee on the securities might do the trick and get credit flowing again. The problem was that banks and lending institutions as we know them were in self-preservation mode. Also, the global network of investors who had been buying asset-backed securities, called the "shadow banking system," was missing in action, if not already annihilated from credit losses. The Fed was creating a program that would hopefully resuscitate the shadow banking system. However optimistic, or perhaps naive, the TALF idea was as a facilitator to bringing the securitization market back from the dead, the Fed had already been intervening in the commercial paper markets through its Commercial Paper Funding Facility (CPFF). The CPFF was an October 2008 move by the Fed to step directly into the commercial paper market and assume the role of creditor to firms such as GE that were trying, but unable, to transact in these near-term maturity credit markets.

Problematically for the Federal Reserve and Treasury, their attempts to restore trust in the financial system actually eroded it further. The American public and the stock market recognized that their leaders did not have clear answers. These unelected officials in the Fed and Treasury who were controlling their hard-earned tax money were engaging in a very public version of throwing spaghetti against the wall to see what might stick. To worsen matters, in October 2008, about a week after the tremendous drama surrounding the bailout of AIG and the extension of $85 billion in funds from the public coffers, AIG executives took off on a retreat to a St. Regis spa in California. The event cost the company—or, shall we say, its new owners—$440,000. Americans ranging from elected members of Congress to Joe Six-pack were livid, and rightfully so. Confidence in bailout mania continued to sink, as did share prices trading on the world's indices. By the end of 2008, Americans had a new president coming on board in 2009, as well as an estimated $8.5 trillion price tag on the assortment of bailouts that had occurred over the course of the year. To bring this $8.5 trillion into perspective, the *entire* dollar amount of mortgages outstanding at the time was around $12 trillion. In other words, with no end in sight to the crisis, the government basically could have bought over 70% of the loans in the market with the amount of money it was throwing at the situation. Based on polling by the Rasmussen Reports in October 2008, 63% of respondents thought Wall Street would benefit more than the taxpayer from the bailouts. Interestingly, within this 63% was an almost perfectly even dissemination across party lines. In the same poll, just 26% of American adults possessed "even a little bit of confidence that the nation's policy makers know what they're doing when it comes to the current problems on Wall Street." December offered a merciful end to a year full of financial shock and awe, and Bernanke cut the Fed Funds rate again to a hail-Mary range of 0% to 0.25%. By now, the Fed was starting to resemble that frustrated man standing behind the curtain in *The Wizard of Oz*, vainly tugging and pulling on an assortment of economic levers. The S&P 500, after a particularly gut-wrenching run through September and October, had fallen for a total return of –37.0% in 2008. From its previous high, set on October 9, 2007, the index had declined –40.6% on a total return basis.

Strategy Number Two: Spend Our Way Out of a Spending Problem

Anyone who possessed the audacity of hope that 2009 would represent a fresh start from the runaway spending on bailouts, and the monetary policy gone wild of 2008, was quickly disappointed. The government that had rushed onto the scene as a formal cavalry brigade in September 2008 was now exposing itself as something closer to a Monty Python movie. One problem, though, was that no one was laughing.

Although it had already slipped through a $168 billion stimulus plan in February 2008, Congress had taken a backseat to the Paulson and Bernanke show up until early 2009. This would not last, though, because this group now had a legitimate excuse to unleash some real spending. The National Bureau of Economic Research, a group that officially records the dates of recessions, released its opinion in December 2008 that the United States had entered a recession in late 2007. This was hardly a keen observation. But its significance for policy makers lay in presenting a more formal opportunity to tap into public funds to pick up the slack in the economy through government spending. With both a Democrat-controlled Congress and White House, it was clear that old projects and causes that had been patiently waiting in the wings could now receive generous sums of money in the absence of any serious resistance. A quote from White House chief of staff Rahm Emmanuel sent a clear strategic message to Congress during late November 2008 about how the executive and legislative branches of government should view the current economic circumstances: "Never let a serious crisis go to waste. What I mean by that is it's an opportunity to do things you couldn't do before."[1] If the things that "could not be done before" referred to taking advantage of a situation in order to spend wild sums of money in the name of aiding a crisis, Congress got the message. Unfortunately for a country with already-shaky finances, Congress took the message to heart. In February 2009, Congress passed the American Recovery and Reinvestment Act of 2009. The bill included what apparently had very little to do with the traditional reinvestment into public works and infrastructure that most Americans anticipate in a Keynesian-style stimulus package. Instead, this bill included $650 million for coupons for digital television set-top converter boxes, $30 million to protect a wharf mouse habitat, 10,000 checks mailed to deceased people, and $600 million for the federal government to buy new cars. To top it all off, the government placed $300 road signs to tout its own road construction stimulus projects. Despite the boastful road signs as evidence that infrastructure was receiving reinvestment, the *Wall Street Journal* estimated that only 5% of the stimulus money was actually going to bridge and road work.[2] Disillusioned by the flagrant political overtones, critical, satirical, or generally lucid pundits quickly redubbed the stimulus package the "spendulus" package. The stimulus package drew criticism from its early 2009 draft through its February passage in Congress. Many onlookers objected to the speed at which it was drafted and ferreted through the legislative process. The use of fear-saturated rhetoric played a substantial role in expediting the bill's passage through Congress. Egged on by Mr. Emmanuel's repugnant battle cry, fear had now become the sharpest rhetorical tool in Washington's efforts to effect policy changes. President Obama, himself a gifted rhetorician, used this tool often and with precision: "If we do not move swiftly ... an economy that is already in crisis will be faced with catastrophe."[3] The stock market, acting as an on-again, off-again judge of the effective allocation of capital and resources, saw the bill and the heavy-handed political maneuvering that was swirling in its midst as unsettling. To be sure, the stock market was now pitched into a selling frenzy in the first quarter of 2009. The fevered pitch of doomsday rhetoric from Washington was accelerating the selling activity to the point where the bear market was now taking its place in history as one of the worst on record. In this respect, no bear market had ever produced such sharp losses in such a short period of time (see Table 4.1).

On March 6, 2009, the S&P 500 touched an intraday low of 666 during trading, which was appropriate, since most investors probably already felt like they were in hell. Three days later, on March 9, the market hit its bottom closing price of 676. Finally, after 17 months of liquidation and deleveraging, the stock market put the finishing touches on a –57% decline from its October 2007 high. Incidentally, stocks had become heavily discounted on nearly every valuation metric imaginable (see Table 4.2). Value investors, despite being kicked around by a steady succession of *even better bargains* than what they had bought the day before, were finally about to be vindicated for their steadfast behavior.

TABLE 4.1 The 2007 Bear Takes Its Place in History

Bear Market Start Date	Length in Months	Total Percentage Decline
November 1916	13	–43%
July 1919	25	–35%
September 1929	34	–86%
September 1932	5	–41%
July 1933	32	–34%
March 1937	12	–55%
November 1938	41	–46%
May 1946	37	–30%
August 1956	14	–22%
December 1961	7	–28%
February 1966	8	–22%
November 1968	18	–36%
January 1973	22	–48%
September 1976	18	–19%
November 1980	21	–28%
August 1987	4	–35%
July 1990	3	–20%
July 1998	3	–20%
March 2000	31	–49%
October 2007	17	–57%

On March 10, 2009, something beautiful was born. All the pessimism that had driven the market into its depths, accelerated by margin calls among the leveraged, and fear of fresh lows among the pessimists, had finally exhausted itself. To begin with, it was becoming clear that despite the terrible economic environment, inventories across the world's economy had been thoroughly liquidated to the point that some rebuilding would be necessary. Given the positive implications for future GDP, it at least seemed possible that the rate of contraction in the world's economy had found a near-term nadir. It was becoming clear that the market, too caught up in its race to the bottom, had gotten carried away. During the summer months of 2009, the market was again off to the races, albeit in a completely different direction.

TABLE 4.2 Fourth Quarter 2008 Stock Market Valuations

Index	Country	Current P/E
Dow Jones Industrial Average	US	10.5x
S&P 500 Index	US	9.3x
NASDAQ Composite Index	US	11.5x
S&P/TSX Composite Index	CA	7.8x
Mexico Bolsa Index	MX	7.9x
DJ EURO STOXX 50 = Pr	EC	6.5x
FTSE 100 Index	GB	6.5x
CAC 40 Index	FR	6.6x
DAX Index	GE	7.0x
IBEX 35 Index	SP	6.6x
S&P/MIB Index	IT	6.2x
AEX Index	NE	5.1x
Swiss Market Index	SZ	9.1x
Nikkei 225	JN	8.8x
Hang Seng Index	HK	6.8x
Shan Ghai SE Composite Index	CH	10.0x
S&P/ASX 200 Index	AU	7.8x
Straits Times Index	SI	7.4x

The Vestigial Effects of the Crisis Come into Focus

Despite the sudden and altogether inevitable reversal in stock prices during 2009, the long-term focused value investor is still left with much to ponder. The years of excesses built up in the U.S. consumer, as well as the overbearing reactions of the U.S. government to the crisis, have created vestigial effects that could linger in the fundamental landscape for years to come. The rest of this chapter explores these fundamentals. The remaining chapters highlight and discuss investment themes that offer a response or solutions to some of the problems facing investors.

As we methodically examined the financial crisis in the preceding pages, we identified several phenomena that are worth ongoing consideration from investors in the present day. First, we witnessed an unbridled attempt by the Federal Reserve to leave no stone unturned in its efforts to restimulate the extension of credit in the economy. Under conventional standards, the Fed typically sets the Fed Funds rate and then buys and sells short-term government securities in the open market to manage the money supply toward its target rate. The Fed had pushed down rates to a range of 0% to 0.25% in December, with little of the desired effect it sought in its efforts to "get credit flowing again." In March 2009, it embarked on its most aggressive policy to date in its fight against deflation and the credit crunch— quantitative easing. Economists debate the definition of quantitative easing, as well as whether the Fed's actions in 2009 replicated the actions of the Bank of Japan by the same definition in the 1990s following its economic meltdown. Rather than get academic, we will cut to the chase. We will denote quantitative easing in the Fed's version as entering the longer-term markets for government debt such as Treasuries, and making purchases to inject further liquidity into the system. The Fed resorted to this measure because it had in no uncertain terms already fired every last one of its usual bullets. Quantitative easing is effectively printing money, but no presses are needed. Instead, the Fed enters a few (actually, many) 1s and 0s into a computer and credits the bond seller's account, and, voila, we have new money. Technology is amazing; a policy maker's ability to destroy your purchasing power has never been easier. In other words, as Mr. Bernanke and company fought off the specter of deflation, they were creating money like never before—or, actually, many times before during the course of human history, for those who study those things. Either way, Mr. Bernanke's problem was and remains how to unwind this activity, if and when the time comes. Given the sheer volume of the preceding activity, the effects of a wrong move could prove seismic. How much money has been created? Figure 4.1 shows the growth in the monetary base of the United States.

4 • Quis Custodiet Ipsos Custodes?

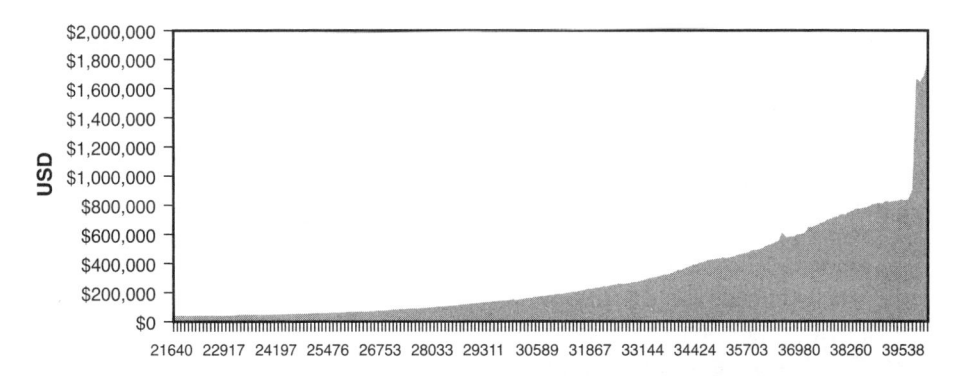

Figure 4.1 U.S. aggregate reserves depository institutions monetary base

Source: Bloomberg, Federal Reserve

As you attempt to digest what is shown in Figure 4.1, we can offer some additional food for thought from the foremost authority on monetary policy and inflation:

> "I know no example in history of a substantial inflation lasting more than a brief time that was not accompanied by a roughly corresponding rapid increase in the quantity of money; and no example of a rapid increase in the quantity of money that was not accompanied by a roughly corresponding substantial inflation."[4]

Milton Friedman, Money Mischief (1994)

Dr. Friedman's words provide little comfort to investors whose financial goal is to accumulate and store their wealth throughout their lives in hopes of consuming at a later date. There can be little question that the U.S. government intends, at least to some degree, to inflate its way out of a good bit of this debt overhang. For anyone who thought the explicit bailouts of Wall Street were bad enough, if allowed to occur by the Fed, the government's efforts in monetary expansion will lead to implicit bailouts of remaining entities carrying heavy balances of fixed-rate debt. This is because their fixed payments remain the same while dollars in the system multiply. No one should be confused by this phenomenon. This form of monetary expansion works, although discreetly, as a form of tax on savers and redistribution of wealth to debtors. The purchasing power of the saver's accumulated wealth is eroded in lock-step with the debtor's eroding balance of fixed payments relative to the multiplying dollars. Since the government is also a heavy debtor, it has an incentive to use some degree of this ploy. So in many ways, if we consider the total amount of money that has been created by the Fed during the crisis, in the name of rescuing failing financial institutions, this is a tax liability hanging over people and entities that store wealth in the U.S. dollar. If and when a likely inflation appears in the U.S. dollar, prices of goods will rise, and future dollars will buy less of those goods than 2009 dollars. This loss of purchasing power can simply be thought of as a tax bill that resulted from the financing of the 2008–2009 rescue activity through the Federal Reserve's printing money.

Clearly, this type of monetary strategy has a shelf life. A government can betray the faith placed in its responsible management of a currency only so many times before people cease to trust the government any further. Eventually, savers see through this shallow game and seek to save in other currencies or assets that retain their purchasing power. The exit from a currency where the holders lose confidence can occur with blinding speed, particularly if the currency in question is not widely used. For countries that control the reserve currency, such as the United States, the process of its partners exiting the game can take considerably longer, because ready alternatives take time, confidence, and trust to develop. Nevertheless, if the United States allowed its monetary growth to lead to inflation, it would only be joining a rich history of countries that over time sought to finance activity through the printing of additional currency. Put another way, this leads to the debasement of their currency (if it is backed by a metal). For instance, Rome was a steady debaser of its currency throughout its history, having reduced a once-pure silver coin to mere alloys by the time the empire fell. For that matter, the United States debased its currency to finance the Civil War, as it removed the greenback from gold convertibility for over a decade. The point is that whether you are talking about England during the Napoleonic Wars or China a thousand years ago, there is ample evidence of humans issuing a currency and then sooner or later abusing their power over that currency. The temptation for government to finance activity by issuing additional currency, or by avoiding an unpopular direct taxation on its citizens, is often irresistible. This is yet another example of timeless human behavior and the search for a shortsighted, easy solution to a difficult problem. Historically, though, the consequences of this behavior have been serious. As soon as trust has been broken, or confidence is lost in a currency, it can be difficult to restore.

Despite the potential for inflationary problems at some point in time, the Federal Reserve still believes it will be able to withdraw these excess dollars from the economy before any serious emergence of inflationary pressure. Although it is possible that the Fed will safely remove this extra supply of money before it can begin to damage purchasing power, it is not probable. First and foremost, appearances and rhetoric notwithstanding, the Federal Reserve faces much political pressure to maintain a loose stance on monetary policy. The Federal Reserve Chairman is not an elected official, but instead is appointed by the president and periodically reports to Congress. So although textbooks or other official documents may say the Fed is independent, most people can view evidence to the contrary by simply turning on their television. In reality, Fed Chairman Bernanke lobbied hard for his reappointment in 2009. In a historically unprecedented but also sensible move for someone looking to garner public opinion in his favor, Bernanke appeared on the televised newsmagazine *60 Minutes*, where he granted a rather warm and fuzzy interview. Perhaps more than anything, he wisely struck a tone of distaste for the bailouts he had helped engineer and broker and successfully couched himself as an advocate for the little man on Main Street. He deftly executed his role of the compassionate central banker. He might have even kissed a baby during the interview had one strolled by on the streets of his hometown of Dillon, S.C. In any event, it proved a successful if not unconventional PR move, and he was reappointed by Obama. Political posturing aside, the point is that it was clear that there *was* political posturing of some variety from the Fed Chairman. This lays bare what most have already surmised: Central bankers like to be reappointed and will curry favor to do so. Whether they are pining for public opinion, the adoration of the president, or the steady approval of Congress, they must stay popular with the powers in Washington. Incidentally, the powers in Washington want as much as anything low interest rates and easy money. Washington certainly does not care much for recessions, since they crimp tax revenues and yield sour voters. To put it in the frankest terms, have you ever heard of a politician in Washington pounding the table for higher interest rates? With that said, the institutional framework does not support a high probability of the Fed exiting its monetary expansion soon enough to avoid a rise in inflation. What makes the situation most difficult is that the rapid acceleration in prices typically is preceded by a period of benign, feel-good economic times. Historically, when inflation first appears, it is recognized by businesses everywhere as a gentle uptick in sales, or the appearance of an economic recovery. These people running their assorted businesses respond in time by purchasing more inventory or expanding their operations, since they are examining the phenomenon mostly from their own perspective. In time, though, costs begin to rise also, and given enough time, the growth in the money supply invades all corners of the economy. Inflation in this sense produces a bit of a sucker punch to the business operator. At first conditions seemingly improve, but after time the business sees that its profits are not much better, or even deteriorating from a margin standpoint. Many businesses see their profitability decline if they cannot adequately respond to rising costs by quickly increasing their selling prices. Nevertheless, at the outset of the feel-good period, as the press, pundits, and policy makers claim victory over the crisis, does it seem likely that the Fed will abruptly step in and crash the party? Even better, would the Fed risk reentering a recession just as conditions were improving? Talk about an unpopular move, made by a group of policy makers that seem to prize popularity! *60 Minutes* would run a far different piece following that policy move. It is possible that the Fed will fall on its sword for the sake of sparing the U.S. economy from these inflationary events. But it seems more likely that the Fed will wait until there is stronger evidence of an economic "recovery." If it does so, it also runs a much higher risk that inflation is already accelerating.

Even so, with all the superlative evidence of potential inflation built into the monetary base notwithstanding, it remains difficult, if not impossible, to forecast when (or if) it might appear. It's possible that the newly created money could stay on the sidelines or in the system for a while. We can attribute this enigma to the peculiar nature of man and what the economist John Maynard Keynes described as "animal spirits." The late economist coined this term to describe a sudden appearance of confidence in human behavior. Animal spirits are observed with little effort in the stock market. In stock market parlance, this phenomenon is often called risk aversion or, even more technically, the "equity risk premium." What makes a P/E ratio suddenly rise from 7x to 10x in a few trading sessions, with only little incremental news having arrived? Confidence in future earnings or, better yet, animal spirits. So it is with the current state of the U.S. economy and the mountain of money lying dormant in banks throughout the system. Currently, spirits remain low, and banks are still largely in a state of self-preservation as they worry over further credit defaults. In other words, all that money remains in an essential lockdown, although the situation is far better than it was in late 2008 and early 2009. Fortunately, a simple equation will save us from wasted ink and fallen trees, because it explains the monetary situation in clear terms. The equation of exchange gives it to us straight: money supply × velocity of money = price level × quantity of goods and services produced (MV = PQ). The idea is that the two sides of the formula must balance. So if you increase the M for money supply and there is no corresponding increase in the P × Q side, velocity, or the number of times a dollar changes hands in the economy, must be declining. Velocity is the key here. The fact that M increased so disproportionately during late 2008 and early 2009 with no corresponding increase in the PQ (Gross Domestic Product) suggests that dollars are not circulating much. Velocity is based on confidence—the confidence to spend, the confidence to lend, the confidence to invest. As we said earlier, animal spirits. Although it's impossible to project, we can at least turn again to the analyst's best friend when pondering an impossible projection: What happened in the past?

For this analysis, we return to the expert on monetary matters, Milton Friedman, as described in one of his many books, *Money Mischief*:

> "Over the past century or more in the United States, the United Kingdom, and some other Western countries, roughly six to nine months have elapsed on the average before increased monetary growth has worked its way through the economy and produced increased economic growth and employment. Another twelve to eighteen months have elapsed before the increased monetary growth has affected the price level appreciably and inflation has occurred or speeded up."[5]

If we accept Dr. Friedman's research of history as a guide, this would mean in general terms that unless demonstrative action is taken to reverse the monetary growth, inflation might be noticeable in late 2010 through 2011. In June 2009, Alan Greenspan offered his own take on the prospects for inflation in an op-ed for the *Financial Times*:[6] "If political pressures prevent central banks from reining in their inflated balance sheets in a timely manner, statistical analysis suggests the emergence of inflation by 2012; earlier if markets anticipate a prolonged period of elevated money supply. Annual price inflation in the United States is significantly correlated (with a 3 1/2-year lag) with annual changes in money supply per unit of capacity." Hopefully, neither of these scenarios will unfold, but in any event, investors should prepare for this risk and plan appropriately with the proper investments that protect their purchasing power while the market still offers opportunities on the heels of the bear market. Historically, investments in companies whose businesses can reset their prices quickly in the market stand the best chance of maintaining profitability. These types of businesses are often tied to the production or sale of a commodity, such as oil or various agricultural goods. We discuss these potential investments in later chapters. Their merits as potential long-term investments extend beyond simple inflation hedges.

In the meantime, we are not quite done with our discussion of risks being created by the U.S. government. Sadly, there is more to discuss. As we return our attention to the spendulus package of early 2009, it raises an important question: How will the government pay for all this additional spending activity? As you know, the U.S. government has substantial debt of its own and does not possess a war chest of savings that it can deploy at will on various public ventures. With that said, when the government spends sums beyond its revenues, it runs a deficit and must finance this activity, just as a consumer or business would have to finance spending beyond its means. To finance this activity, the government borrows money by selling Treasury bonds to raise the funds to support its spending. All this activity is typical and has been occurring off and on since the country gained its independence and established a federal government. In particular, it is a fact of history that governments run large deficits during wars to finance the activity. However, large peacetime deficits are a relatively newer phenomenon that emerged in the 1980s. In the present day, since policy makers use the excuse that drastic times call for drastic measures, the government ramped up its spending, and hence its deficits, to historically unprecedented levels. Figure 4.2 shows how the top-level powers in Washington, consisting of Congress and the White House, continue to steer the country's finances into uncharted territory.

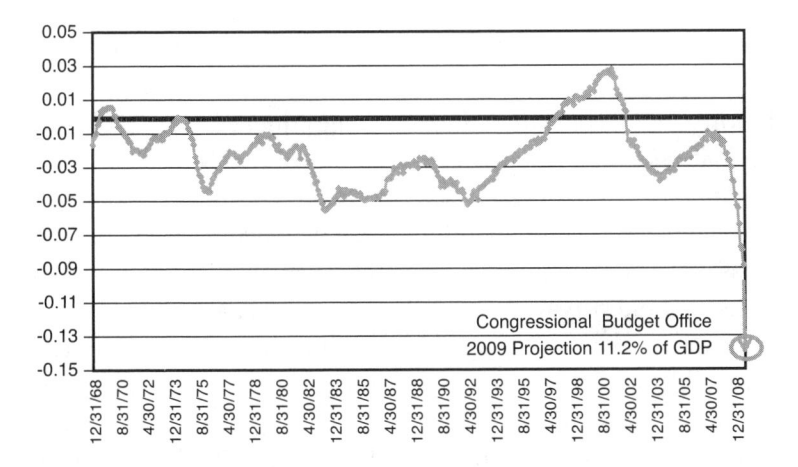

Figure 4.2 U.S. federal budget deficit as a percentage of GDP

Source: U.S. Treasury, Congressional Budget Office, Bloomberg

Figure 4.2 shows pretty well how the U.S. government has attempted, in a no-holds-barred Keynesian fashion, to pick up the spending slack in the economy left by the indebted consumer, who is missing in action. In effect, the U.S. government has picked up the baton from the fallen consumer and is trying to keep the spending race alive. As with the consumer back in 2003, the government is spending beyond its means from a revenue standpoint and is racking up too much debt in the process. All this spending behavior is being performed in the name of "getting credit flowing again" and "creating or saving much-needed jobs." As the government tries to induce more spending among its steadfast sidekick, the consumer, it resembles the two hacks from the campy movie *Weekend at Bernie's*. These characters ridiculously prop up the corpse of their wealthy boss and continue having a good time. Of course, the ploy in the movie ultimately fails. A similar outcome for the government's efforts to foster consumerism is also probable. Unfortunately for the U.S. government and its efforts, the consumer who spent and borrowed willy-nilly during the past two decades has retreated into a state of self-preservation alongside the banking system. For all intents and purposes, the U.S. consumer is entering a phase of balance sheet repair that will be initiated by spending much less and saving much more. Two solid reasons underlie this behavior. The first is a tangible fear and recognized probability of financial failure and hardship. With their balance sheets already stretched with debt, and the value of their lynchpin real estate and equity assets still well off levels from years before, many consumers fear the consequences of a pink slip and have altered their spending habits appropriately. Second, the shadow banking system of credit securitization that funded the heavy borrowing and fueled the spending has been deeply impaired by credit losses. This change in consumer behavior is evident in the short term. It could very well establish a behavioral pattern stretching over years rather than months. This is analogous to the generation who emerged from the Depression and preached a message of saving and living within one's means. While presenting a paradigm shift, this development would not be all that bad should it persist. First, getting the U.S. consumer on better financial footing is essential to the economy's long-term health. Second, many exciting areas of consumerism have considerably higher growth prospects and hence offer investors better potential rewards. In fact, participating in the construction of a middle class of consumers in emerging-market countries will provide ample opportunities for investors in the years to come. Put another way, knowing what we know now about the history and economic progress of the United States, would anyone pass on an opportunity to invest in the U.S. stock market back in the early twentieth century? If you can recognize the opportunity the U.S. stock market presented at that point in time, you should recognize the present opportunities lying in China, India, and Brazil, to name a few.

The U.S. consumer aside, the current spending deficits from the U.S. Congress are complicating matters on a number of fronts, including the ability of the Federal Reserve to unwind its wildly stimulative policy of quantitative easing. The Federal Reserve took the unprecedented step of purchasing long-term Treasuries in an effort to directly impact the level of mortgage rates (to keep them low by putting buying pressure on Treasuries to help mortgage rates). It also injected staggering amounts of liquidity into the U.S. economy. Therefore, at some point, the Fed has to sell these same Treasuries to unwind its loose policy. In other words, selling these Treasuries withdraws the cash the Fed created earlier from the economy. However, with the U.S. Congress running deficits well over $1 trillion for the next ten years according to CBO projections, the Fed will have to tread carefully so as not to add to the selling pressure of U.S. Treasuries in the market. This creates a delicate situation. With the Treasury already selling more bonds than normal to finance its outsized deficits, this added selling action by the Fed could create additional market pressure for lower prices on these Treasuries. As you know, lower bond prices spell higher interest rates, and rising rates on Treasuries affect everybody. Higher interest rates would potentially crush all those poor souls still stuck in ARMs as their rates continued to reset at higher levels. The irony of the situation is that the government's actions to rescue these borrowers with aggressive policy created a potential risk that could undermine the same people in a foreseeable chain of events. Likewise, higher interest rates in the bond market get the final say and would act to override anything the Fed or politicians could devise. Ultimately, the bond market creates the interest rates that proliferates all other financial contracts denominated in that currency. So whether we are discussing the potential deluge of Treasury sales or the arrival of inflation, it appears that a discernible risk exists for potentially higher interest rates. Either way, we can say with relative certainty that one of the two parties must change its current behavior to lower the risk of future inflation and higher interest rates. For instance, since the Fed is primarily concerned with keeping interest rates low in key financial contracts such as mortgages, it does not want to see its policies unraveled by a deluge of Treasury sales. With that said, the Fed would benefit if Congress and the White House would back off of their spending also. Based on all available information at the moment, this is unlikely. Applying the Congressional Budget Office's deficit projections for the coming ten years (see Figure 4.3), we can find little hope for a sharp reversal in current spending levels.

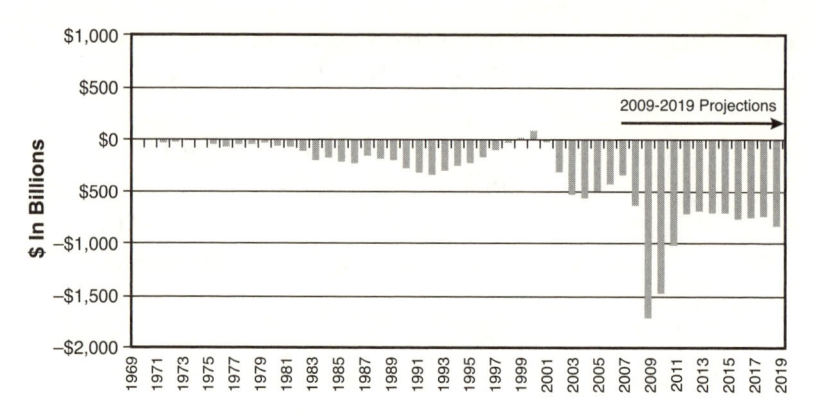

Figure 4.3 U.S. federal budget deficits

Source: Congressional Budget Office

We have already discussed the complications that this spending creates for the Fed, but there are further long-term considerations also. First, this deficit activity also represents a large change in the structure of the government's balance sheet. Under the current projections, the nation's debt-to-GDP ratio would rise from 41% in 2008 to around 70% of GDP in 2019. If these numbers taken as a percentage of GDP seem abstract, let's add another perspective. Figure 4.4 shows the CBO's debt projections resulting from proposed deficits out of White House estimates. Because a deficit translates into debt, we can see that the projected debt will more than double. Put another way, beginning when George Washington took office in 1789 through George W. Bush's presidency in 2008, it took the U.S. government 219 years to accumulate $5.8 trillion in debt. Based on the current president's spending plans, it will take only about six years to run up a comparable amount of debt. This spending path is untenable, because under these current projections, close to 90% of the budget deficits in 2017 through 2019 will be comprised of interest payments on the debt itself.

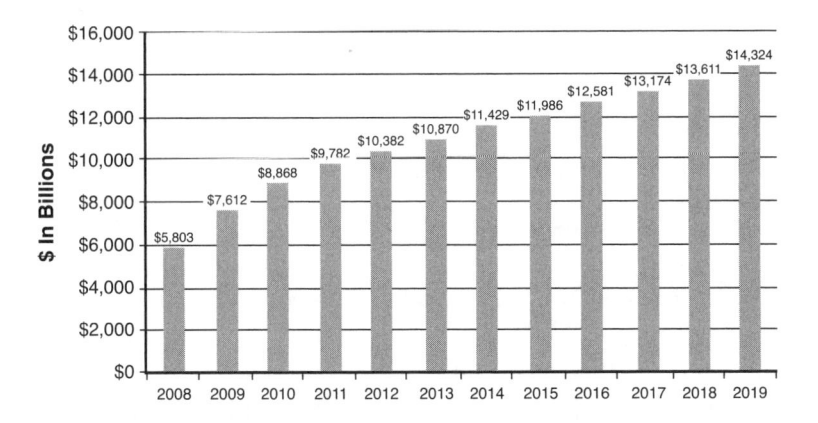

Figure 4.4 U.S. government debt held by the public

Source: Congressional Budget Office

Unfortunately for the roughed-up U.S. consumer, if this deficit plan comes to pass, well over 3% of GDP will already be spoken for through interest payments on government debt. Assuming that U.S. consumers did repair their balance sheet in the coming years, they must do so knowing that taxes may rise as these deficits persist. We can only hope that sometime during the coming years, this deficit path will be reversed, and these levels of spending are never recognized. Otherwise, the purchasers of U.S. debt—which back around World War II were entirely American citizens but now are almost half comprised of foreign governments such as China and Japan—may start demanding higher interest rates. They would want to be compensated for a weaker balance sheet and rising inflation expectations, just as any lender would in that circumstance. Although it is true that a U.S. Treasury obligation carries no default risk, there is substantial risk of a loss of purchasing power, and these bondholders recognize this risk. Likewise, there is a much smaller but still identifiable risk that the largest holder, China, could threaten to sell its Treasury holdings faster than the market could absorb them to avoid falling prices and rising rates. This act, although a very unlikely scenario, would effectively send Treasury rates much higher and the value of the U.S. dollar lower, forcing a significant standard of living adjustment on Americans (for the worse). As mentioned, this scenario is unlikely, but its possibility should be respected by policy makers and not *ignored*. The United States successfully threatened this same strategy on Great Britain in 1956 during a dispute over whether to engage in military action over the Suez Canal. Although the United States did not sell its substantial pound holdings, the threat alone was enough to send the pound's value plummeting. Many observers cite this event as a defining moment in Great Britain's loss of its status as an empire. Fortunately for the United States, China still needs the U.S. as a trade partner and does not have much incentive to undermine a key customer for its economy. However, this economic position will change over time as China continues to develop and builds a larger domestic economy. It is important that the United States get its financial house in order during that time span. When taken in sum, the potential consequences of all these behaviors by the U.S. government present a basket of unique risk factors to Americans who seek to protect their purchasing power. At the same time, investors can potentially lessen these burdens by seeking long-term investments in countries that manage their finances in a far more responsible manner. As ironic as it may be following the Asian Financial Crisis, many emerging-market countries currently are in better fiscal shape, and are more responsible stewards of public finances, than the developed-market countries that rescued them from financial turmoil in the late 1990s.

The Visible Hand Is Coming into View, and It's All Thumbs

It might be reasonable to assume that after covering so many potential risk factors introduced by the U.S. government, we have exhausted the topic. Not exactly. We have yet to tackle the replacement of Adam Smith's invisible hand with the big clumsy hand of the U.S. government. Actually, to say that the United States was guided by an invisible hand in its financial markets is unjust. To be frank, having a Federal Reserve that actively controls the money supply and sets interest rate policy is not laissez faire. For that matter, neither is having a Congress that forces banks through policy to lend money to less-than-creditworthy borrowers. Although it is true that Alan Greenspan gained street credibility by hanging out with Ayn Rand, the U.S. system has been a mix of free markets and interventionism from the outset. The two forces have worked alongside each other since the beginning. Over the course of the twentieth century, regulation and deregulation have waged bitter turf wars. During late 2008 and early 2009, Americans saw these forces remanifest their ongoing clash as the financial system nearly collapsed under the weight of too much borrowing and unbridled risk taking. On one hand, the excesses of Wall Street and risk taking that spilled over into the main economy were credited to the ills of deregulation. But regulators incentivized this behavior by creating public-private market devices such as Fannie and Freddie. Rather than laying the blame wholly on an inanimate idea such as deregulation, one could argue just as easily that regulators are simply ineffective. We all know that Bernie Madoff was a crook, and onlookers tried to tell regulators the same, years before the collapse of his Ponzi scheme. The facts show that the SEC was warned by more than a few observers that the firm smelled fishy. The SEC was even provided arithmetic evidence that Madoff's strategy was incompatible with his assets under management. It is not a novel idea that regulators fall short of expectations. Although most people recognize this reality, human behavior is to still consistently seek more regulation in the wake of a crisis. This pattern is too well established in the history of the United States. Policy makers can be counted on to increase their dominion over the public when given the least opportunity, much less a glaring one such as 2008.

Most people are familiar with the correlation between crises and the impending introduction of further government regulation. No less than 16 government agencies were created in response to the Great Depression. Likewise, many more people have come to recognize that regulation grows of its own volition if left unchecked, because government bureaucracies generally expand over time. One simple way to examine this phenomenon in growing regulation is to measure the number of pages printed in the Federal Register over time. The Federal Register is a lengthy book dedicated to printing the rules, proposed rules, and notices of Federal agencies, organizations, and executive orders. In one rough brushstroke it can be used as a proxy for the growth in United States regulation over time. Figure 4.5 shows the annual page count for the Federal Register since its first printing in 1936. It is often cited by Milton Friedman and regularly scrutinized by a publication produced by the Competitive Enterprise Institute called the "Ten Thousand Commandments." The Federal Register has ascended from its humble beginnings of 2,620 pages in 1936 to a staggering 79,435 pages in 2008.

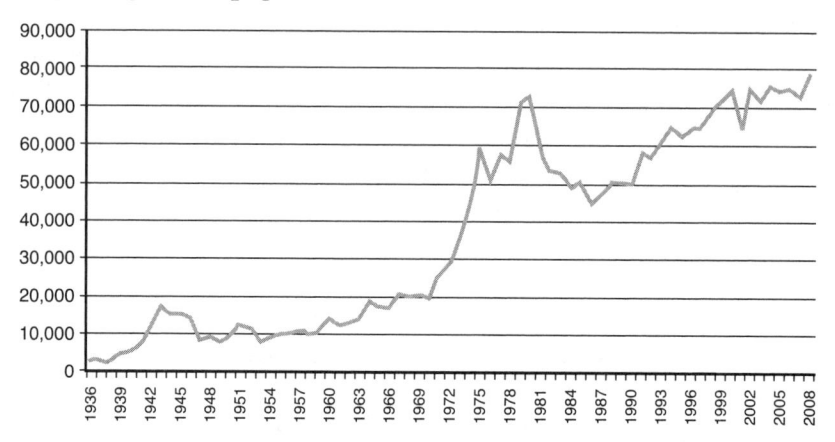

Figure 4.5 Annual page count in the Federal Register

Source: Competitive Enterprise Institute, "Ten Thousand Commandments"

As you can see in Figure 4.5, the Federal Register has displayed fits and starts over time in its growth rate. Although not a perfect measure, these growth rates have corresponded quite well to different regulatory regimes and their accompanying economic growth rates. Most noticeable is the tremendous rise in the annual page count during the 1970s. To bring these growth rates into better focus, Figure 4.6 shows the same data as in Figure 4.5 on a ten-year compound annual growth basis by decade.

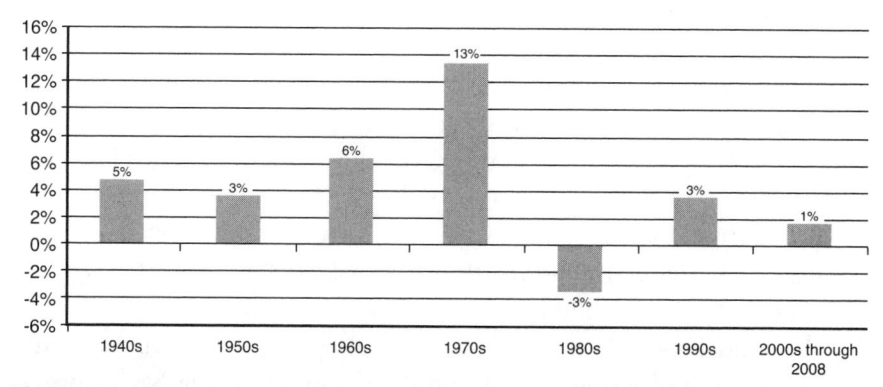

Figure 4.6 Ten-year compound annual growth in the page count of the Federal Register

Source: Competitive Enterprise Institute, "Ten Thousand Commandments"

The assorted growth rates in regulation demonstrate the runaway regulatory behavior of the 1970s. As you might have guessed, economic growth faltered in the U.S. economy as it became overly burdened by the substantial growth in regulations, and their associated costs that were ultimately passed along to the consumer. In Milton Friedman's 1980 book, *Free to Choose*, he offers an assessment of the 1970s regulatory environment and its deleterious effects on economic growth:

> "Government expenditures on both older and newer agencies skyrocketed—from less than $1 billion in 1970 to roughly $5 billion estimated for 1979. Prices in general roughly doubled, but these expenditures more than quintupled. The number of bureaucrats employed in regulatory activities tripled, going from 28,000 in 1970 to 81,000 in 1979. During the same decade, economic growth in the United States slowed drastically. From 1949 to 1969, output per man-hour of all persons employed in private business—a simple and comprehensive measure of productivity—rose more than 3 percent a year; in the next decade, less than half as fast; and by the end of the decade productivity was actually declining."[7]

Dr. Friedman's comments on the growth of regulatory agencies in the 1970s are illuminating, but this phenomenon is far from a historic relic. The collective budgets of federal regulators have increased at a steady compounded growth of 9.8% in nominal terms during the past 49 years. Put another way, the whole of regulators' budgets, and their drag on economic resources, have been doubling nearly every seven years for the past 49 years, as shown in Figure 4.7.

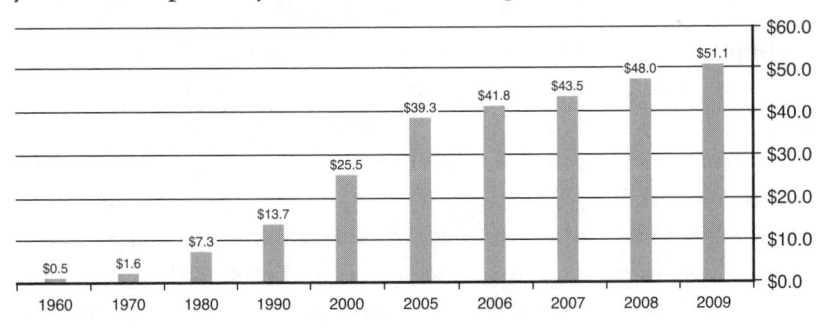

Figure 4.7   Regulators' budgets, in billions of dollars

Source: fiscalaccountability.org

The conundrum is that everyone can agree that some amount of regulation is necessary. In its simplest form, the United States requires some authoritative enforcement of the right to own property, if it is to function as it was originally designed. Problematically, when regulation tries to do too much, adverse effects set in. Businesses waste their precious resources filling out paperwork, attempting to understand legalese, and spending money to comply with certifications, tax preparation, or purchasing new equipment that meets specific guidelines, to name just a few distractions. In some industries businesses must hire employees whose only purpose is addressing and complying with regulations. This has two effects: It makes the cost of running a business higher, and it distracts businesses from their core objectives. Even worse, it pulls businesses away from their most beneficial societal externality—innovation. This wasted activity, although difficult to measure, is estimated to range from $1.2 to $1.5 trillion in the United States. Put another way, businesses waste a sum equivalent to approximately 9% of GDP (or the economy's total output) on regulatory costs. Since this money flows toward the government and its myriad agencies, we can fairly call this another form of taxation. Likewise, since businesses pass along these costs through higher product prices, consumers ultimately bear these regulatory costs. So although regulations are often constructed with good intentions, it is nothing short of ironic that their negative consequences of higher prices and forgone productivity create a perverse by-product that works against a society when taken too far. When regulation gets taken to an extreme, people seek to circumvent it and operate in the informal economy. In these instances everyone loses, because governments receive less revenue, and people's rights are not protected.

Importantly, regulations tend to unduly punish the small business—in particular, the entrepreneur. First and foremost, a large organization is far better equipped to absorb the monetary costs that result from meeting regulatory burdens. Second, as regulations increase, government effectively increases its oversight of and direct involvement in business practices. In this sense, large firms have the financial resources to lobby policy makers and protect their interests. In this paradigm, however, the small firm has no say and can be subjected to various forms of de facto protectionism as larger firms seek to influence policies and steer government initiatives that protect their interests above all else. These policies typically evolve into serving two interests: the incumbency of the firm doling out the money, and the politician receiving the money. In the end, new entrants into the given industry become disadvantaged or discouraged from entering by these self-protective measures. Politicians are amenable to these lobbying efforts for several reasons. These include financial rewards, reciprocation by the company to enact government industrial policies, the small number of large companies (easier for politicians to deal with) versus many entrepreneurs, and the higher number of jobs (employed voters) controlled by the company.

One striking example of this behavior at work can be found in the U.S. government's rescue of General Motors. For starters, GM was a large employer in a heavily regulated industry. Much worse, but not by accident, once the company received its billions of dollars of taxpayer money to retool, it announced that it would start producing more "green cars." Not coincidentally, this production plan matched a core industrial policy that the Obama administration has peddled in its efforts to create "green jobs." Never mind that GM could not profitably produce run-of-the-mill gasoline-powered vehicles, much less these fuel-efficient vehicles with their higher breakeven costs. Unfortunately, these relationships between regulators and large corporations have been shown to breed corruption in countries where regulation overreaches.

Another related and worrisome development in the United States that stemmed from the financial crisis was the government's intervention in the banking industry through the conditions imposed on the TARP funds that were used to rescue ailing institutions. At the time the government initiated its investments, there was widespread concern in the American public that the government would nationalize the banks. What most observers missed were nuances derived from accounting rule APB 18 under U.S. GAAP. It states that in instances of less than 20% ownership, an entity should be consolidated into the acquirer's balance sheet where control is exercised. Any observers focused on who was exercising control over the country's largest banks would have unmistakably concluded that Uncle Sam was calling the shots, irrespective of the absence of common equity ownership. During a February 11, 2009 Congressional hearing, the heads of the large commercial banks, including Citi, J.P. Morgan, and Bank of

America, were called to Capitol Hill and publicly browbeaten like miscreant kids yanked off the playground. No one should have—or did, for that matter—shed a tear for the bankers. However, there should have been some sorrow for private businesses around the country, given that banks subordinate to politicians soon become allocators of capital to politically-driven objectives. Fortunately, several banks have repaid their TARP money, but many have yet to do so. Those that have not repaid their loans, including Citigroup currently, have seen a large increase in telephone calls from their new bosses in Washington, DC. According to reports on the Bloomberg newswire in July 2009,[8] Senator Charles Schumer of New York telephoned Citigroup's CEO, Vikram Pandit, to protest the withdrawal of a mall developer's credit. After Mr. Pandit had executives review the credit line for a mall in Syracuse, N.Y., Citi stuck with its prior decision. Bank of America reported that calls from lawmakers in Washington increased fivefold from a year earlier. If the banks have resisted calls from politicians to direct their business, sadly, GM has not. In June 2009, Congressman Barney Frank of Massachusetts asked with success to delay the closure of a plant in Norton, Mass. for 14 months. Translation: The U.S. taxpayer should subsidize a loss-making activity on behalf of a lawmaker's constituents. Taking all this into consideration, the evidence of the government's attempted involvement in capital allocation for political objectives has already been shown, even if the bankers have resisted it.

We cannot be sure what the future holds. But based on available information, including the tremendous growth in federal spending and deficits, as well as the introduction of legislation attempting to cap and trade carbon emissions, and even possibly provide universal healthcare, intentions are known. We can be sure that the U.S. government is posturing toward a dose of bigger government and interventionism. What is most odd about these policies that are being pursued is that they are often promoted in the name of progress. However, if the U.S. government pursues its budget deficits on the current course it has suggested, it will introduce the risk of a rise in long-term interest rates and an effect of crowding out private firms' access to capital. Among all the adverse regulations and policies that could impact small businesses and entrepreneurs, an inability to access capital due to punitive interest rates would be particularly damaging. In turn, the withdrawal of the small business or entrepreneur due to these factors would truly halt progress. The free-market system of commerce's success relies on many factors. But for a society to truly progress, it needs to foster the creative destruction that is borne on the back of highly competitive small business. Societies that promote the freedom of individuals to pursue these goals will continue to progress faster than their counterparts over time.

We have discussed many potential risks to consider over the coming years, ranging from inflation in the U.S. dollar, to runaway spending deficits, to a sharp rise in regulation and government intervention. Again, no one knows the future. We may be weighing risks whose importance will fade in time. However, wise investors will always watch the watchers and prepare for potential risks they introduce accordingly. The following chapters discuss investing alternatives that seek to avoid many of the risks discussed in this chapter. They target areas with strong long-term opportunities and the ability to help protect purchasing power over time.

Endnotes

[1] Review & Outlook. "40-Year Wish List." WSJ.com, January 28, 2009.

[2] Ibid.

[3] Susan Davis. "Obama Praises Democrats for Quick Work on Stimulus." WSJ.com, February 5, 2009.

[4] Milton Friedman. *Money Mischief*. Orlando: Harcourt Brace, 1994.

[5] Ibid.

[6] Alan Greenspan. "Inflation — the real threat to sustained recovery." *Financial Times*, June 25, 2009.

[7] Milton Friedman and Rose Friedman. *Free to Choose*. Orlando: Harcourt, 1980.

[8] Alison Fitzgerald. "Pandit Defies Schumer as Lawmakers Flex Muscles." Bloomberg, July 22, 2009.

5

A New Landscape for Investors

Since the world began to recover from the extreme stress of the financial crisis, it has become increasingly important that investors in search of the highest long-term returns over the coming years distinguish from among the world's thousands of publicly traded companies some of the more attractive opportunities. Without a structure or framework to draw on, this could prove a difficult, if not daunting, task. On the other hand, depending on your perspective, there are tens of thousands of stocks to choose from in the world's markets, so the possibilities are numerous.

If all investors have come to recognize one phenomenon (and, if not, this chapter may help), that phenomenon is the entrance of several new players onto the global stage of capitalism during the past 30 years. We must use the word capitalism in a broader sense, because few countries seem to apply the exact same regimen of the term from top to bottom. However, we can acknowledge that an unprecedented number of people are now competing in the global marketplace for goods and services. Perhaps this is the most important element of globalization as it relates to investing—which nations are becoming increasingly competitive, and what markets, businesses, and investments stand to benefit from this competition. Most importantly, the centerpiece of this phenomenon lies in the one word: *competition*.

During the twentieth century, the world bore witness to a wide dichotomy in the argument over how best to eliminate poverty and create prosperity. Among the many approaches were ideologies embraced by fascists, communists, and freedom-seeking capitalists, who were all vying for the top position in the world's rank of prosperous societies. These ideologies clashed with each other in economic wars, military wars, and cold wars, but in the end, only one system was left standing in a form close to resembling its original design. The United States, and its institutional bias toward promoting freedom across all aspects of its society, ultimately triumphed in these battles. It empirically displayed from top to bottom the most prosperous civilization the world has ever seen. This display coincided with the dissolution of many competing ideologies, because ultimately they could not compete in the war waged on the commercial battlefield. Without question, the standard of living progressed in the United States at rates, and to levels, that few could have imagined in the ages leading up to the creation of this country. One of the most striking periods of this rise in economic productivity and the standard of living occurred in the decades following the end of World War II. This stretch of time defined by rising productivity lasted until the standard of living became temporarily derailed during the heavy onset of regulation and low growth of the 1970s. From the late 1940s until the early 1970s, productivity per worker increased at a rate of approximately 3% per year. Although this sounds modest, it means that productivity and the standard of living per worker were doubling at a rate just under every 25 years. In other words, if you were a child during this period, you could reasonably expect to have a standard of living twice that of your parents by the time you reached adulthood. Of course, there were conditions. To achieve this goal, an individual was expected to enter the workforce and compete for a good salary or wage, and save their money to store and build wealth for retirement. This practice can be distilled even further: Work hard and save your money. In the true free-market capitalist system, these two components must be successfully combined for an individual or society to continually advance.

While Americans were working hard, saving, and prospering during the post-war boom of the twentieth century, many other countries in the world remained under the grip of oppressive regimes. Far from prospering, the citizens of these countries routinely dealt with hunger, famine, low wages, and corrupt rulers. One of the biggest problems these regimes faced in their ability to create prosperity was that their economies never reached anything close to their full potential. These countries were routinely guided by ruling factions who actively steered resources. Just as managing a large company can become too complex for any one CEO or small group of executives, directing an entire country's economic resources is a hopeless endeavor. One of the key reasons the citizens of these countries could never prosper under these governments was because resources were routinely misallocated, assets hardly ever received reinvestment, and innovation atrophied. That is about the only way to explain a country with the wheat production of Russia lacking enough bread to go around, as was the case by the early 1990s, when the wheels were coming off the Soviet Union. As these countries began their transition away from their closed-market, centrally planned economies, they transferred state-owned assets into private hands, even if incompletely. This helped unleash some of the human potential that had been lying dormant for decades. More specifically, governments in countries like China, Russia, India, and Brazil, while all starting from different relative positions and all going at their own pace, began to step out of their people's way. They let their citizens compete in the global markets for producing manufactured goods, services, energy, information technology, and commodities.

Arguably, over this time period beginning in the 1980s, no country has unleashed so much raw human potential through institutional guidance toward greater commercial competition than China. The effects of this Chinese policy are clear if we examine the country's GDP per head taken on a purchasing power parity basis over that time horizon. It is readily apparent that over the past three decades, or since its de facto ruler Deng Xiaoping was rumored to say, "To get rich is glorious," the Chinese have been improving their standard of living at a breakneck pace of 12% per year. Forget doubling your standard of living every generation; in China, the pace has been every six years or so (see Figure 5.1). Naturally, this rate of growth also has a lot to do with starting from a low base; nevertheless, the phenomenon is real.

It would be easy to look at these figures and discount their meaning due to their low base. But if we examine this growth alongside the country's institutional reforms, illustrated by the continual opening of its economy, we can see that this phenomenon is being driven by a fundamental change in the economy. Quite simply, the government, although still authoritarian, has been allowing its people to compete and fulfill their hopes for a better life. For example, if we examine China's rank over time in the Global Competitiveness Index, shown in Figure 5.2, this dynamic becomes more evident. From just the year

2000 through the 2009 rankings, China raced from the bottom 30% of the ranking in 2000 to the top 20% of the ranking for the 2009–2010 publication. More succinctly, in just nine years, China went from having one of the world's least competitive economies to one of the most.

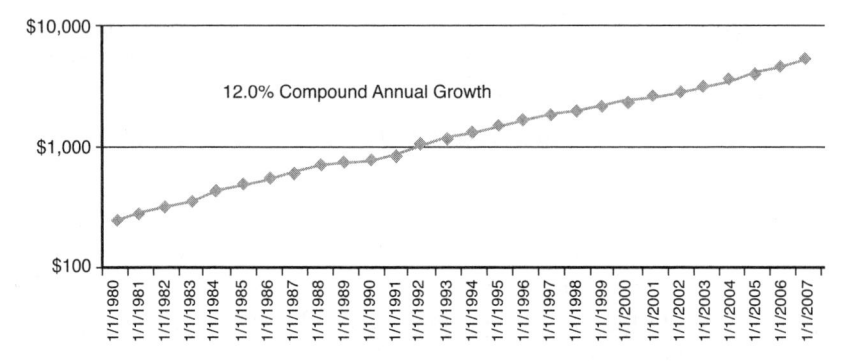

Figure 5.1 China per capita GDP (purchasing power parity)

Source: World Bank

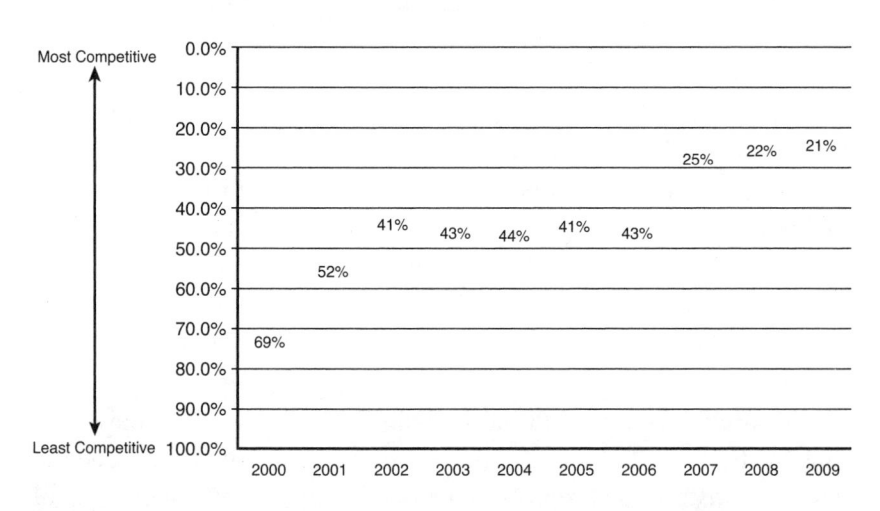

Figure 5.2 China's decile ranking in the Global Competitiveness Index, 2000 to 2009

Source: World Economic Forum

Entrepreneurialism Is Thriving in Many Key Emerging Markets

Competition leads to innovation, innovation leads to progress, and progress leads to wealth. We should hasten to acknowledge that wealth can be measured in numerous forms, extending beyond the financial manifestations. Heavy competition, innovation, and progress are the key ingredients of the Chinese economic miracle, not the cheap labor that some pundits cite. Cheap labor can take a nation only so far before it ceases to step forward any further. The truth is that China's adoption of freer market principles unleashed a wave of competition as its people took advantage of the opportunity to improve their lives after decades of oppression. The country is teeming with entrepreneurs (see Figure 5.3). China ranks among the top five countries in the world for its percentage of entrepreneurs who are all actively engaged in a constant state of competition with each other. It also has multinationals who have set up shop in China, seeking to participate in the new wealth that is being created. Clearly, succeeding at this level of competition, where local businesses are hungry for the opportunity to become wealthy, and the most successful multinational companies in the world have ventured into your backyard, requires a great deal more than cheap labor to thrive.

In addition to the large presence of entrepreneurs in China, the prospects for more entrepreneurs to enter the workforce and compete remain strong. Based on polls conducted by Gallup in China during 2006,[1] the Chinese actually rank starting and owning a business as the most desired vocation. This was well ahead of the old regimen of joining the ranks of the government or working for a state-owned enterprise. In fact, the poll found that just under 30% of respondents desired to start and own a business, versus a modest 8% who sought employment in a government or state-owned enterprise.

The Chinese drive toward entrepreneurialism is backed by a general dissatisfaction with their standard of living and their career, as shown in Table 5.1. As it turns out, many Chinese citizens are dissatisfied with their current state and see launching a business and taking control of their own prospects as the best solution. This disposition among the Chinese makes for a deep and broad pool of competitive businesses across the economy, which in turn spurs progress.

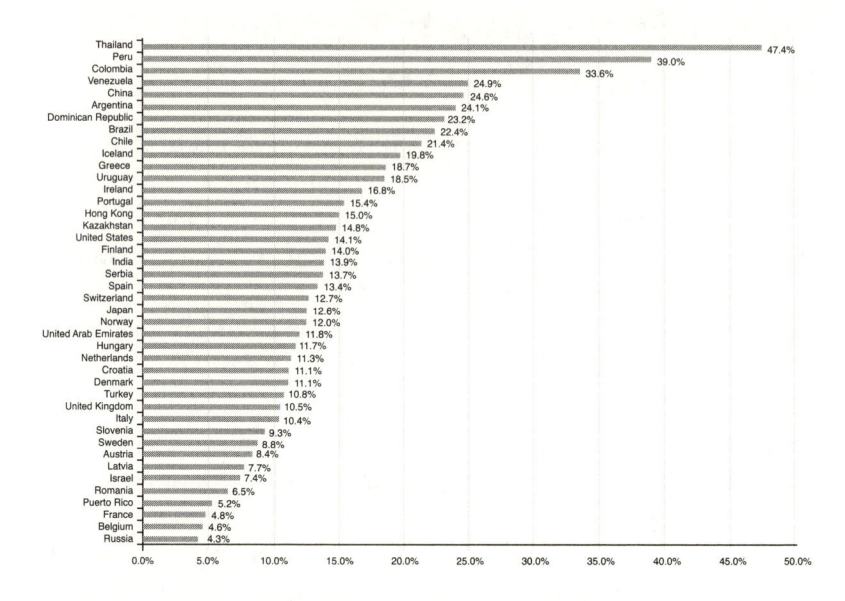

Figure 5.3 Overall entrepreneurial activity ages 18 to 64

Country	%
Thailand	47.4%
Peru	39.0%
Colombia	33.6%
Venezuela	24.9%
China	24.6%
Argentina	24.1%
Dominican Republic	23.2%
Brazil	22.4%
Chile	21.4%
Iceland	19.8%
Greece	18.7%
Uruguay	18.5%
Ireland	16.8%
Portugal	15.4%
Hong Kong	15.0%
Kazakhstan	14.8%
United States	14.1%
Finland	14.0%
India	13.9%
Serbia	13.7%
Spain	13.4%
Switzerland	12.7%
Japan	12.6%
Norway	12.0%
United Arab Emirates	11.8%
Hungary	11.7%
Netherlands	11.3%
Croatia	11.1%
Denmark	11.1%
Turkey	10.8%
United Kingdom	10.5%
Italy	10.4%
Slovenia	9.3%
Sweden	8.8%
Austria	8.4%
Latvia	7.7%
Israel	7.4%
Romania	6.5%
Puerto Rico	5.2%
France	4.8%
Belgium	4.6%
Russia	4.3%

Source: Global Entrepreneurial Monitor

TABLE 5.1 Satisfaction with Aspects of Life

How Things Are Going in Your Life	
Very Satisfied	8%
Very/Somewhat Dissatisfied	26%
Your Household Income	
Very Satisfied	3%
Very/Somewhat Dissatisfied	49%
Your Job (the Work You Do)	
Very Satisfied	4%
Very/Somewhat Dissatisfied	34%

Source: Gallup

The way China competes is simple: It is a nation of savers who expend the majority of their energy trying to excel in business. Since the opening of the economy in the 1980s, a great many Chinese have competed in the highly competitive export market for global goods and services. The United States did the same during its industrial boom that spanned the twentieth century, as Japan did as it emerged from World War II and took the world by storm in the 1980s, and as South Korea did as it emerged from the shambles of the Korean War to culminate its rapid ascent into the OECD. Therefore, China and its fellow emerging markets have joined a commercial environment that now includes an unprecedented number of competitors from across the globe. This had not been the case over the course of the twentieth century. In other words, China entered a highly competitive environment that requires its best efforts to succeed. Aside from top-down surveys, further evidence exists of China's ascent into the highest competitive stratospheres of the global business landscape. Bottoms-up surveys also provide empirical backing to China's competitive drive and its dividends as Chinese companies have begun to appear in the widely read business rankings published by *Forbes* and *BusinessWeek*.

Beginning with the Forbes Global 2000, perhaps the most simplistic ranking of the top 2,000 companies in the world, measured by a composite ranking of size based on sales, assets, profits, and market value, China's rapid advance into this group is notable. In 2003, the country contributed only 13 businesses to the entire 2,000-member ranking. By the publishing of the 2009 ranking, however, China's list of companies joining this group had risen sevenfold to 91, as shown in Figure 5.4. This advance provides increasing evidence of the country's commitment to competing among the best companies in the world, and its relative success as its businesses expand their operations and gain market share.

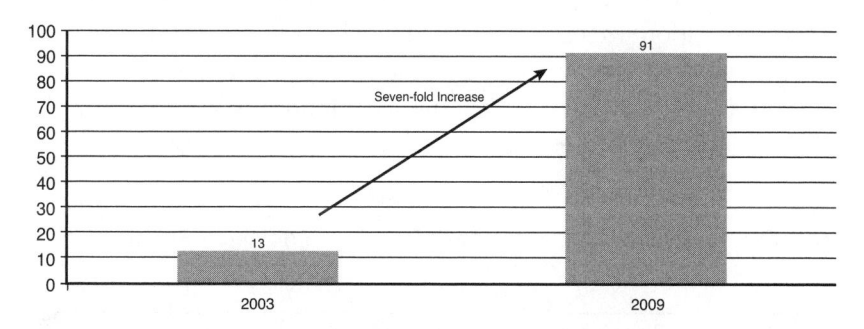

Figure 5.4   Chinese countries in the Forbes Global 2000

Source: Forbes

Not only have Chinese companies grown to the point of penetrating a greater portion of the largest 2,000 companies in the world over the past six years, but they also have been successful in penetrating the upper reaches of the ranking. For example, in the 2003 ranking, not a single Chinese company was among the top 50 in the world. But by 2009, five were in the top 50, and three had actually climbed into the top 25. Table 5.2 shows the number of Chinese companies placed by quartile in the top 100 companies on the list.

TABLE 5.2 Chinese Companies in the Top Quartiles of the Forbes 2000

	2009	2003
1–25	3	0
26–50	2	1
51–75	2	1
76–100	0	1
Total Top 100	7	3

Source: Forbes

This evidence of China's increasing competitiveness in the global business world is fortified by the increased recognition of its companies' ability to innovate on its path to financial success. As you know, innovation comes from competition, so China's increasing innovation is the direct result of its intensely competitive base. Let's return to the Global Competitiveness Ranking, published by the World Economic Forum (see Table 5.3). If we examine the subindexes, one of which ranks innovation, we can see that China's level of innovation has risen with its increasing competition in the world's markets. In 2006, the country ranked just 57th among the most innovative countries in the index, but by 2009 this ranking had leapfrogged almost 30 spots to number 29.

TABLE 5.3 Global Competitiveness Ranking: Innovation Subindex

	2006	2009
China Innovation Ranking	57	29

Source: World Economic Forum

Coinciding with this advance in innovation chronicled in the Global Competitiveness Ranking is some bottoms-up evidence of the same phenomenon. Using the annual *BusinessWeek* ranking of the top 50 most innovative businesses in the world, a Chinese computer manufacturer, Lenovo, cracked this elite company in 2009. As we compare the rankings from 2009 to the 2007 rankings, it is clear that, only two years ago, this list was confined to a group of iconic household-name developed-market companies (see Table 5.4). Since then, however, four emerging-market companies have cracked this enclave of innovative firms—Lenovo and three Indian companies: Tata Group, Reliance Industries, and Infosys.

TABLE 5.4 *BusinessWeek*'s 50 Most Innovative Companies for 2009 and 2007

	BusinessWeek's 50 Most Innovative Companies 2009			*BusinessWeek*'s 50 Most Innovative Companies 2007	
1	Apple	USA	1	Apple	USA
2	Google	USA	2	Google	USA
3	Toyota Motor	Japan	3	Toyota Motor	Japan
4	Microsoft	USA	4	General Electric	USA
5	Nintendo	Japan	5	Microsoft	USA
6	IBM	USA	6	Procter & Gamble	USA
7	Hewlett-Packard	USA	7	3M	USA
8	Research in Motion	Canada	8	Walt Disney	USA
9	Nokia	Finland	9	IBM	USA
10	Wal-Mart Stores	USA	10	Sony	Japan
11	Amazon.com	USA	11	Wal-Mart	USA
12	Procter & Gamble	USA	12	Honda Motor	Japan
13	**Data Group**	**India**	13	Nokia	Finland
14	Sony	Japan	14	Starbucks	USA
15	**Reliance Industries**	**India**	15	Target	USA
16	Samsung Electronics	South Korea	16	BMW	Germany
17	General Electric	USA	17	Samsung Electronics	South Korea
18	Volkswagen	Germany	18	Virgin Group	UK
19	McDonalds	USA	19	Intel	USA
20	BMW	Germany	20	Amazon.com	USA

TABLE 5.4 *BusinessWeek*'s 50 Most Innovative Companies for 2009 and 2007 (continued)

BusinessWeek's 50 Most Innovative Companies 2009			*BusinessWeek*'s 50 Most Innovative Companies 2007		
21	Walt Disney	USA	21	Boeing	USA
22	Honda Motor	Japan	22	Dell	USA
23	AT&T	USA	23	Genentech	USA
24	Coca-Cola	USA	24	Ebay	USA
25	Vodafone	Britain	25	Cisco Systems	USA
26	**Infosys**	**India**	26	Motorola	USA
27	LG Electronics	South Korea	27	Southwest Airlines	USA
28	Telefónica	Spain	28	Ideo	USA
29	Daimler	Germany	29	Ikea	Sweden
30	Verizon Communications	USA	30	Daimler Chrysler	Germany
31	Ford Motor	USA	31	Hewlett-Packard	USA
32	Cisco Systems	USA	32	Nike	USA
33	Intel	USA	33	BP	UK
34	Virgin Group	Britain	34	Research in Motion	Canada
35	ArcelorMittal	Luxembourg	35	AT&T	USA
36	NSBC Holdings	Britain	36	Citigropu	USA
37	ExxonMobil	USA	37	Verizon	USA
38	Nestle	Switzerland	38	Royal Philips Electronics	Netherlands
39	Iberdrola	Spain	39	Nintendo	Japan
40	Facebook	USA	40	Costco Wholesale	USA
41	3M	USA	41	Volkswagen	Germany
42	Banco Santander	Spain	42	Pfizer	USA
43	Mole	USA	43	Best Buy	USA
44	Johnson & Johnson	USA	44	Johnson & Johnson	USA
45	Southwest Airlines	USA	45	Amgen	USA
46	**Lenovo**	**China**	46	Merck	USA
47	JP Morgan Chase	USA	47	News Corporation	USA
48	Fiat	Italy	48	McDonalds	USA

TABLE 5.4 *BusinessWeek's* 50 Most Innovative Companies for 2009 and 2007   (continued)

BusinessWeek's 50 Most Innovative Companies 2009		*BusinessWeek's* 50 Most Innovative Companies 2007	
49 Target	USA	49 LG Electronics	South Korea
50 Royal Dutch Shell	Netherlands	50 Exxonmobil	USA

Source: *BusinessWeek*

Emerging nations, including China, India, Brazil, and several others, have already examined and successfully implemented the key factors that lead to successful competition in the capitalist system of commerce. Much proof already exists that these countries have developed key institutional biases toward free-market competition, as well as sound fiscal policies. Most importantly, as we place these factors of increasing competitiveness and sound fiscal policies into the context of the recent financial crisis, it seems probable that businesses from these countries will actually see their competitiveness accelerate over the coming five to ten years as they benefit from the crisis.

Crisis Is an Opportunity for Those in a Position to Seize the Opportunity

Simply put, firms from these countries were already competitive heading into the financial crisis. As the world economy recovers, these firms have a clear opportunity to emerge from the wreckage as even stronger entities.

China is far from alone in its emergence onto the global business stage due to its embrace of global competition. An old, if unfortunate, joke states that "Brazil is the country of the future, and it always will be." Ironically for this country with blessed resources, and now an enviable fiscal scorecard, the future may be now. In the past, the country was prone to widely swinging cycles of boom and bust that were both punctuated and accentuated by its sloppy finances. To place its economic history into context, a quick review of its annual rate of inflation judged by its year-over-year percentage increase provides an ample illustration of its constant financial turmoil. Brazil's heavy use of debt and loose monetary policy had taken inflation into the sphere of hyperinflation, or an outward manifestation of financial imprudence, that had reached an artistic level. During the course of the 1980s and 1990s, hyperinflation spiraled into growth rates approaching 3,000%, as shown in Figure 5.5. At these levels of inflation, consumers would have been wise to buy groceries as soon as a store opened in the morning rather than waiting until the afternoon.

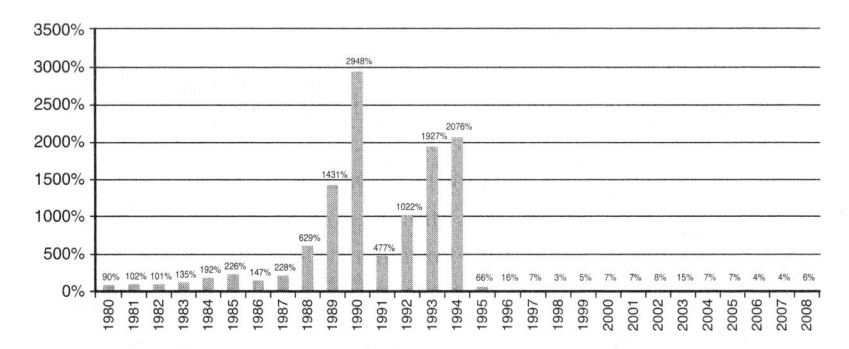

Figure 5.5 Brazil's annual year-over-year percentage change in inflation
Source: IMF

Still, the country eventually repaired its finances and inflation abated, eventually into the low single-digit rates seen during the past several years. Having gone from the emerging market's largest debtor nation to a creditor nation, Brazil received notable upgrades in its debt ratings, including an increase to investment grade by Standard & Poor's in 2008. Brazil successfully executed a strategy that would open its economy and stabilize its longtime Achilles heel of weak finances. The result has been that Brazil can also count itself among the nations that have an opportunity to improve their competitive positioning in the wake of the financial crisis. The clearest illustration of the country's newfound financial strength is its becoming a creditor to the International Monetary Fund through the purchase of IMF bonds. This represents a sharp reversal from its traditional position as the heaviest borrower of IMF resources during its various crises. More importantly, this shows that the country is attempting to take its financial strength and translate it into additional clout in world affairs. This reversal has not gone unnoticed by observers. Following a poll among business economists conducted by the World Economic

Forum, Brazil received the highest ranking in the world among countries expected to benefit from the crisis and recession. All told, only five countries received a ranking that predicted an improved forecast following the recession, including, in order, Brazil, India, China, Australia, and Canada. One large reason for this confidence in Brazil's prospects comes from its diligent reversal of its prior financial weakness. Brazil, which had accumulated over $200 billion in reserves during the boom preceding the crisis, was able to implement a number of fiscal and monetary measures in response to the financial crisis without weakening its financial position in the process. In the meantime, Western developed nations, such as the United States, had to push their fiscal balances and public debt levels into nearly uncharted territory in their attempts to counteract the financial crisis. Moreover, Brazil had also entered the crisis less dependent on Western developed nations for its exports. It had actually diversified its export base substantially into fellow emerging-market countries such as China. This offset some of the worst possible exposures to the initial shock. It also meant that exports would stand on stronger future footing, because many of Brazil's key trade partners were not left financially hobbled by the crisis and their risk-laden responses. One case in point comes from Brazil's deeper relationship with China as a key trading partner. For instance, in 2005 only 6% of Brazil's exports went to China, but more recently China became a larger partner than the United States, accounting for nearly 14% of Brazil's exports. There can be no question that the financial crisis at least temporarily negatively affected Brazil. But its financial prudence leading up to the crisis, in addition to its further diversification of its trading partners to more creditworthy nations, has provided a tremendous advantage to the country as it emerges from the financial crisis.

The New Landscape

In sum, we have discussed an ongoing paradigm that could have residual effects in the years to come, following the financial crisis and recession. This paradigm is simple because several of these developed countries that we have already mentioned did not expose themselves to the heavy use of borrowing and credit extension that ensnared developed markets, such as the United States and many in Europe. Therefore, for these fiscally sound economies, the global recession is a cyclical phenomenon whose effects will pass. On the other hand, the debtor nations encompassing the developed world must deal with the lasting consequences of substantial public and private debt loads, and the possible risks introduced by the institutional responses from their governments. This ultimately increases the financial burdens of all stakeholders of the indebted economies, because taxpayers must redress these imbalances over time. We cannot be sure how long it will take the United States and other developed markets to repair their balance sheets. But no matter the time period, it seems probable that a secular trend of saving and paying down debt balances will come at the expense of historic levels of consumer spending that occurred in the years leading up to the crisis. Likewise, any ill effects from the government response of a massively expanded monetary base, unprecedented budget deficits, and increased regulation implies that the United States economy has introduced possible further distractions from uneventfully resuming a solid rate of growth. We have seen so far that a new investment landscape is separated by a clear divide between countries, economies, businesses, and consumers who lie on the financially sound side of the chasm. Those that remain must traverse the divide from their current land of debt burdens, impaired financial systems, impending regulations, and risky sovereign finances. It is likely that the latter side will cross the divide in time and rejoin the former side in financial health. Until then, investors will find better growth among those inhabiting the healthy land.

With that said, investors looking ahead need to consider the long-term attractiveness of companies operating in these increasingly open and competitive nations. Just as important, investors need to consider the various methods through which they can participate in this growth, ranging from natural resources such as oil to consumer goods. More than 80% of the world's population lives in the emerging markets that are in the process of constructing a middle class of consumers. The remainder of this book discusses several investment themes that should capture this potential growth and reward investors who have the patience of long-term focus. Furthermore, because these themes surround long-term phenomena, they should afford lasting opportunities that can be taken advantage of at future points of maximum pessimism.

Endnote

[1] William J. McEwen, Ph.D. "The Chinese: a New Wave of Entrepreneurs?" http://www.gallup.com, December 26, 2007.

6

China: Ready for Prime Time

In 1975, the U.S. television network NBC created a program of skits aired on Saturday nights that came to be known as *Saturday Night Live*. The program featured a cast of talented comedians known as the "not ready for prime time players." These comedians were initially relegated to a bleak, late Saturday night timeslot that was all but ignored, but they beat the odds and went on to become legends in their craft. Over time, these original cast members and later cast members benefited from their growth in the entertainment industry through movies and their own television shows, rather than remaining confined to their live skits on Saturday nights. In many respects, if we trace the rapid ascent of the Chinese economy from its opening up in the 1980s under the leadership of Deng Xiaoping, we can find similarities between these two phenomena. China, although widely watched and even admired for its economic progress in the past couple of decades, has continually been cast as the economic version of the "not ready for prime time players." That is, up until the global financial crisis of 2008 and 2009. In the years following the crisis, the world will continue to see more of the Chinese influence turning up in the prime-time slots of the global economy that had been previously dominated by the United States, Europe, and Japan.

To grasp why the financial crisis marks an inflection point in China's modern history, we need a brief and modest historical context. Broadly speaking, during the past 4,000 years, China has developed a relatively continuous national identity. Perhaps due to the Confucian principle of studying history, many Chinese can appreciate their country in a larger historical context. Many understand that approximately 300 years ago China, alongside its Asian neighbor India, controlled 60% of the world's GDP. In the 300 years that followed, paced by the

Industrial Revolution, the world seemingly reversed hemispheres as it came to be dominated by the Western nations of Europe and the United States. These countries leveraged their industrial capabilities into military and commercial power. Meanwhile, during the twentieth century, as Western society achieved its heights, China suffered one setback after another. Invasions, occupations, civil war, political upheavals, natural disasters, famine, persecution, civil strife, and widespread poverty were all part of the Chinese experience of the twentieth century. In the time continuum of Chinese history, the majority of the twentieth century represented a low point. Even so, the fabric, national identity, and pride of the Chinese never wavered. Late in the twentieth century, Deng Xiaoping eventually assumed leadership of the country after the passing of Mao and the political defeat of his cronies in the late 1970s. He undertook the difficult chore of rebuilding China from decades of institutional mismanagement. In his search for answers, he examined several other Asian nations that had successfully constructed powerful economies, widespread prosperity, and peaceful, law-abiding environments that were still thoroughly controlled by their respective governments. Deng found in his travels and research that he wanted China to model itself after Singapore, South Korea, and Japan. In particular, he pointed out Singapore as the model China would both emulate and, in his mind, improve upon. The surprise of this one-time communist revolutionary singling out Singapore—Asia's most sparkling example of the success of free-market enterprise and capitalism—as the model for China's future cannot be overstated. Upon closer inspection, however, the Singaporean model was a natural fit for Deng and China. For starters, at one time Singapore was itself a microcosm of China when Deng came into power. In the 1960s, Singapore was a city-state that, after breaking off from Malaysia in 1965, basically had to find its place in the world. It did so by embracing the Western ideals of free markets, property rights, and capitalism in an attempt to join the global economy. Incidentally, this plan not only worked, but worked on an unprecedented scale. Importantly, based on the public accounts of Singapore's original Prime Minister, Lee Kuan Yew,[1] Deng was impressed with the use of the capitalist model to create widespread home ownership, especially in the context of an authoritative government and large presence of ethnic Chinese (77% of the population).

China was in a similar situation in the late 1970s when Deng came into power. It had been cut off from the rest of the modern world for half a century under Mao and was starting from scratch in a world that had left it behind. China too had to find its place if it were to restore its once-powerful place in the world order. According to Yew, after Deng's 1978 visit to Singapore, he left to return to China with the comment, "You made use of capitalism to build a more egalitarian society; everybody owns their own home. I will do the same."[2] As we now know, Deng returned to China and set his country on a path toward unparalleled economic growth. Productivity ascended from an exceptionally low economic base following decades of neglect due to social chaos and Maoist economic blunders. In the decades that followed, this growth accelerated and began lifting hundreds of millions of people out of poverty. This was based on the simple Asian tiger model of export-led growth, emphasis on education, and high savings rates. We also must recognize that although China embraced capitalism, it fashioned its own form of capitalism to meet Chinese ideals, rather than forcing the Chinese into an entirely Western model of society that includes democracy. In other words, China has possessed a long-standing backdrop of central authority, including both the Communist Party and the succession of dynasties leading up to the communist takeover. Although we should think of China as capitalists, the influence of government policy should continue to play a role in this growth.

A Culture Well Suited for Capitalism

Irrespective of government influence, the ancient Chinese saying that "The hills are high and the emperor is far away" remains in effect. Despite the central authority, the Chinese are also accustomed to self-reliance. In this regard, capitalism has been a natural fit for the Chinese. It assimilates nicely with Chinese customs such as thrift that have been around for thousands of years. The simple fact is that the Chinese possess such a high savings rate because it is embedded in their culture. China, unfortunately, is a vast expanse of land that has been prone to some of the worst natural disasters ever recorded, as measured in the number of fatalities. Earthquakes, floods, fires, and famine have occurred often enough over time in China that they have been remembered, recalled, and warned against from generation to generation. To provide some perspective, we can see from U.S. Geological Survey earthquake data that China's history is littered with well-recorded events of natural disasters that exacted horrific death tolls. See Table 6.1.

TABLE 6.1 China's History of Major Recorded Earthquakes

Date	Location	Fatalities
09/27/1290	Chihli	100,000
01/23/1556	Shensi	830,000
02/13/1918	Nan'ao, Guangdong	1,000
12/16/1920	Haiyuan, Ningxia	200,000
03/24/1923	Near Luhuo, Sichuan	3,500
03/16/1925	Yunnan	5,800
05/22/1927	Tsinghai	40,900
08/10/1931	Xinjiang	10,000
08/25/1933	Sichuan	9,300
08/15/1950	Tibet	1,526
03/07/1966	Hebei	1,000
03/22/1966	Hebei*	1,000*
07/25/1969	Guangdong	3,000
01/04/1970	Yunnan	10,000
05/10/1974	China	20,000
02/04/1975	Haicheng	2,000
07/27/1976	Tangshan	255,000
05/12/2008	Eastern Sichuan	87,587

Source: USGS
* Not a typo

As bad as these earthquakes have been, China's history of devastating floods is equally shocking. Home to two of the world's longest rivers, the Yangtze and the Yellow, China has always been plagued by floods. It is believed that throughout China's history, the Yangtze River has flooded over 1,000 times. But in spite of this track record, it must concede the title for the most severe floods to the Yellow River, which has become known among outsiders as "China's sorrow." For instance, in 1887 the Yellow River flooded and took the lives of an estimated two million people. In 1931, a flood from the Yellow River is believed to have taken four million lives. In 1938, another million were lost to flooding from this river. Taking into account these shocking records of natural disaster, and China's tremendous land mass, it has always been difficult for the central authorities to respond to these events in any sort of timely fashion. In the past, without motorized craft, routes were buried underwater, thus preventing travel. Over centuries of these collective experiences, the Chinese have conditioned themselves to prepare for catastrophe. Back in the time of imperial dynasties, this behavior was manifested in the form of searching for high ground on which villagers could stockpile grains and other provisions for when a flood eventually arrived. In modern Chinese society, based on the exchange of currency for goods and services, this behavior manifests itself through a high personal savings rate, as shown in Figure 6.1. Instead of floods and earthquakes as their primary concerns, though, the Chinese are more focused on saving for healthcare and retirement, to name a couple categories. The Chinese save for a number of practical reasons, but a large portion of this behavior ties back to a conditioned anxiety and a healthy respect for the risks tied to future emergencies.

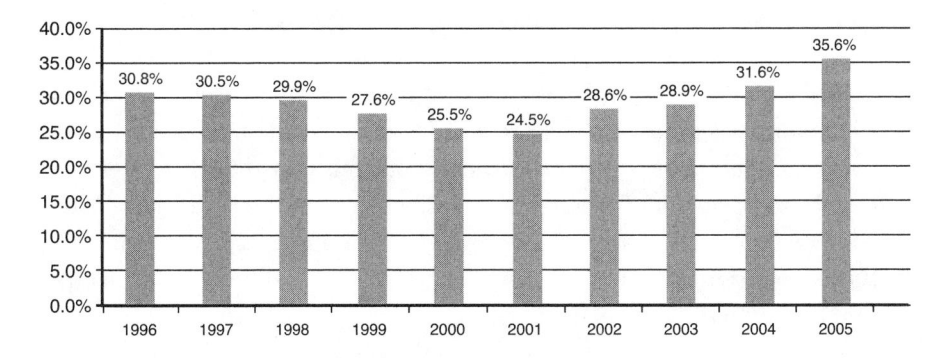

Figure 6.1 China's household savings rate

Source: Asian Development Bank

The point of this discussion of history and culture is to provide a context for what is occurring in the aftermath of the financial crisis. Since the Chinese moved into the global village of commercial trade and have been assimilating themselves into the world's business scene since the 1980s, they have been well prepared for the metaphorical flood that nearly wiped out entire developed-market economies. In other words, China's long-standing habit of preparing for calamity has served it extremely well in the capitalist system. For that matter, the behavior held in common among the most astute capitalists ever known in the West has been a common practice of thrift coupled with a sharp eye for opportunity in the wake of a crisis. The Rothschilds, Pierpont Morgan, Sir John Templeton, Warren Buffett—all these financial legends have practiced the art of possessing heavy savings that were ready to be deployed in the wake of a financial calamity. In this regard, as the capitalist system was shaken to its core in late 2008, China was safe from financial ruin. Now the country is realizing the rewards that flow to a saver when nearly every asset in the world goes on sale, all at once. So, just as all these capitalists increased their fortune in the wake of a crisis, China will do the same.

Putting Those Rainy-Day Savings to Work in the Worst Storm of the Past Century

The relevant question that follows is this: What will China buy with its massive hoard of rainy-day funds? Activity through the first three quarters of 2009 has left little doubt that China, a country hungry for commodities, has been gorging in the natural resource space. The country is interested in this space for many reasons. Rather than parade all the data points on China's voracious consumption of copper, iron, oil, cement, scrap metal, and so on, suffice it to say that China is bereft of natural resources. It must import large amounts of these materials to continue growing its economy. During the years that led up to the financial crisis, China was beginning to feel the pain of requiring these materials in the midst of relatively limited supply and competing demand from other countries. These economic tensions were on vivid display in the iron market during the years leading up to the crisis. China basically had to accept whatever pricing the Western-controlled, three-firm oligopoly of BHP, Rio Tinto, and Vale imposed. This record of steeply rising iron ore prices, which China had little choice but to accept, was punctuated by an 86% increase negotiated for 2008, as shown in Figure 6.2.

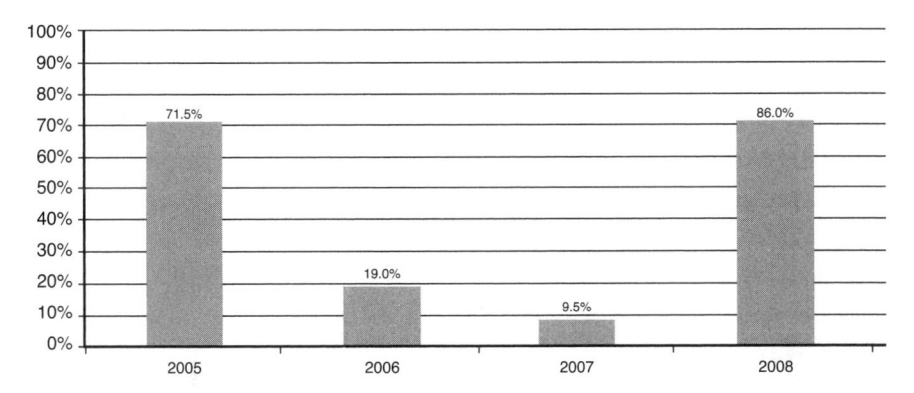

Figure 6.2 Year-over-year iron ore price increases
Source: Oligopoly Watch; Ministry of Commerce, People's Republic of China

Values: 2005: 71.5%; 2006: 19.0%; 2007: 9.5%; 2008: 86.0%

China has spent heavily on mergers and acquisitions (M&A) in 2009. This is unsurprising in light of what happened in the years prior to the financial crisis and global recession. Another factor was the subsequent collapse in commodity prices that precipitated sharply lower valuations and even some financial distress among the companies in this space. Nor is it surprising to find that the bulk of the major transactions announced by Chinese firms have occurred in the natural-resources space, with a handful in iron ore companies. Table 6.2 and Figure 6.3 show the sharp decline in commodity prices as defined by the CRB commodity index, as well as the subsequent M&A transactions by Chinese firms.

Based on the evidence so far, China has executed the role of an opportunistic capitalist close to perfection. This statement also is based on the strong probability that these types of transactions will continue underpinned by China's lack of internal natural resources, combined with its $2 trillion war chest of foreign exchange reserves. In short, China has used the financial crisis as an opportunity to improve on what had been a key weakness for a country in great need of natural resources but possessing few of its own.

TABLE 6.2 China's Buying Spree by Major Deal Announcement Through the Third Quarter of 2009

Acquirer	Target	Date	Country	Industry	Value
Shenzhen Zhongjin Lingnan Nonfemet	Perilya Mining	05 Feb '09	Australia	Metals	$29.8M
Hunan Valin Iron & Steel	Fortescue Metals Group	24 Feb '09	Australia	Iron	$438M
China Minmetals	OZ Minerals	01 Apr '09	Australia	Iron	$1.21B
China Nonferrous Metal Mining Group	Lynas Corp	30 Apr '09	Australia	Metals	$186M
PetroChina	Singapore Petroleum Corp	24 May '09	Singapore	Oil	$1.02B
Haier Group	Fisher & Paykel	26 May '09	New Zealand	Appliances	$29M
Sichuan Tengzhong Heavy Industrial Machinery	Hummer	03 Jun '09	US	Auto	(est) $100M
CIC	Morgan Stanley	03 Jun '09	US	Financial	$1.2B
Wuhan Iron & Steel	Consolidated Thompson	09 Jun '09	Canada	Iron	$240M
CIC	Goodman Group	15 Jun '09	Australia	Real Estate	$585M
CIC	Blackstone Group	19 Jun '09	US	Financial	$500M

TABLE 6.2 China's Buying Spree by Major Deal Announcement Through the Third Quarter of 2009

Acquirer	Target	Date	Country	Industry	Value
CIC	Diageo	21 Jul '09	UK	Beverages	$396M
Suning Appliance	Laox	24 Jun '09	Japan	Appliances	$8.4M
Sinopec Group	Addax Petroleum	24 Jun '09	Switzerland	Oil	$7.24B
CIC	Teck	06 Jul '09	Canada	Coal	$1.5B
Sinochem	Nufarm	30 Jul '09	Australia	Chemicals	NA
Beijingwest Industries	Delphi	08 Aug '09	US	Auto	NA
Yanzhou Coal Mining	Felix Resources	17 Aug '09	Australia	Coal	$2.95B

Source: ChinaStakes.com

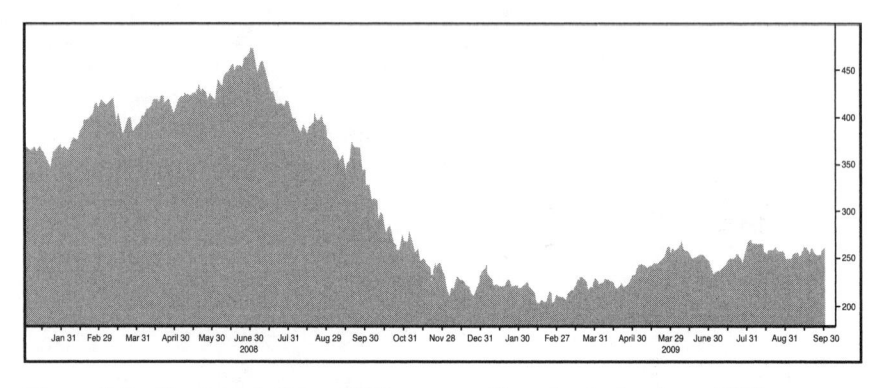

Figure 6.3 Reuters Jeffries CRB commodity price index from 2008 through the third quarter of 2009

Copyright 2009 Bloomberg Finance LP

Urbanization Is the Growth Engine

This still leaves the question, What does China want with all these natural resources? The answer leads us into the heart of our discussion. China is in the midst of a multidecade construction of an economy that more closely resembles the developed world. To accomplish this feat, the Chinese are constructing numerous cities to house all the migrants who have yet to enter its developed economy from the countryside. To construct these cities and hopefully show its lower-income citizens a new, modern way of life, China must have access to all the raw materials that are necessary to build up a city, such as cement, steel, alloys for steel, iron, aluminum, and copper. Without access to these materials, the construction projects will slow, and the country's rapid ascent to prosperity will sputter. Taking this knowledge, we can easily surmise that the significant bull market in commodities that occurred prior to the financial collapse has plenty of cause to resume in the coming years, and likely will. Despite the large run in commodity prices from the early 2000s through 2008, and all the economic incentive to expand mining production in copper, bauxite, and nickel, the havoc wreaked by the crisis through a commodity price collapse and tight credit stopped and in some cases reversed these mining expansions. As compelling as the commodity space may be, those discussions are saved for the chapters on protein and agribusiness, as well as oil and energy. This discussion instead focuses on the urbanization trend in China as it relates to the country's domestic economy, and the manifest opportunities that will be presented to investors over the coming five to ten years.

Before we jump into the areas that investors will want to consider as they look for opportunities presented by the growing middle class of Chinese consumers, let's quickly look at the size of the opportunity at hand. Chinese President Hu Jintao stated at the 17th Congress that he would like to quadruple China's per capita GDP by the year 2020 from its 2000 level.[3] This means that the standard of living in China is targeted to continue growing at just over 7% a year in the coming decade. The simplest way to replicate the growth of the past twenty years over the next ten is to keep doing what you have been doing. What the Chinese have been doing is relatively straightforward: They continue to incentivize the migration of citizens out of the countryside and into the urban centers. This recipe for economic progress has been cooking since the 1980s. In 1980, only 190 million people, or 20% of the population, were living in cities. But by 2000, this number had increased by 270 million, or to 36% of the population, based on World Bank estimates. As this migration has happened, the standard of living has risen sharply for the new urbanites as they are effectively assimilated into the global economy through China's trade and local domestic businesses. The simple fact is that city-dwellers in China have incomes that are more than three times as large as rural inhabitants, as shown in Figure 6.4.

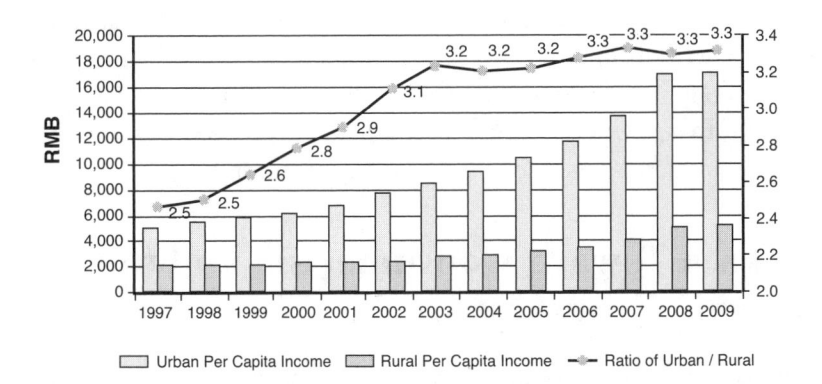

Figure 6.4 Urban and rural per capita incomes in China

Source: China Statistical Yearbook

Because about 46% of the population in China is urban, it is easy to see that the rural workforce has latent capacity and that this proportion can and will change in the coming years. In fact, based on estimates by the consulting firm McKinsey,[4] China's urban population already accounts for 75% of the country's GDP. This means that there is ample incentive to grow this economic engine and reduce the slack in the economy from the less productive rural areas of China. The same study from McKinsey estimated that by 2025, well over 926 million people will live in China's urban centers, or an additional 350 million from the 2005 level. With two current megacities of more than 10 million people, these estimates suggest that six more cities of this scale will emerge in the coming 20 years. By 2030, 1 billion people will live in China's cities, or over 60% of the population. Likewise, the World Bank estimates that by the year 2020, China will have between 70 and 100 cities with over 1 million inhabitants. These numbers are staggering by developed-market standards. For all intents and purposes, the Chinese are in the process of constructing a new urban population over the coming 15 years that is greater than the entire population of the United States. As this demographic shift continues from the rural areas to China's cities, it will bring with it new markets and a need for new goods and services to match urban consumption patterns. Again, the scale for urban consumption trends presents a large market opportunity. We are talking about adding an urban market that, based on the earlier McKinsey projections, represents a level of aggregate consumption that will be twice the size of Germany's entire economy by 2025. So although all this urbanization will drive continued demand for commodities and raw materials for infrastructure construction, the real sea change and new opportunity will unfold in the emergence of increased consumerism.

The Path Toward Consumerism and the Domestic Economy

Of course, before we make over the Chinese economy into a nation of spenders, we must address the long-standing tradition of Chinese saving. This phenomenon represents a perceived speed bump of sorts for Westerners who associate consumerism with the runaway levels of spending that have been witnessed in developed markets, such as the United States, during the past few decades. We should not expect the Chinese to ditch their custom of thrift anytime soon. But it is entirely reasonable to suspect that as the economy develops, these citizens might save less than their current run rate, while still maintaining ample financial security and long-standing customs. The government also wants to direct the nation toward a larger domestic economy. Therefore, one initiative it is pushing is to strengthen the country's social security system in an effort to alleviate fears and induce less saving and more consumption. The prospective success of these efforts remains to be seen, but other trends may also precipitate less anxiety and more consumption. One development comes from the private market, where the growth in insurance products has been remarkably high, thanks to the low base of penetration and continued popularity. Insurance products and the companies that provide them in China play a significant role in the development of higher consumption levels since they effectively take over the traditional role of self-insurance from the Chinese household. In other words, rather than the Chinese household keeping cash deposits at the bank as reserves against life events related to health, retirement, or death, instead they can purchase an insurance product that accomplishes the same. In turn, this method frees up additional current income for consumption purposes, or saving for other items. Importantly, the scope of continued growth in the Chinese insurance market is easily recognized, with insurance premiums in China representing 3% of GDP compared to 10% to 12% in the OECD countries. Additionally, the insurance industry in China has become a growth market, with 95% controlled by three Chinese firms: China Life, Ping An, and China Pacific. Thanks to financial products such as insurance, there is additional room for the savings rate to loosen up through these private-market solutions. Aside from a stronger safety net from the government and private-market solutions, some of the high savings rate may erode from its current levels based on demographics.

Another factor is the growing generational divide between the adults who lived through the establishment of the People's Republic and the Cultural Revolution, and the most recent generation. They are products of China's one-child policy and are known as "Little Emperors" or the "Me Generation." Based on available reports and surveys, a generational divide has appeared between the country's older citizens, who survived Mao's China, and the new generation of single-child youths. They have been exposed to advertising, branding, multiculturalism, rock and roll, hip-hop, video games, and everything else the consumer companies can throw their way. The society of the Me Generation has been loaded with consumer stimulus since it grew up alongside Deng's globalization beginning in 1980. Because this culture is littered with only children, these young people are accustomed to receiving attention and gifts from their parents and grandparents. The urban youth of today have departed from the over-50 crowd insofar as they have not engaged in politics much, whereas the lives of their parents and grandparents were dominated by epic political battles and civil strife. Instead, the young Chinese of today are far more tuned into the good life that globalization has spawned, including the prevalence of consumer technology and the ability to travel. The emphasis that the Me Generation places on material goods among their top purchasing priorities is widely reported on an anecdotal basis. It's also revealed in statistical surveys, such as MasterCard's Worldwide Index of Purchasing Priorities. In the most recent available survey conducted in China for the first half of 2009, the disparity between consumer habits for Chinese older than 30 versus those younger than 30 was clear. For instance, measuring the top three categories for purchasing priorities, the survey showed that, for fashion and accessories, 71% of the crowd below 30 prioritized this expenditure versus 59% in the above-30 crowd. In the consumer electronics category, a similar trend was apparent, with 73% of the respondents younger than 30 prioritizing this purchase versus 51% in the above-30 group. Further evidence of the Me Generation's relative tilt toward consumerism versus their parents and grandparents can be seen in the overall sophistication of the Little Emperors in the marketplace. This demographic has gained a reputation for brand awareness and being attuned to quality, and they obtain their knowledge through heavy online research and social networking, including blogging on products. Surveys among young shoppers suggest that 70% of Chinese youth use an Internet search engine before making a major purchase. This behavior is not surprising, because the youth in China spend far more time on the Internet than even their American counterparts. According to several estimates, young people in China spend approximately 20 hours per week on the Internet versus just 12 hours for the same age group in the United States. Taking these factors into consideration, the young shoppers of China are far more inclined to shop online as well. Based on recent surveys from MasterCard, 15% of Chinese people under the age of 30 perform 10% to 20% of their shopping online versus 6% in the above-30 age group (see Figure 6.5).

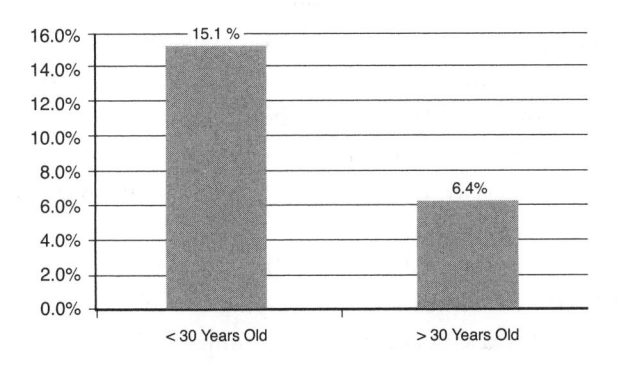

Figure 6.5 10% to 20% of shopping is conducted online
Source: MasterCard Worldwide Index of Purchasing Priorities

These data points underscore a demographic trend in China in which the youth are far more comfortable, if not altogether obsessed, with technology. Recognizing trends such as these is critical for consumer goods companies that hope to sell or expand their businesses in China. It is widely forecast that much of the rapid growth in future urbanization may occur in what are called "second-tier" cities in China. The largest cities will increase too, but at a slower rate. When speaking of tiers, some disagreement has arisen over how to classify Chinese cities. In general, the first-tier cities are the four largest: Beijing, Shanghai, Guangzhou, and Shenzhen. The second-tier cities include the province capitals, and the third-tier cities include big, economically developed cities in the provinces such as Qingdao and Xiamen. We should exercise some caution in respect to the terms "second tier" and "third tier" when applying a Western perspective, because some "towns" in China hold three quarters of a million residents. Irrespective of what they are called, these smaller cities by Chinese standards have been growing faster. In particular, their retail sales growth has been outpacing growth in the first-tier cities by two to three percentage points during the past several years.

More growth has occurred in the second- and third-tier cities because these consumers start from a lower economic base. The first-tier cities, while still possessing very low per capita incomes by developed-market standards, are saturated with people. For that reason, the second- and third-tier cities will see better growth from people migrating out of the countryside, as well as an upward drift in their own per capita income levels toward the first-tier levels of income. For these reasons, and nationwide growth in consumerism notwithstanding, the second and third tiers should continue to see higher rates of growth. This has important implications for consumer companies and the investors who would like to own their shares. First, the second- and third-tier cities are less globalized and, therefore, less export-driven than the first-tier cities in many cases, which in turn means that their economies are more domestically led. This presents an opportunity for a consumer goods company, but it can also make the waters a bit trickier to navigate due to the less multicultural influences and stronger native Chinese taste preferences. In this regard, although the growth in these markets is promising, it is even more essential that companies understand their markets and consumer tastes. These distinctions are important for all consumer goods companies—in particular, for the Western multinational firms that are attempting to sell into these markets. For Western firms, the challenge can be even more daunting, because customs and taste preferences can vary by province and region. Some examples of Chinese taste preferences and how they may substantially differ from Western preferences can be most clearly seen in the grocery aisles. The first significant difference a Western food executive might find is that the Chinese are obsessed with fresh products when it comes to food. If you walk into a Walmart in China, you will find many of the customers crowding around large open-air fish tanks going after live carp, eels, and crabs with handheld nets. This may seem odd from a Western perspective, but Walmart would be unable to sell its fish in filets behind glass. The Chinese insist on freshness to the point of personally obtaining their fish and having it cleaned live, right before their eyes. This process might be too much for the American soccer mom, who desires considerably less knowledge of the preparation process. Likewise, Westerners might be confused by the large open case of turtles crawling over each other. But if you want to attract food shoppers in China, it is important that they can get the necessary ingredients for the traditional dish of turtle soup. Want to sell skin moisturizer in China? You would sell more if it contained sheep's placenta. The point of these illustrations goes beyond highlighting distinctive consumer preferences among the Chinese. It shows that for a business to be successful in the consumer market, it is imperative to understand the Chinese consumer. In this respect, and from what we can easily see in the local practices of Walmart, a large Western multinational (or any firm, for that matter) cannot waltz through the Chinese consumer market without first studying and adapting to local tastes and preferences.

For the reasons discussed, it is easy to appreciate that when it comes to selling products to the Chinese consumer, local firms that understand Chinese tastes and customs have an edge. The good news for all competitors in the Chinese consumer market is that these purchasers prize quality above all else and have no qualms about paying more for premium products. Because of these behaviors, the market is indeed open to all competitors rather than only local Chinese companies. Evidence of meritocracy in the Chinese consumer is abundant in light of consumer surveys on branding in China. As it turns out, the Chinese are not against Western products, but the products must be of good quality to attract their discretionary income. Another positive sign for Western consumer goods firms is that perceived quality of American-made goods is high, especially among the younger demographic, who represent the key opportunity for consumption. Judging from the results of surveys conducted by Gallup, 44% of Chinese citizens aged 18 to 24 rate the quality of American goods as excellent, compared to only 22% for Chinese-made goods (see Table 6.3).

TABLE 6.3 Ratings of Goods Manufactured by the Chinese

	Years of Age		
	18–24	25–29	60+
Produced in China			
Excellent	22%	30%	35%
Good	27%	23%	13%
Poor	51%	44%	40%
Produced in USA			
Excellent	44%	32%	19%
Good	16%	21%	14%
Poor	8%	8%	6%

Source: Gallup

This perception carries through into even more tangible measures that survey individual brand names and their ranking among the Chinese. Table 6.4 shows the first 25 names from a consumer survey conducted in China by the Asian-focused brokerage firm CLSA, which polled for the top 100 brands. In light of the earlier taste preferences we mentioned, it might be surprising that many firms outside China are on the list, including a good many Western names, such as Coca-Cola, Nokia, and Nike.

Table 6.4, and its inclusion of iconic Western brands, underscores a few simple threads of consumer behavior in China that are important to grasp. The first important realization is that the Chinese are obsessed with brand names. The second is that the Chinese utilize the personal display of these brand names as the most visible outward manifestation of their success in business and having achieved a higher income. In other words, although the Chinese are savers, they are also materialistic, and high-quality brand names are status symbols. The purchase and display of premium brands represent aspirational consumption that serves as a calculated projection of one's standing in society to other Chinese.

TABLE 6.4 Top Consumer Brands in China

	Segment	Brand
1	Mobile Services	China Mobile
2	Instant Messaging	Tencent QQ
3	Instant Noodles	Master Kong
4	Mobile Handset	Nokia
5	Search Engine	Baidu
6	Carbonated Drinks	Coca-Cola
7	Milk, Yogurt & Dairy	Mengniu
8	Property Developer	Vanke
9	Juice	Huiyan
10	Supermarket	Carrefour
11	Milk, Yogurt & Dairy	Yili
12	Sportswear	Adidas
13	Banking	ICBC
14	Washington Machine	Haier
15	Beer	Tsingtao Brewery
16	Camera	Canon
17	Bottled Water	Nongfu Spring
18	Wine	Great Wall Wine
19	Aircon	Gree
20	Carbonated Drinks	Pepsi
21	Insurance	Ping An
22	Sportswear	Nike
23	Supermarket	Walmart
24	Insurance	China Life Insurance
25	Tea Beverages	Uni-President

Source: CLSA

Prime-Time Products

Given our better understanding of the behavior of Chinese consumers, including their tastes and preferences, we can now turn our discussion toward the actual products they are consuming. We also can look at some of the consumer goods that investors may want to target as areas of growth for future consumption. We can consider this discussion in two ways. We can assess what consumers profess to purchase or even plan to purchase from a discretionary perspective. We also can assess what we can expect consumers to purchase in the context of increased urbanization. In other words, we can look at this equation from what consumers want to buy and what they do buy as they move from rural to urban areas.

Beginning with the discretionary discussion, the Chinese consumer is nearly rabid for consumer technology, including cell phones, computers, televisions, and music players. In many cases, it is not unusual to see these purchases come before household appliances such as refrigerators, microwaves, and vacuum cleaners in order of importance for planned purchases. As you can see in Table 6.5, as shown in a Gallup poll, Chinese consumers aged 18 to 24 ranked purchasing a cell phone above all other categories, as did consumers aged 25 to 29. Perhaps not surprising in this context, the poll also found that more Chinese households owned computers than vacuum cleaners. In keeping with our earlier comments, the cell phone is yet another product where Chinese consumers often try to distinguish themselves with a premium product. This device is a status symbol in China, as are the brand and model within the product category. In fact, a 2008 study by McKinsey[5] found that young Chinese consumers are sometimes willing to pay as much as three times their monthly income for the latest cell phone. Finally, young Chinese are also believed to upgrade or switch their cell phone every 9 to 12 months, versus their developed-market peers, who average 18 to 24 months.

With all this emphasis on technology, it should be unremarkable that online shopping in and of itself is an important consideration when discussing the Chinese consumer. We already know the Internet usage habits of young Chinese people and their 20-hour-per-week habit. We should also point out that approximately 145 million of these users are registered with TaoBao, the most popular online shopping site in China. Online shopping in China is a growing secular trend that has been helped in part by better connectivity between Internet users and retailers. Despite all China's infrastructure spending, its roads to some second-tier cities are still poorly developed. These physical impediments make establishing an already difficult distribution system even harder for retailers that don't have a local

TABLE 6.5 Plan to Buy in the Next Two Years

| | Years of Age | | |
	18–24	25–29	60+
Mobile phone	52%	36%	10%
Color TV	38%	27%	15%
Air conditioner	37%	26%	3%
Refrigerator	36%	27%	8%
Computer	36%	26%	5%
Video camera	31%	19%	3%
Microwave	31%	19%	7%
Digital camera	27%	12%	3%
Motorcycle	22%	17%	5%

Source: Gallup

presence, but online shopping has helped bridge this gap. In this respect, online shopping circumvents the lack of physical retail presence that many firms possess in the second- and third-tier cities. Additionally, the Chinese are open to shopping online to obtain the item they desire. Online shopping is also important to meeting the Chinese consumer's need for market research on a particular product before making the purchase. This pursuit of market research and demand for technology devices coalesce in a detectable appetite for information and the speed at which information can be delivered. In the Gallup study shown in Table 6.6, Chinese people aged 18 to 24 consume more information across more media and also record far higher exposure and access to the Internet.

TABLE 6.6 Media Consumption in China

| | Years of Age | | |
	18–24	25–29	60+
In past 12 months:			
Read a book	76%	64%	32%
Played music/CDs	84%	76%	24%
Took photos	63%	58%	25%
Attended Western language movie	35%	24%	6%

TABLE 6.6 Media Consumption in China (continued)

	Years of Age		
	18–24	25–29	60+
Bought Western records/CDs	54%	34%	2%
Bought Western brand clothing	27%	17%	1%
Ever read:			
Newspapers	86%	73%	50%
Magazines	81%	64%	34%
Have access to a computer	62%	43%	7%
Ever used a computer	66%	41%	2%
Ever used the Internet	51%	26%	1%

Source: Gallup

These discretionary trends are interesting in the ranks of the Me Generation, and so are their implications for future consumer purchases over the coming five to ten years. We can also appreciate that when a consumer relocates from a rural environment to an urban setting, certain new consumption patterns may also follow. Table 6.7 shows the tremendous disparity between goods and services that are owned by city dwellers versus rural citizens of China.

TABLE 6.7 Ownership Among First-Tier Cities and Rural Chinese

	Tier 1 City	Rural
Mobile phone	90%	49%
Computer	72%	4%
Medical insurance	68%	40%
Life insurance	52%	12%
Privately owned automobile	13%	1%

Source: Gallup

In Table 6.7, it is not hard to see that within large cities such as Beijing, ownership levels of some specific goods such as cell phones and even computers start to resemble developed-market benchmarks. This is supported by two phenomena: the higher level of income that accompanies urban residence in China compared to rural income levels, and the commonsense necessity of some of these items when living in a faster-paced urban environment filled with modern businesses. One product that stands out in particular is the low number of automobiles owned in both environments. This category has tremendous room for growth across the board in China as its standard of living rises over time. For example, when measured by automobile ownership per 1,000 people in China, approximately eight people own cars, compared to 750 in the United States.

Irrespective of the potential, and China's emergence in prime time, it remains a work in progress. The long-term picture is promising, but to be clear, there are always bumps along the way in any developing nation's progress. The prospects for future turbulence in the country's financial or real estate markets as China comes of age should not be disregarded. At the same time, the occurrence of these events are always the case rather than the exception, as we witnessed during U.S. development suffering through a depression and the Asian Tigers who were temporarily sidetracked by the Asian Financial Crisis. The key question an investor must consider, though, is how he will take advantage of similar events should they unfold in China. In the prior cases of the United States and the Asian Tigers, investors were heavily rewarded for purchasing stock in the wake of these events or, as we say, at a point of maximum pessimism. With that said, should one occur in China, the same rewarding results may likely hold.

In any event, over the coming several years, China will have an important opportunity to leverage its strong potential for growth and its record of financial prudence into even greater economic rewards and higher standards of living. In short, the country is entering a phase of its economic progress that will continue to shift toward increasing levels of domestic demand and consumerism. One key will be the steady push by the central government to continue opening its economy to greater globalization and transparency. Nothing has done more for this country to date than its leaders allowing its people to enter global trade and compete with the rest of the world. We can take comfort in the fact that the Chinese understand this reality well. In an early 2009 interview with the *Financial Times*,[6] Chinese Premier Wen Jiabao quoted in admiration the wisdom of a Western economist whose teachings had impacted more Chinese people than any other economist in history. This economist was not Karl Marx, but Adam Smith.

Endnotes

[1] Lee Kuan Yew. Interview by Charlie Rose, October 24, 2009. *The Charlie Rose Show*.

[2] Ibid.

[3] Xinhua. "Hu sets goal of quadrupling per capita GDP under environment, resource restrictions." http://english.people.com.cn, October 15, 2007.

[4] McKinsey Global Institute. "Preparing for China's urban billion," March 2009.

[5] Insights China. Annual Chinese Consumer Survey 08. McKinsey & Co.

[6] Lionel Barber, Geoff Dyer, James Kynge, and Lifen Zhang. "Interview: Message from Wen." *Financial Times*, February 1, 2009.

7

Proteins and Agribusiness: Billions and Billions to Be Served

Since the beginning of human existence, every man, woman, and child has required nourishment to embrace another day of life. This began with the hunter-gatherer method, which involved intense day-to-day pressure to skillfully acquire whatever sustenance one could find by foraging and scavenging. Later, around 9000 B.C., humans first planted and successfully domesticated grains in the Mesopotamian region of the Tigris and Euphrates Rivers. This development marked a profound inflection point and likely changed the course of mankind forever, as well as for the better. Through generations of practice and innovation, people honed their farming skills and eventually produced more stock than they could consume, with the difference available to trade for other goods or services. It soon followed that those who were disinclined or unable to farm could instead negotiate their skill sets in exchange for a share of the crop surpluses. This simple innovation of domesticating crops unified people beyond the tradition of tribes or bloodlines and led to coordination between people who could farm and those who wanted access to food production. In turn, the nonfarming people would spend their days in various pursuits that their neighbors valued. These pursuits took many forms, whether crafting goods or providing services to the remaining people who had assembled in these bountiful areas. In time, society based on commerce was born.

Fast-forward 11,000 years, and this simple paradigm remains alive and well. Perhaps most interesting and relevant to our discussion is that the rapid spread of globalization since the 1980s, resulting from intensified economic coordination among the many nations of the world, led to an age of prosperity that could hardly have been imagined in earlier centuries. In practical terms, this means that an increasing number of people have improved and continue to improve their lot by successfully joining the global economy. For lack of better words, entire nations that had previously been shut off from the world due to overbearing governments or dictators suddenly reversed course and joined what amounts to a new model for a global village. In particular, the people of China and India have done a remarkably good job of assimilating into the global markets after their governments rescinded policies that heavily enforced the allocation of resources by the state. As the people of these countries have sought opportunity in any number of ventures, such as operating manufacturing plants, writing computer code, attending universities, and launching their own businesses, their standard of living has increased dramatically. Returning to our simple example, these global villagers create goods and services that their neighbors value and in turn trade money for. We can use GDP per head, adjusted for purchasing power parity, as a proxy for the standard of living in China and India. Figure 7.1 shows that since 1980 the general prosperity of the two countries has been doubling every six and ten years, respectively. These advances in the standard of living are unprecedented and have been rapidly altering consumer behavior in these countries as well.

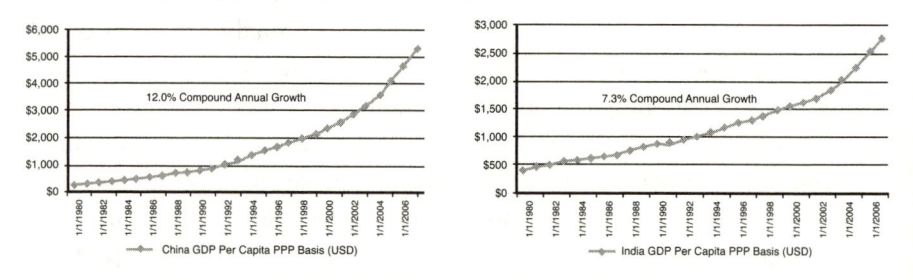

Figure 7.1 China's and India's GDP per head since 1980

Source: World Bank

Where's the Beef (and Chicken and Pork, Too)?

During the past three decades, this growth in prosperity has affected the citizens of these countries in a multitude of ways. In particular, it has enabled them to improve their lifestyles, including their diets.

More specifically, as the citizens of China and India have improved their standard of living during the past 29 years, their protein intake has also risen substantially. So although inhabitants of the developed markets may take for granted the daily availability of protein sources such as beef and poultry, these goods in China are still transitioning from special occasion and holiday meals into the mainstream daily diet. In effect, many urban coastal region Chinese are already consuming protein in a similar fashion to Western developed-market consumers. But the phenomenon is in a nascent stage from a broader economic perspective, and the scope for adding new consumers to this fray remains considerable. In other words, despite all the rapid progress, these countries still have a long way to go in their development toward Western standards of living. To bring this relationship into better perspective, Table 7.1 examines the rate of per capita consumption in China compared to a developed market such as the U.S. Taken on a per capita basis, China's consumption of poultry is only 25% of the U.S. level, and its consumption of beef is only 11.6% of the U.S. average.

TABLE 7.1 China's Per Capita Consumption Levels Taken as a Percentage of Those in the United States

	1997	1998	1999	2000	2001	2002	2003	2004	2005	2006	2007	2008
Beef	8.2	8.8	9.1	9.1	9.2	9.2	9.9	10.0	10.1	10.1	10.9	11.6
Butter	4.0	3.7	3.7	3.9	3.9	4.2	4.6	4.7	4.9	5.6	5.7	6.1
Cheese	1.3	1.2	1.2	1.3	1.3	1.3	1.4	1.6	1.6	1.6	2.0	2.1
Poultry	18.8	20.3	19.8	21.2	20.8	20.2	21.0	20.7	21.1	21.8	22.8	25.0
Sugar	21.3	21.2	21.6	20.7	23.3	26.8	28.9	28.1	28.3	34.3	37.2	37.7
Vegetable Oil	23.2	22.5	24.3	24.7	25.3	30.1	40.3	41.6	41.2	41.3	41.9	43.7

Source: FAO, OECD, Maximum Pessimism Report

Expanding on the poultry example, this means that China's current level of per capita consumption in poultry is on par with the U.S.'s dating all the way back to 1942 (18 pounds per capita). With that said, reading modern Chinese accounts that describe meat dishes as still part of a holiday or special-occasion menu sounds like childhood accounts from Americans of the Depression/post-World War II generation. Most modern Americans can appreciate that their standard of living exceeds levels from their grandparents' generation. Some may even take for granted their relatively easy access to cheap meals of poultry and beef.

However interesting the historical context may be, the prospects for continued growth in consumption deserve our focus. Returning to the per capita GDP growth rates, in Figure 7.2, we can now better see the approximate relationships between rising GDP per head and its effects on the consumption behavior of its citizens.

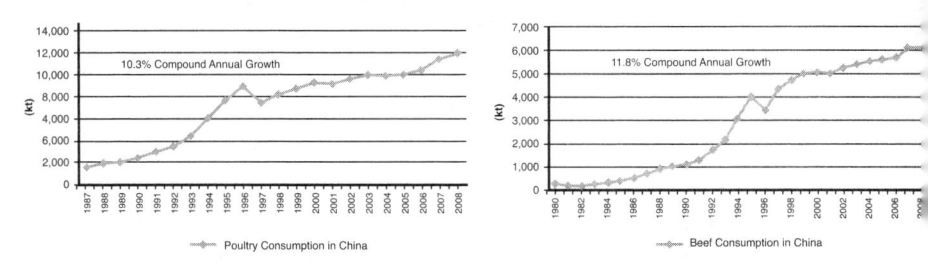

Figure 7.2 China's poultry and beef consumption
Source: USDA

As evidenced in the Figure 7.2, consumption growth for both poultry and beef in China has increased at an annualized rate of 10.3% and 11.8%, respectively. This suggests that both goods have trended in line with the long-term growth in GDP per head of 12.0% since 1980. The basic takeaway from these data points is that protein consumption is indeed scaling with the broader economic phenomenon of rising incomes and standards of living. The other key point is that these citizens do not have to wait a generation, unlike the postwar Americans, for their standard of living to double, and their consumption habits are adapting in comparatively real time. All protein consumption is growing sharply in these countries. However, the growth prospects for poultry consumption in China may possess the most interesting potential if consumer behavior patterns follow the market paradigms witnessed during the twentieth century in developed markets such as the U.S. More specifically, poultry is one protein that has demonstrated an accelerating demand trend as an economy becomes wealthier and more health-conscious. In other words, poultry receives yet another demand catalyst when higher incomes prevail and people can afford to take better care of themselves. In Figure 7.3, which shows the per capita rates of consumption during the second half of the twentieth century in the U.S., the trend toward higher poultry consumption at the expense of beef consumption is apparent. Again, the underlying cause of this substitution can be found in the greater attention paid to healthy diets among higher-income consumers. Another important driver is the low price of poultry relative to other meat proteins in the market.

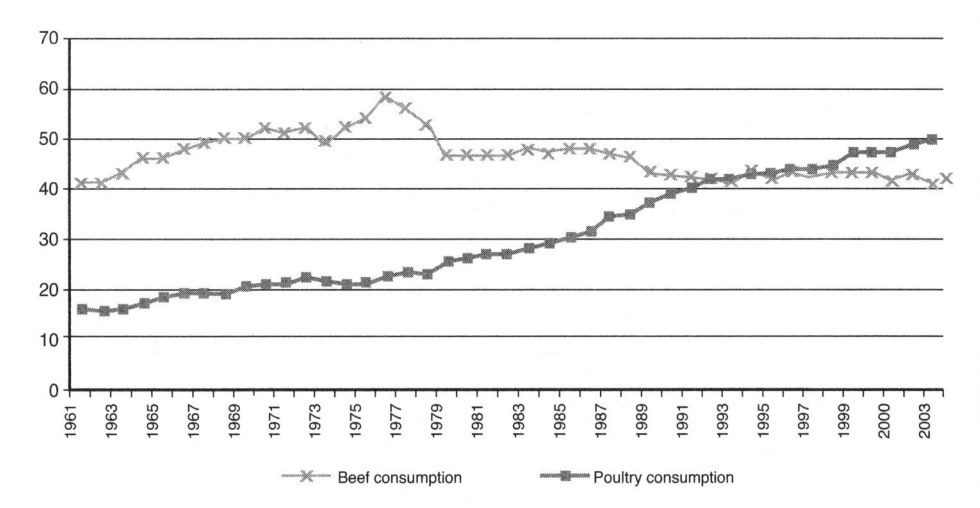

Figure 7.3 U.S. per capita beef and poultry consumption
Source: FAO

So in the case of poultry, it might be reasonable to expect this protein in particular to experience a solid long-term growth pattern thanks to its low cost and healthier attributes relative to beef. In addition to the health trend in poultry consumption, another significant demand driver that is currently under way in China comes from the increasing need for convenience—in particular, ready-to-eat meals in the Chinese diet. Since the opening up of the Chinese economy and its pull on greater workforce participation and employment, the percentage of women in the workforce has steadily climbed. For example, the most recent data suggests that over 45% of the urban workforce was composed of women, compared to just 37% during the mid 1990s. This greater participation by women has created some departure from traditional Chinese meal preparation, which typically has involved several hours of cooking, in favor of more Westernized trends that prize little preparation and greater convenience. The ready-to-eat meals category experienced a sharp growth trajectory in the United States during the second half of the twentieth century through the proliferation of the iconic TV dinner. Now China appears to be following a similar trend. This trend toward ready-to-eat meals, and even eating out more in restaurants, creates additional demand for protein in the form of processed meat through the packaged foods category.

At the same time, this dietary phenomenon toward a heavier protein content covers more goods than just meat items. As we turn to other simple proteins such as soybean oil, we can see the same trend at work. Soybean oil has also experienced a high and sustained rate of growth over time, as shown in Figure 7.4.

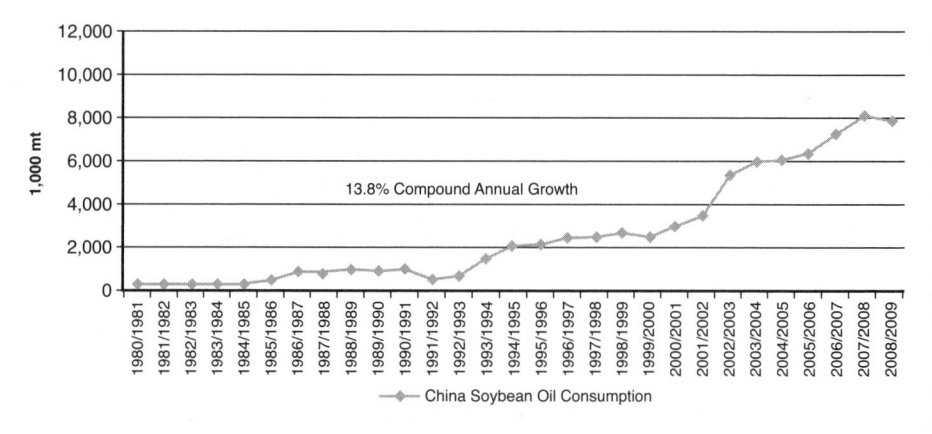

Figure 7.4 China's soybean oil consumption
Source: USDA

At this point, it seems fair to say that China—which appears to be on a trajectory to become the world's largest economy in a matter of decades—has demonstrated a steadily increasing appetite for proteins.

Eating Good in the Global Neighborhood

This still leaves the most important question in our discussion unanswered: Can China supply its growing demand for protein through internal production? In many cases, the answer is no.

Figure 7.5 shows the internal supply and demand balances for China in the protein categories we have already mentioned: poultry, beef, and soybean oilseeds (which are crushed into oil).

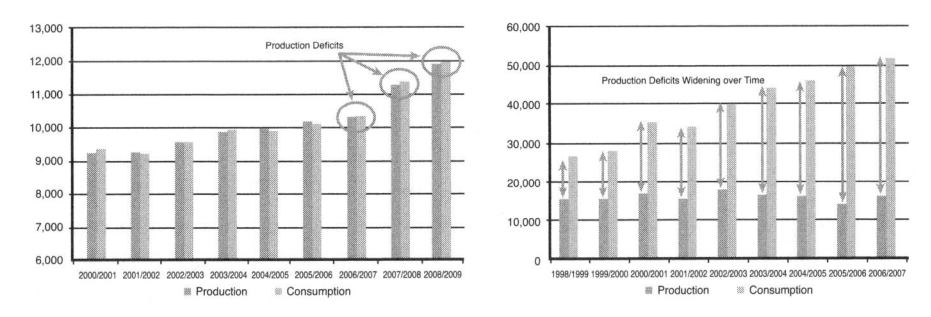

Figure 7.5 China's poultry (left) and soybean oilseed (right) production and consumption

Source: USDA

Judging from the recent data shown in Figure 7.5, Chinese producers have not met the internal demand for poultry and soybean oilseeds (imported for crushing). Meanwhile, the internal supply and demand balance for beef has not pushed into a deficit, but the balance has tightened enough to spur a twentyfold increase in beef imports from 1992 through 2008. The problem at hand is that China does not possess the natural resources to underpin this level of growth in the consumption of proteins. For starters, growing proteins, whether through poultry, cattle, soybeans, swine, or any other land-farmed variety, requires available arable land, water, and other resources, including feed. In this respect alone, China is struggling, because its level of arable land is already critically close to what officials consider a danger zone where food security becomes jeopardized. Chinese officials believe that their country possesses 1.83 billion mu (mu is a Chinese measure of acreage: 1 mu equals 6.07 acres) of arable land (300 million acres) compared to a "red-line" level of 1.8 billion mu. Recently, the Ministry of Land and Resources in China stated that it has halted a program of allowing marginal farmland to return to its natural state through reforestation because of these food security issues.[1] Additionally, the government has enacted punitive measures in an attempt to discourage any further transfer of arable land to commercial use. For example, the central government has stated that any use of farmland must receive official approval first, and that no water, power, or loans can be provided to this development without approval. These policies are meant to protect what is left of the shrinking amount of arable land in China. This has been a consequence of industrialization in the country, which has led to increasing acreage dedicated to manufacturing and commercial sites. Local officials protecting their own interests have been quick to rezone or seize farmland during this period of economic expansion, because the prices commanded by the commercial end users can be a quick source of revenue for these government officials. This trend of commercialization and urbanization has persisted to the point of creating a food resource problem borne out of China's rapid ascent toward prosperity. The problem is obvious, if not paradoxical. China's increasing standard of living due to its commercial success is driving new consumption patterns in proteins. But the same commercial success comes at the expense of being able to internally supply these new consumption trends for protein in the country. China's arable land resources taken on a per capita basis highlight its weak ability to supply its internal needs. The country holds a modest 80 hectares (1 hectare equals 2.47 acres) per 1,000 people, ranking it 144 out of 199 countries according to the World Development Indicators published by the World Bank. This compares unfavorably to other large nations such as the U.S., which has seven times more hectares per 1,000 people.

Another important point about China's inability to internally supply its growing protein demand is its terribly weakened water resources. Although it is bountiful by other countries' standards, with China having three of the world's ten longest rivers, China's water supply is insufficient for its large population. The basic problem that China and India share comes down to simple arithmetic: The two countries combined make up 73% of the world's population but possess only 47% of the water available. This poses a remarkable contrast to the Western Hemisphere, where the Americas have 14% of the world's population but 40% of the world's water. The key takeaway is that the Americas have far more water to spare than Asia (see Figure 7.6). To get a better sense of the status of China's water resources, consider that its per capita rate is approximately 25% of the world average. Even within the country itself, tremendous disparity exists.

In northern China, the rate drops from the national average of over 2,000 m³ per year to only 757 m³ per year, which is well below the designated "water scarcity" threshold of 1,000 m³ per year.

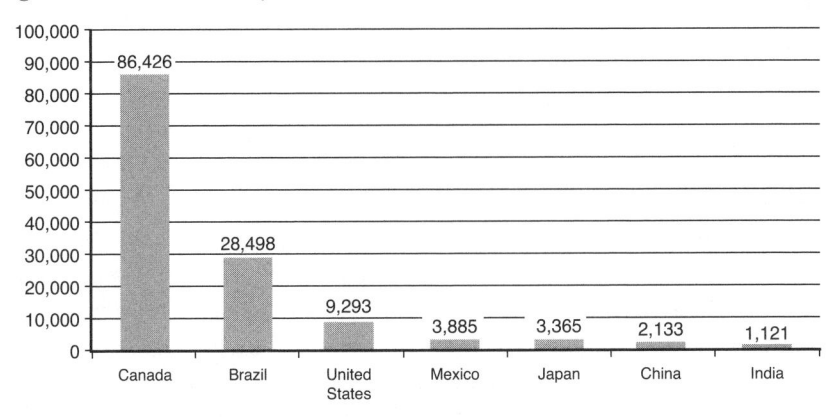

Country	Per capita water (m³)
Canada	86,426
Brazil	28,498
United States	9,293
Mexico	3,885
Japan	3,365
China	2,133
India	1,121

Figure 7.6 Per capita water resources by country

Source: World Bank

The comparative bounty of water in the Americas is critical for protein production and, for that matter, agricultural production. When we reduce these relationships to their barest elements, China and India are importing water from the West through these agricultural goods. The reality is that agricultural production is the largest consumer of water on the planet, because irrigation alone is estimated to take up to 70% of all freshwater used for human consumption. In simpler terms, it requires a great deal of water to produce agricultural items such as grains, meat proteins, and dairy items (see Table 7.2)—water, it turns out, that Asia cannot spare.

TABLE 7.2   Water Use by Liter of Kilogram of Product

Wheat	1.2
Rice	2.7
Corn	450.0
Potato	160.06
Soy	2.3
Beef	16.0
Pork	5.9
Poultry	2.8

TABLE 7.2 Water Use by Liter of Kilogram of Product

Eggs	4.7
Milk	865.0
Cheese	5.3

Source: ONU Water Report 2006, Sadia

China's water problem in particular has been deeply impacted by the urbanization and industrialization of its economy. So although the economy has been progressing, and its citizens have experienced a higher standard of living, negative consequences have resulted through increased demand on its strained water resources, in addition to more wide-scale pollution. From a simple demand perspective, China's annual demand growth for water during the 2000s has been just under 1%, while the growth in supply has been half that rate at approximately 0.5%. There is an obvious mismatch between supply and demand. Before we get too carried away, though, we should emphasize that at least some of these water issues are brought on by wasteful practices by the Chinese themselves that need to be and, over time, can be corrected. One clear example is the amount of water recycling in the industrial sector. Industry accounts for 24% of water consumption in China and is estimated to recycle only about 40% of its intake compared to 75% to 80% in developed countries. Rather than beat up on industry, however, the real culprit in China's water issues comes from the domestic front. Since 2000, the domestic sector has been the principal wastewater contributor to pollution, because only 56% of municipal sewage is treated before finding its way back into the water system. Comparatively speaking, the industrial sector looks like environmentalists for treating 92% of its waste discharges. The water treatment shortcomings have led to severe consequences. Studies conducted in 2004 revealed that in China's river system 28% of the water was in the Grade V standard, meaning that it was not fit for any use. Another 32% of the river system fell in the Grade IV category, which means it is suitable for industrial and irrigation use, but not human consumption. This means that a full 60% of the country's river system should not be consumed or probably even handled by people. In the lake system, the numbers only go downhill; 48% is Grade V and 23% is Grade IV, meaning that 71% of the lake system should be avoided for human use. So as we absorb these data points, we can better understand some of the factors behind China's water shortage, because some of this water, but not all, is intentionally held back by producers. Even so, according to World Bank estimates around 300 million people in China drink water that is unsafe. All told, World Bank estimates suggest that between the effects of pollution and shortages, China's water situation costs the country around 2.3% of its GDP annually. In any event, the problem of too little water to meet demand can be helped with better practices and treatment methods. However, these improvements will still not solve the outsized need for water to meet agricultural uses as incomes rise and citizens consume more protein.

Although the land and water issues in China present a problem, insofar as the problem relates to meeting protein demand, the problem is easily solved. The solution has been, and will likely continue to be, bridging the supply deficits by importing the goods from external markets (see Figure 7.7).

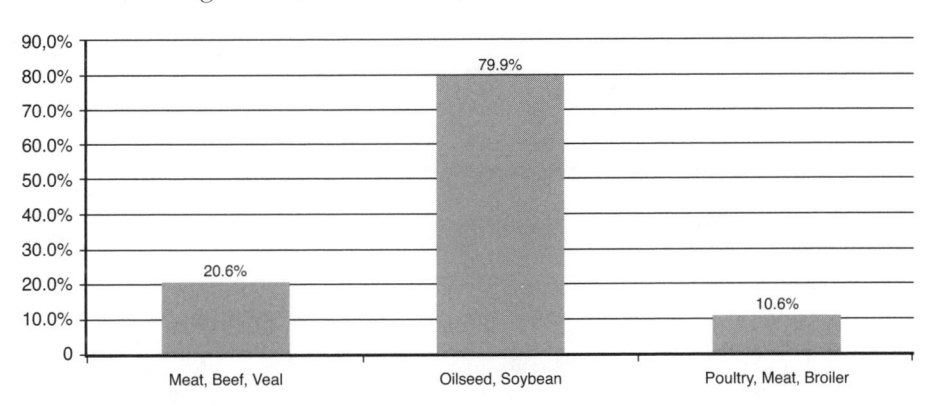

Figure 7.7 Compound annual growth in Chinese imports since 1990 (Beef begins in 1992)

Source: FAS, USDA

The relationship between production and consumption in China for various protein goods creates a situation where the country must access markets that can readily supply its growing demand. Just as ancient man had to resort to capable farmers, as mentioned at the beginning of the chapter, the Chinese and many other Asian emerging markets must look toward a similar global producer that can produce large surpluses of agricultural goods.

Brazil Has the Competitive Advantages in Agribusiness

Based on mounting evidence contained in years of global trade statistics, this producer is Brazil. Brazil has been winning in the global agribusiness trade for two simple reasons: its world-leading low cost of production, and its ability to expand production. Figure 7.8 helps you understand Brazil's ability to expand its production in agribusiness. The figure illustrates a plotted time series of the expansion of arable land in three countries: Brazil, the United States, and China. It is readily apparent that Brazil has expanded its arable land, and thus its agricultural capacity, by a much faster rate than the U.S. The figure also shows the relative decline in China we discussed earlier.

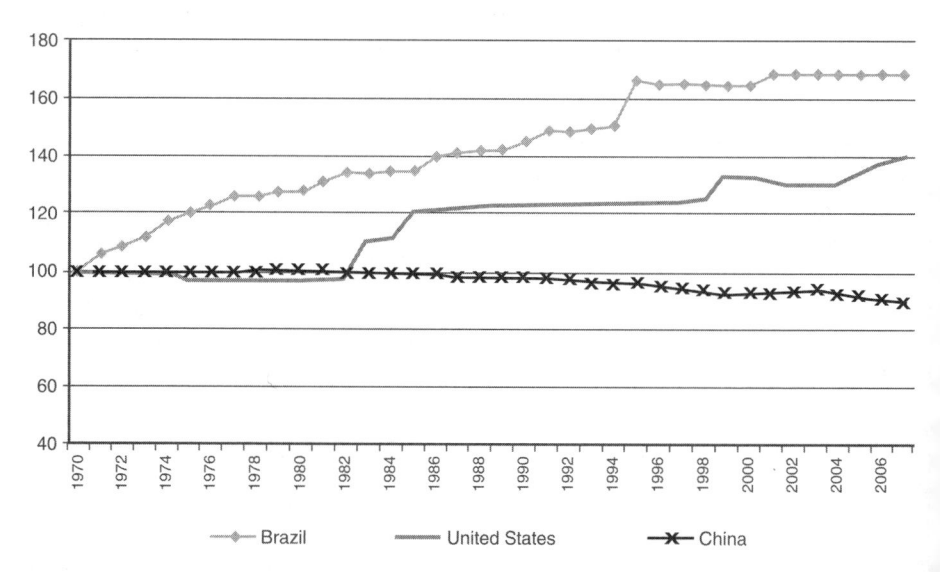

Figure 7.8 Growth in arable land since 1970 (baseline 100)
Source: FAO

Just as important as Brazil's historical track record for expanding its production is its scope for future expansion. Brazil ranks first among the major producing nations for possessing the largest amount of unutilized arable land, with well over 400 million hectares, even excluding rain forest, available for further development (see Figure 7.9).

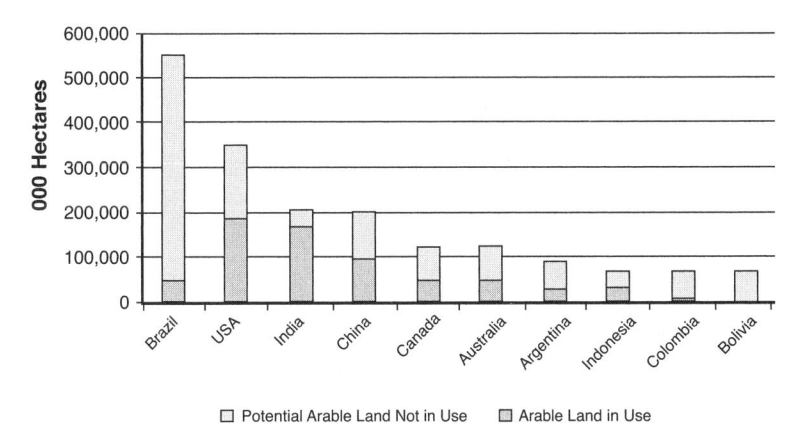

7 • PROTEINS AND AGRIBUSINESS: BILLIONS AND BILLIONS TO BE SERVED 153

Figure 7.9 Spare capacity among largest holders of arable land
Source: FAO

Turning to the cost of production in Brazil, if we take soybeans as an example, on average the cost of producing a ton of soybeans in the Mato Grosso region of Brazil is only half as much as producing a ton in the U.S. Two reasons underscoring the lower cost of production in Brazil versus the U.S. are the country's access to vast land resources and cheap labor. The importance of these cost advantages spills over into the remaining protein markets, because soybeans comprise feedstocks, and feedstocks comprise a good portion of the cost of production in meat goods. Put more simply, Brazil's cost advantages are prevalent throughout its agribusiness and food product value chain. These cost advantages have translated into sharp growth rates and market share gains in the global market for proteins, as shown in Figures 7.10 through 7.12.

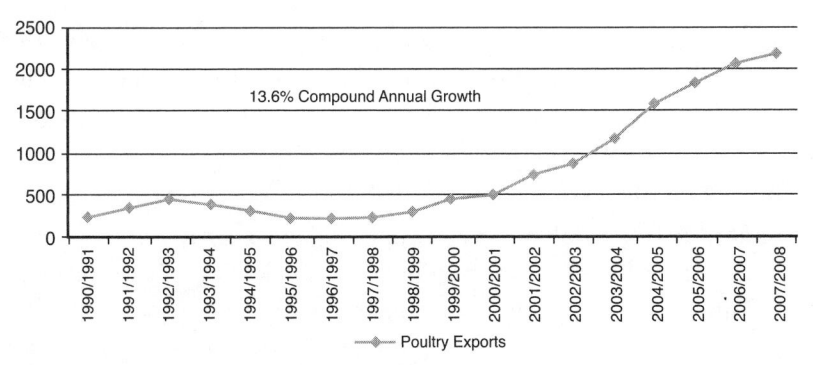

Figure 7.10 Brazil's poultry exports
Source: USDA

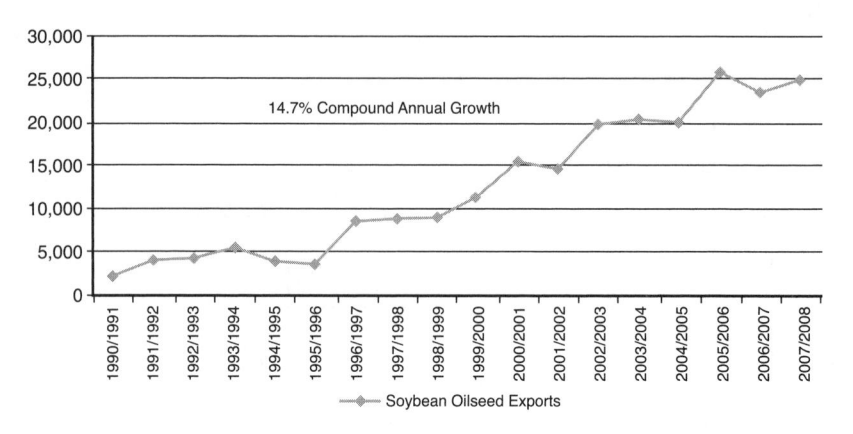

Figure 7.11 Brazil's soybean oilseed exports

Source: USDA

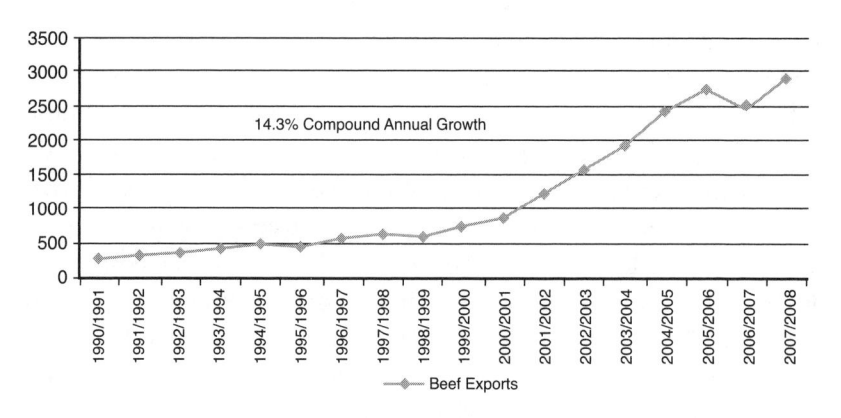

Figure 7.12 Brazil's beef exports

Source: USDA

Brazil's consistent double-digit growth rates in exports over the past two decades are impressive, but the easiest way to detect a true competitive advantage in a producer is to examine its ability to gain market share over time. On this measure Brazil again demonstrates its prowess in the protein space, as shown in Figure 7.13.

Based on the available evidence, it appears that Brazil has established itself as the dominant producer in the global trade for protein, and China appears to be the key demand driver.

POULTRY

1990 pie chart:
- Brazil: 6.4%
- USA: 3.5%
- Rest of World: 90.1%

2008 pie chart:
- Brazil: 28.6%
- USA: 8.5%
- Rest of World: 62.9%

SOYBEAN OILSEEDS

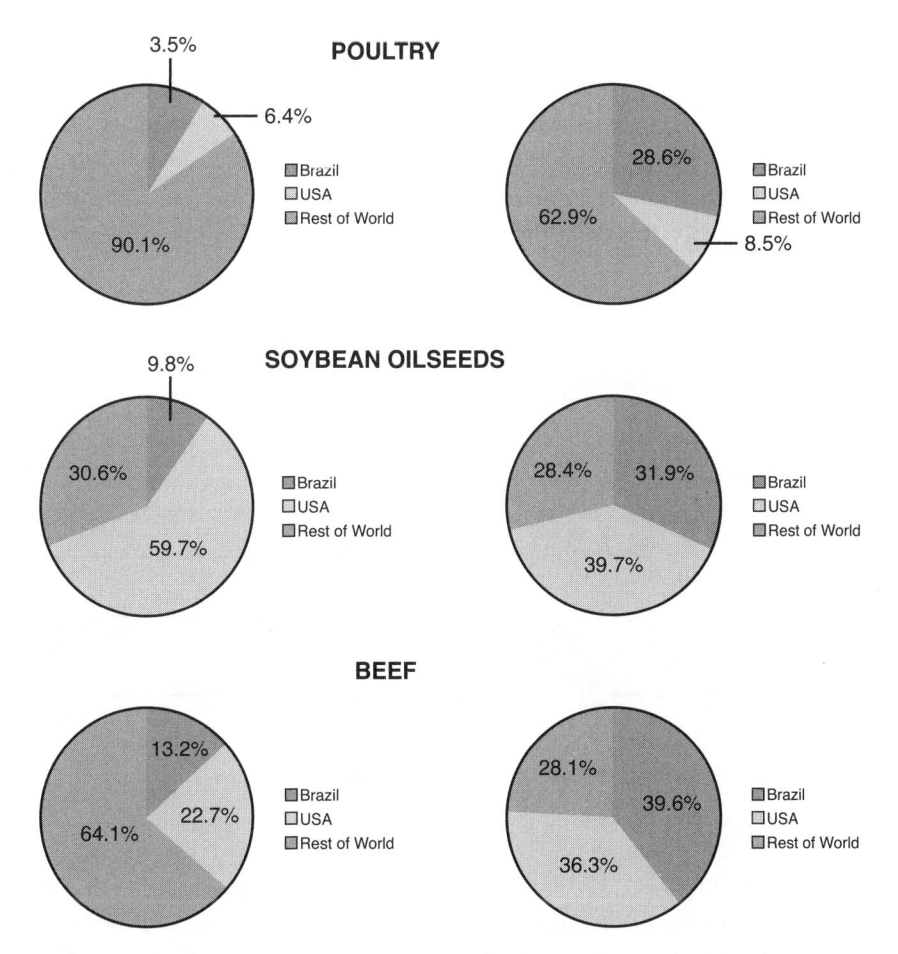

1990 pie chart:
- Brazil: 9.8%
- USA: 59.7%
- Rest of World: 30.6%

2008 pie chart:
- Brazil: 28.4%
- USA: 39.7%
- Rest of World: 31.9%

BEEF

1990 pie chart:
- Brazil: 13.2%
- USA: 22.7%
- Rest of World: 64.1%

2008 pie chart:
- Brazil: 28.1%
- USA: 36.3%
- Rest of World: 39.6%

Figure 7.13 1990 and 2008 export market shares for poultry, soybean oilseeds, and beef

Source: USDA

Our discussion thus far has focused on the interplay between rising per-head GDP levels in the emerging markets and the effect this has on the global protein end market. But we should also note that the protein demand driver has a broader effect on the value chain for food consumption, because proteins require a substantial amount of grains in the production process. For better or worse, each kilogram of protein meat produced in the livestock business is supported by a disproportionate amount of grains that must be supplied as feedstock. This is known as a feed grain multiplier. It can actually take up to

7 kilograms of feed to produce 1 kilogram of beef, as shown in Figure 7.14. This is one reason why the beef industry in Brazil has such a strong competitive advantage in its cost of production versus other markets. In Brazil, with its abundant arable land, beef is grass-fed and circumvents this onerous cost to production. However, turning to the other proteins, it is still necessary to dedicate a fair amount of costs to feedstock.

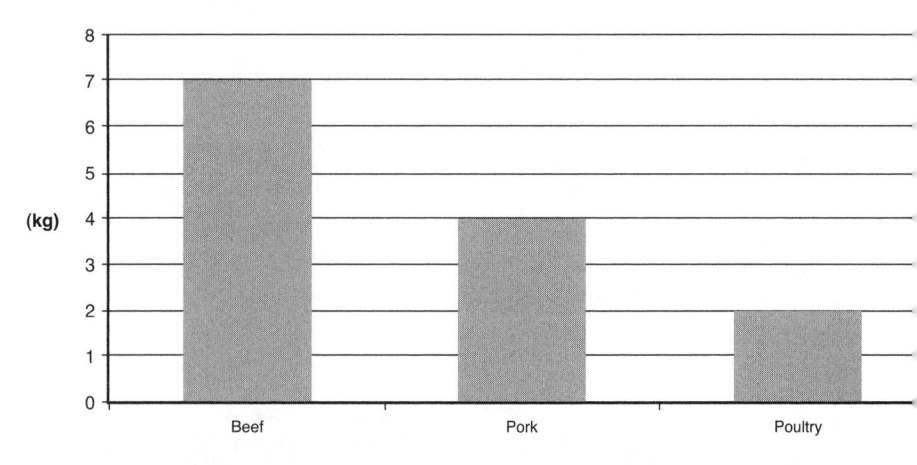

Figure 7.14 Kilograms of feedstock per kilogram of meat
Source: FAO

As you can see in Figure 7.14, which shows the disproportionate amount of feed grains that must be dedicated to livestock production, when protein demand accelerates, so does demand for the grains that are used in the production process. Furthermore, when demand rises for grains and prices react by rising, farmers in turn react by trying to maximize the amount of grain they can produce to bring to the market for sale. Farmers can produce more grain in two ways. They can add fertilizer in an attempt to raise crop yields, or they can expand their operations. When the process sets in, demand for fertilizer rises in the effort to increase yields, and demand for farming equipment such as tractors increases in the effort to expand operations.

Starting with grains, this space carries compelling fundamentals in and of itself. Irrespective of the cyclical impact from the global recession, there is a surprising long-term growth story to back steady grain consumption. We are not referring to the defensive nature of grain consumption, which is well known. We are instead referring to the growing demand for protein consumption discussed earlier, as well as institutional sources of demand owed to energy regulation. As it turns out, the U.S. government's insistence on incorporating corn-based ethanol into its energy policies has placed corn at a focal point for rising demand in proteins, rising demand for biofuels, and low grain stocks, when taken on a historical basis. To add perspective to the supply characteristics of corn on a worldwide basis, it is apparent from Figure 7.15 that stocks relative to consumption are as low as they have been in 30 years. This is occurring in spite of the financial crisis and the worst recession in at least a generation.

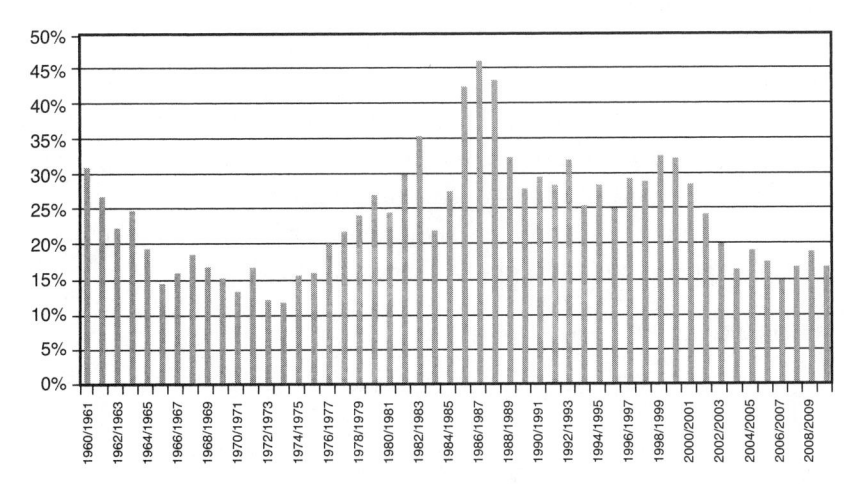

Figure 7.15 Worldwide corn stocks to consumption
Source: USDA

These relationships suggest that when demand improves from the cyclically depressed factors, supply is still in a position that could lead to a resumption of rising prices. In any event, government policies are ensuring a steady backdrop for continued corn consumption through the ethanol demand driver in the U.S.

In particular, the Energy Independence and Security Act of 2007 has created an ambitious goal for the United States: consuming 36 billion gallons of renewable fuel compared to the recent run rate of approximately 11 billion gallons in 2009 (see Figure 7.16). Put another way, the U.S. government has mandated 9.5% growth in these renewable fuels over the coming 13 years. Placing this into a more comprehensive time series of past and present, we should note that it seems likely that the lion's share of rapid growth in ethanol consumption has already occurred. This is due to the installed base of vehicle technology. Motor vehicles (with the exception of flex-fuel vehicles) can operate with only a 10% blend of ethanol in their tanks and still meet the manufacturer's warranty. This means that absent any technology changes (flex-fuel engines that could accept E85 ethanol blends), the rapid near-term growth in ethanol consumption has likely run its course. The blend of ethanol found in gasoline has already increased from 1% in 2000 to 7% in 2008 based on USDA estimates. However, the long-term demand trajectory remains in place thanks to the 2007 bill, and all things being equal, the market still has an artificially created but all too real source of demand for corn to be processed for ethanol. For example, in 2000 just 6% of the U.S. corn crop was utilized for ethanol. This number rose to 24% in 2008 and is expected to stay in the range of 30% to 35% over the coming decade, based on USDA estimates. This means in a sense that over the coming years perhaps about one third of corn production is already "spoken for" through these ethanol mandates.

Figure 7.16   U.S. ethanol consumption

Source: USDA, ERS

Reprinted with permission from Paul C. Westcott, *Amber Waves*, Volume 7, Issue 3.

An artificial source of demand is consuming a significant portion of the world's largest corn producer's crop, set against an already low stock backdrop. It is not hard to imagine that more corn will need to be added in outside markets over time to meet the world's growing demand for protein and, by extension, grains. If we return to the numbers, it is clear that world demand for grains has been increasing during the past several years at a rate that is outpacing production (see Figure 7.17). This dynamic has occurred in both the corn market and the broader market of coarse grains, which can be seen as a more comprehensive view of feed grain. These production deficits have been the real driver behind the declining stocks-to-consumption ratios that have persisted even in light of the cyclical collapse in business conditions during late 2008.

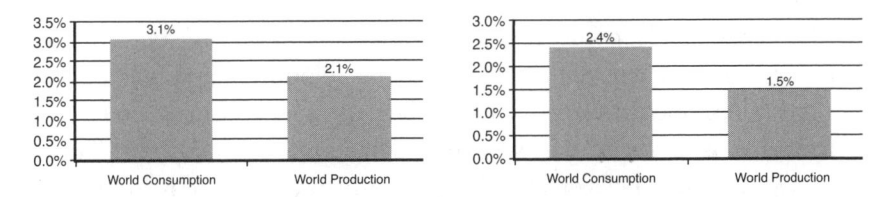

Figure 7.17 Corn (left) and coarse grains (right) worldwide production and consumption compound annual growth rate (CAGR) 2004 to 2009

Source: USDA, FAS

Just as its ability to supply the growing demand for meat protein in the market has been demonstrated, Brazil has been stepping up its production to meet this growing demand. For that matter, Brazil's ability to increase its production of these goods at a much faster rate than the other major players in the market is underscored by its deep competitive advantages in the agribusiness market (see Figure 7.18).

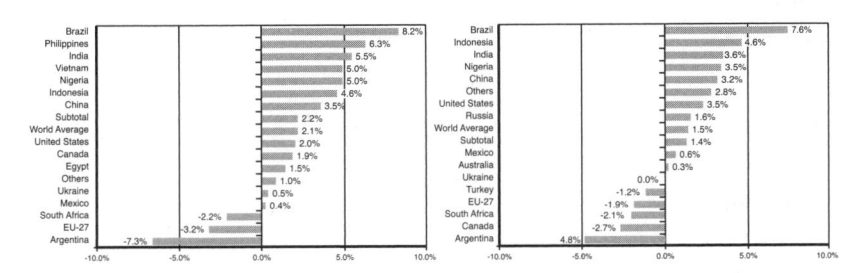

Figure 7.18 Corn (left) and coarse grain (right) production CAGR 2004 to 2009

Source: USDA, FAS

Tying all this together, as the continued demand for protein drives further grain production, pitched against the backdrop of low grain stocks leading to rising grain prices, this price incentive should support stronger production growth in the grains. In turn, this will require further fertilizer application. Further fertilizer application will be necessitated on two fronts: farmers looking to increase their existing yields, and farmers who increase their overall plantings. The demand for fertilizer should occur in both the developed and developing worlds' grain markets. But with arable land already near capacity in developed markets, the long-term demand drivers for fertilizer will likely come from the expansion of agribusiness in the emerging markets such as Brazil. The developing markets have considerable scope for fertilizer usage, because many farmers do not use fertilizer at levels on par with their developed-market peers. This is partly due to a lack of knowledge of the benefits, or resources, of doing so. Either way, there is significant room for the use of fertilizer to increase, based on how little is applied compared to developed-market standards. Table 7.3 shows that farmers in the United States use exponentially more fertilizer per hectare than their developing-market peers.

TABLE 7.3 Rate of Fertilizer Application (Kilograms Per Hectare)

	Nitrogen	Phosphorus	Potassium
Brazil	40.0	35.0	33.0
India	41.7	14.7	3.8
Indonesia	5.0	25.0	8.0
Mexico	80.0	20.0	10.0
Nigeria	5.9	1.4	0.0
Philippines	58.0	16.0	10.0
United States	150.0	70.0	90.0

Source: Fertistat, FAS

These shortcomings in fertilizer application highlight an important divide between crop yields in the United States and those in the developing world (see Figure 7.19). There is little doubt that crop yields in the developing markets could be raised well above their current levels through better use of fertilizer.

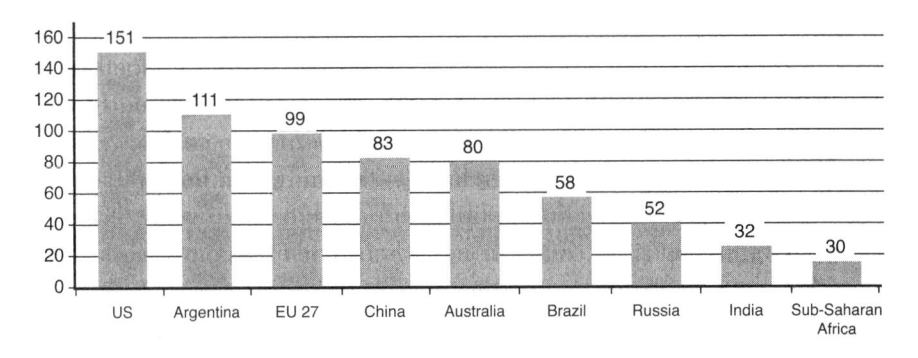

```
160 ┬ 151
140 ┤
120 ┤      111
100 ┤            99
 80 ┤                  83    80
 60 ┤                              58
 40 ┤                                    52
 20 ┤                                          32   30
  0 ┴─────────────────────────────────────────────────
    US  Argentina  EU 27  China  Australia  Brazil  Russia  India  Sub-Saharan
                                                                    Africa
```

Figure 7.19 Corn bushels per acre
Source: FAS, USDA, World Bank, AGCO

Strong Fundamentals Across the Value Chain

In addition to the protein demand growth driver, we should keep in mind the role of the oil market in this overall feed grains equation. Rising oil prices will pull additional corn away from U.S. food and livestock and toward ethanol. Likewise, in Brazil farmers may also favor sugar plantings given the robust and relatively well-developed sugar ethanol market in that country. More simply put, during the past several years, when oil prices have stayed above $50 per barrel, there has been a much stronger correlation between oil prices and grain prices. This relationship is due to the favorable economics presented to farmers selling their product into the fuel market as fuel prices rise. With that said, government policies have created a dynamic for crops that did not materially exist prior to the 2000s: When oil prices are high, corn and sugar can be thought of as petrocommodities. The bottom line is that high oil prices stimulate potentially higher grain prices, as well as fertilizer demand to match the pursuit of increased yields and plantings.

As you can imagine, fertilizer alone will not get the job done. Farmers also require equipment such as tractors, harvesters, combines, and sprayers to raise their yields and expand their operations. The need for additional equipment across the developing markets creates the same relationship we just reviewed in the fertilizer space.

To summarize, the use of farming equipment is far more advanced and prevalent in the developed world, which is not that surprising. When we examine the use of tractors per hectare in the markets that are poised for the most long-term growth, thanks to their ability to expand production, we can see that, in particular, the South American growth markets of Brazil and Argentina use far less equipment than their developed-market peers. In fact, tractor use in these countries is below the world average, as shown in Figure 7.20.

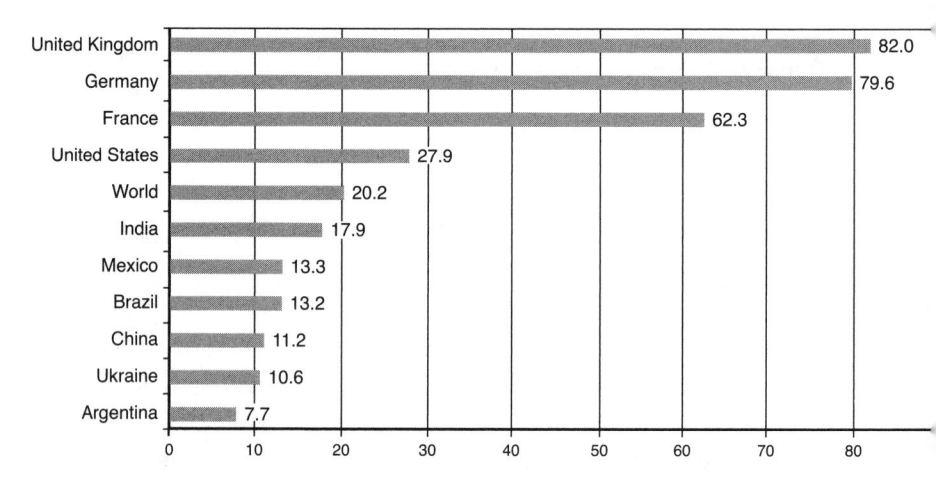

Country	Tractors per 1,000 hectares
United Kingdom	82.0
Germany	79.6
France	62.3
United States	27.9
World	20.2
India	17.9
Mexico	13.3
Brazil	13.2
China	11.2
Ukraine	10.6
Argentina	7.7

Figure 7.20 Tractors per 1,000 hectares
Source: FAOSTAT

Figure 7.20 shows that the emerging markets have much room for growth in tractor use over the near, medium, and long term. As this dynamic unfolds over the coming years, it should provide a key market opportunity for a short list of oligopolistic producers in the farm equipment space. In the meantime, we should be careful not to overlook the large role that the developed markets play in the overall farm equipment industry. These developed-market farmers also play a critical role in the farm equipment market. The good news on this front is that, despite the recession and financial crisis, developed-market farmers are actually in the best financial shape they have been in during the past 30 years, as shown in Figure 7.21.

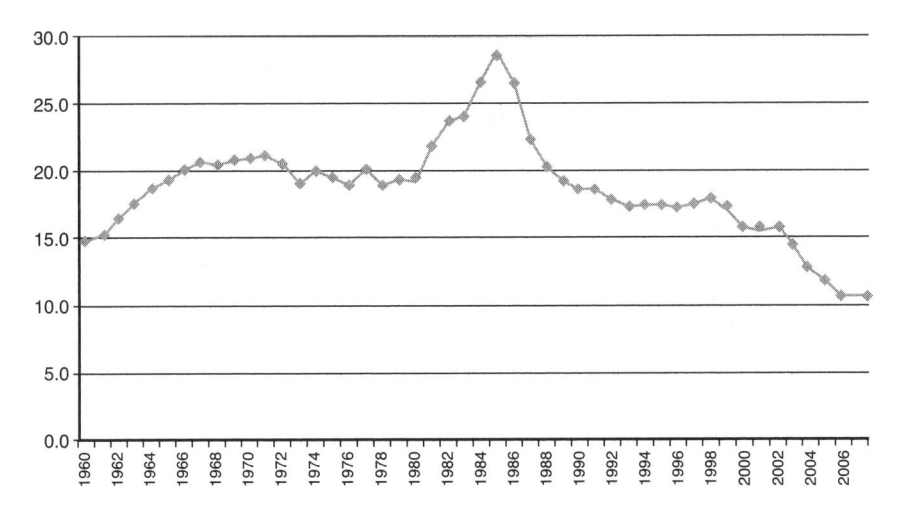

Figure 7.21 Farm debt-to-equity ratio, 1960 to 2007
Source: USDA

The healthy financial condition of the U.S. farmer is yet another positive story in the agribusiness space. It means that farmers have the balance sheet to purchase more fertilizer and equipment or to expand their operations, because conditions appear ideal. Taken as an industry, farmers in the U.S. may possess one of the cleanest aggregate balance sheets among all industry groups. Although the overall debt-to-equity ratio stands at approximately 12%, it is also estimated that around 70% of farmers carry no debt. So although many sectors of the U.S. economy are in the midst of a deleveraging process, the U.S. farm industry has not become encumbered by the debt overhang. This is an important factor, because it clears the industry for a resumption of growth and the ability to respond to demand signals from the emerging-market consumer, as well as the energy markets.

Finally, even with the compelling supply and demand factors notwithstanding, the agribusiness space possesses other beneficial attributes that investors may prefer over the coming years. To reiterate, the agribusiness value chain is supported by relatively inelastic demand, all things considered. That is not to say that demand is impervious to the business cycle, but we can all appreciate the importance of food to our everyday existence. For this reason, many of these businesses can take on relatively defensive attributes compared to other pro-cyclical businesses. Furthermore, because the industry is tied to food commodity prices from the demand side, these businesses can also provide some buffer from inflation, because food and grain commodity prices store value during episodes of inflation. Still, all stocks carry risks, but it does appear that producers in the agribusiness value chain have an opportunity to make hay in the coming years.

Endnote

[1] Xinhua. "China's arable land barely above critical minimum: report." http://www.chinadaily.com.cn, February 29, 2008.

8

Formula for Success: Rise Early, Work Hard, Strike Oil

The chapter's title contains a quote from oil tycoon J. Paul Getty. This formula for success is as true today as it was in the early to mid-twentieth century, when Getty made his billions as an oilman. During late 2008 and early 2009, however, oil and energy stocks were relegated to a sideshow in the deflationary aftermath of the financial crisis and ensuing global recession. Mostly attributable to myopic behavior and analysis, mainstream investors saw little opportunity in energy and oil after the substantial crash in oil prices from $145 per barrel in July 2008 to $31 per barrel in December 2008. The consensus response to the 78% decline in the West Texas Intermediate benchmark for oil prices was fear and apathy regarding the sector. Despite the obvious near-term effects of weaker cyclical demand from around the globe, there is little reason to turn away from oil as a long-term investment, because the secular trend is what counts in this equation.

As most hard asset investors realize, investing in commodity stocks has a particular nuance. The investor in any commodity stock takes on two components in his or her purchase: the future price of the commodity, and the skill set of the business manager combined with his or her productive assets. It is relatively easy for an analyst to determine the business manager's competence and ability, because these traits usually reveal themselves in the financials or other conventional forms of analysis. Turning to the other question, the future price of a given commodity, the picture can quickly become complicated. Rather than trying to explicitly forecast the future prices of commodities such as oil, it is more productive to examine the relevant and discernable factors affecting supply and demand. Then we can determine whether these factors portend a bullish or bearish backdrop for future prices over the coming years. Again, the focus remains on long-term price determinants. For example, it is more pertinent to weigh lasting variables such as the nationalization of energy assets across the globe and their potential effects on supply and production levels. It is not as effective to use a technician's view on an oil chart, or even a near-term fundamentalist's view on oil prices over the next 6 to 12 months. This chapter does not forecast exact price levels. Instead, it espouses reaching a 5- to 10-year conclusion about why investors should maintain oil and energy stocks in their holdings over this time period, and may perhaps even thrive by doing so.

With that said, let us discuss oil. Fortunately, any discussion of the price of oil rests on the simplest concept in economics—supply and demand. From a global perspective, oil has been a relatively steady, low-single-digit growth commodity over the past 40-plus years. Since 1965, global oil consumption has grown at a 2.3% compound annual growth rate (CAGR), compared with a 2.2% rate of production. On average, demand has slightly outpaced production by a modest 10 basis points. However, digging deeper into the global figures, we can find evidence that demand may continue to outpace supply over the coming decades. This should lead to higher prices over time and increasing profits for these companies.

Our examination of global demand factors begins with a dividing timeline of two economic periods delineated by the free-market reforms in the Asian economies of the 1980s and '90s. Our assertion is that we can view global oil demand in two slices of time highlighted by the economic reforms that took hold in the 1980s and '90s in China, India, and Asian tigers such as Singapore, Thailand, and South Korea. Prior to the 1980s and '90s, Asian oil demand outside of Japan was driven primarily by China. But during the emergence of market reforms in India and the Asian tigers, oil demand from the Asian Pacific region accelerated sharply. Since the 1980s, many of these economies have maintained oil consumption growth rates compounding in the mid single digits. Table 8.1 shows representative growth rates and their sharp contrast to developed-market and world averages.

TABLE 8.1 Oil Consumption CAGRs 1980–2007

China	5.6%
China Hong Kong SAR	3.6%
India	5.3%
Indonesia	3.8%
Malaysia	4.1%
Pakistan	4.8%
Singapore	6.1%
South Korea	5.7%
Taiwan	3.7%
Thailand	5.0%
United States	0.6%
Europe	–0.8%
World Average	**1.1%**

Source: BP Statistical Review

The impact of Asia's economic growth on oil consumption is at least somewhat appreciated by long-term investors or those with experience in the emerging markets. Perhaps what is less well known or, at a minimum, is underappreciated is the rapid acceleration in oil consumption among the oil-producing nations themselves. In a sense, the importance of oil as a worldwide commodity and its success in the marketplace have come full circle. Organization of the Petroleum Exporting Countries (OPEC) nations such as Saudi Arabia have continuously raised their standards of living based on this product's economic proliferation. Not surprisingly, because these societies also have begun to prosper from dominating the world trade in oil, they too must consume increasing amounts of oil to maintain their newly industrialized and advancing societies. Essentially, the loss of oil production in the developed world coincided with increased world demand from Asia. The Middle East assumed this market share from the developed world, which propelled it to higher incomes, wealth, and standards of living beginning in the 1980s. These economic changes spurred a sharp acceleration in the growth rate of oil consumption in these oil-producing nations to fuel their rapidly growing economies, as shown in Table 8.2.

TABLE 8.2 Middle East Oil Consumption CAGRs

	1965–1980	1980–2007
Kuwait	–1.1%	4.4%
Qatar	NA	7.8%
Saudi Arabia	1.7%	4.5%
United Arab Emirates	NA	5.4%

Source: BP Statistical Review

The coalescing of these developing-market demand fundamentals, coupled with a long-term slowing of growth in developed-market consumption from the United States and Europe, culminated in a subtle shift. Production outpaced demand from 1965 to 1980, but then demand outpaced production from 1980 to 2007 (see Table 8.3). As shown in Figure 8.1, the balance of oil between consumption and production did not register a worldwide deficit until the early 1980s. Essentially, this was when the onus of production fell sharply onto the

TABLE 8.3 Oil Market Shifts from Subtle Surplus to Subtle Deficit

	1965–1980	1980–2007
Consumption CAGR	4.5%	1.1%
Production CAGR	4.6%	0.9%

Source: BP Statistical Review

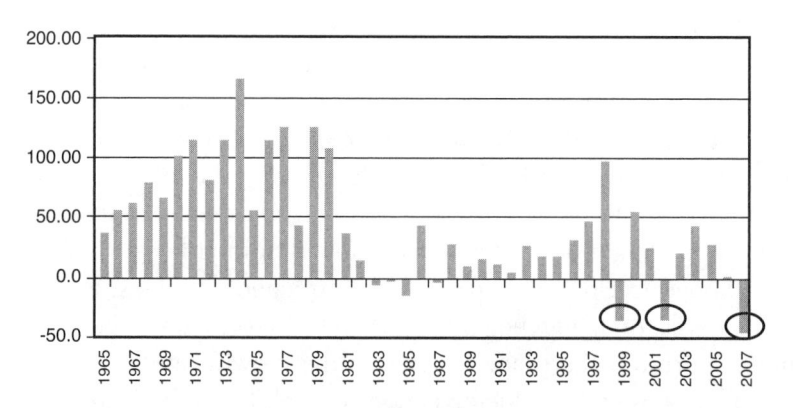

Figure 8.1 Oil market balance: surplus/deficit in tons

Source: BP Statistical Review

Saudis and other OPEC producers. The same supply deficit phenomenon appeared again in 2007, setting the stage for the sharp rise in oil prices that ended in 2008. During 2007 and 2008, the balance between supply and demand fell into deficit from nothing more than anemic growth in production in the preceding four years.

From 2004 to 2008, production increased at a paltry 0.4% compounded rate. This small growth in annual production was matched against a compounded growth in consumption of 0.8%, or a rate of consumption that was twice the rate of production over a four-year span. On the surface, these appear to be subtle mismatches in small numbers. But if we look at what happened to the price of oil over this four-year stretch, the result was anything but subtle, as shown in Figure 8.2.

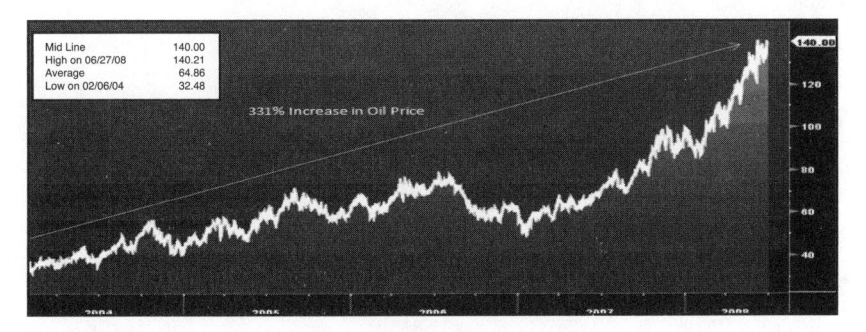

Figure 8.2 West Texas intermediate crude oil price
Source: Bloomberg

These figures demonstrate the driving force that has emerged in the past couple of decades from an assortment of emerging-market nations and their strong demand for oil. Likewise, worldwide production constraints have combined with this growth to create periodic deficits and a sharp rise in prices in response. Nevertheless, we have only described phenomena that have occurred up to this point. Now let's shift our discussion to the future.

In the Long Term, Healthy Demand Meets Higher Cost Supply

As we focus on this discussion, we can find more reason for optimism in respect to future demand, because many of the nations in question are rising from a surprisingly low base of consumption. Table 8.4 shows that despite the rate of prosperity (gross domestic product [GDP] per head) compounding at 8.8% and 4.9% in China and India, respectively over the past 27 years there remains a substantial divide between the standard of living in these countries and a higher standard-bearer such as the United States.

TABLE 8.4 GDP Per Capita in U.S. Dollars in 2007

China	$2,560
Hong Kong	$29,775
India	$940
Indonesia	$1,921
Iran	$3,990
Malaysia	$6,956
Pakistan	$912
Saudi Arabia	$15,724
South Korea	$21,655
Taiwan	$16,760
Thailand	$3,743
United States	$45,778

Source: International Monetary Fund (IMF)

So although myopic observers may argue over the inflection points of business cycles in China and India (including the recent one), the bigger picture from a secular perspective is that substantial room exists for continued growth in these economies. Importantly, oil consumption has increased nearly in lockstep with the rising levels of GDP per head in China and India during these time periods. To bring these relationships between oil consumption and rising levels of prosperity into better focus, we can reference a key driver of oil consumption—automobile ownership. If we look at the number of cars owned per 1,000 people in both China and India (see Table 8.5), we can again see the tremendous potential for economic development and, hence, oil consumption that may lie ahead.

TABLE 8.5 Automobiles Per 1,000 People

China	8
India	6
United States	750

Source: World Bank

With only about eight cars per 1,000 people in China, this country is about where the United States was in 1910. Although we cannot count on the world to remain static regarding its methods of energy consumption, it is clear that the United States in 1910 was on pace to steadily increase its oil consumption over the remainder of the century as its economy matured and reached heightened levels of prosperity. Likewise, in a developed market such as the United States, approximately 70% of oil consumption comes from transportation.

The sum of these demand factors is clear on a forward-looking basis. The primary engines for oil consumption from the emerging markets still have decades of strong demand for oil on tap. The underlying factors for future oil demand are a critical component to consider. The emerging demand from developing markets over the past few decades has become the centerpiece of the demand story. However, any discussion of future oil prices must include the remaining side of the equation—future supply.

Many people have taken for granted the safe, accessible, and cheap supply of oil in the world market. Except for temporary supply shocks created by the occasional embargo or natural disaster, cheap oil became a way of life in the twentieth century. However, for those paying attention, the sharp run-up in oil prices during the first decade of the twenty-first century revealed in no uncertain terms an inability for supply to meet surging demand. Part of the problem is a multi-decade decline in production from developed markets, such as the United States and Western Europe.

From 1965 to 2007, oil production from the United States and Western Europe fell by more than 50%, as shown in Figure 8.3. The numbers cannot speak any more clearly: the supply of oil has been steadily declining for nearly 50 years in the developed markets.

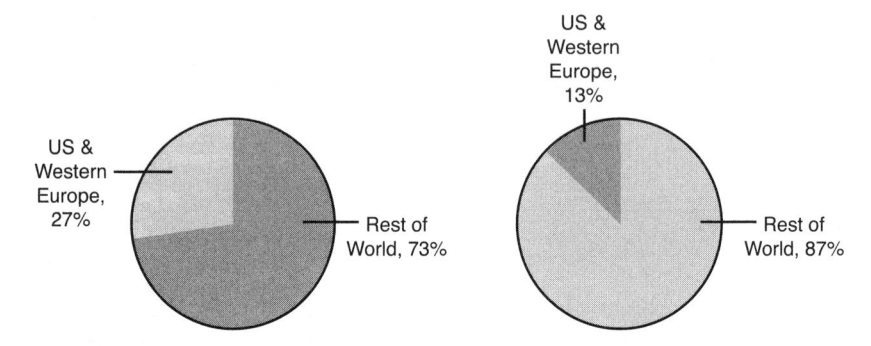

Figure 8.3 Global oil production by source in 1965 and 2007

Source: BP Statistical Review

From a long-term perspective, it is not hard to see that various secular trends are at play in the global oil market. More specifically, the oil market and the upward trend in prices over the past seven years has reflected the growing influence of new sources of demand from the developing world pitted against declining supply in the developed world. These factors have not only ongoing implications for the future long-term direction of oil prices, but also for what will come to define the profile of a potentially successful investment in the oil and energy space.

The story of supply and declining production in the developed markets is straightforward. For all intents and purposes, industry players have spent the past 144 years exploring for, discovering, and exploiting oil reserves. The basic translation is that current reserves are more geologically complex, found in smaller accumulations, deeper water, or even arctic regions. What this means in a modern context is that benefits accrue to exploration and production (E&P) companies that can obtain a competitive advantage in their application of technology and/or efficient production. Taking this thought process one step further, we can see that in the absence of innovation, reinvestment, and the efficiency gains that follow, the price of oil could rise from a mere stagnation in productivity gains. During the past several years, growing evidence has shown that firms across the industry have found it difficult to drive costs lower. Taken on a comprehensive basis, including both finding and development costs, total costs per barrel of production have risen at an annualized rate of 17.5% since 1998, as shown in Figure 8.4. The bottom line is that the price of oil in the market will follow the production costs over time. If production costs continue to rise over the long term, the floor for oil prices will rise as well. The latter years shown in Figure 8.4 probably reflect some cost inflation from heightened activity at the top of the recent cycle. However, the long-term trend is still upward over time because of the relative difficulty surrounding finding and developing new sources of oil.

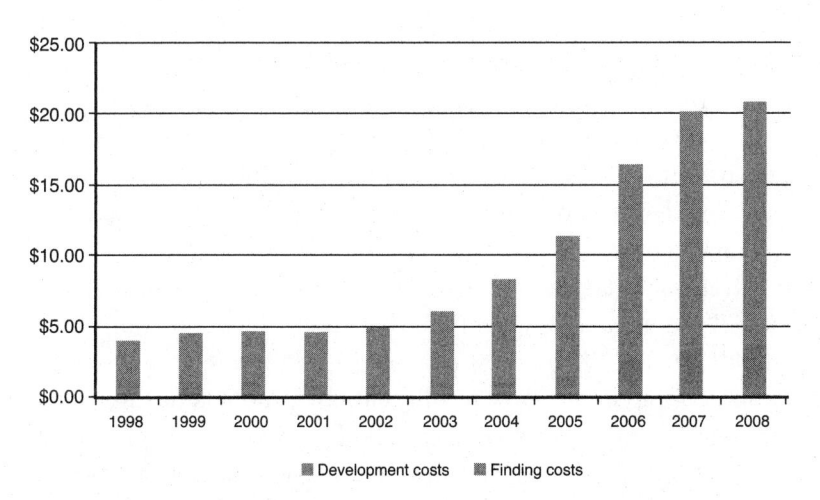

Figure 8.4 Finding and development costs per barrel
Source: Company reports, Credit Suisse First Boston (CSFB)

This geographic risk and its effects on the cost of production is an important trend to realize because it accompanies another widespread secular trend of geopolitical risk in the energy industry. We use the term geopolitical risk because an overwhelming majority of oil-producing nations have nationalized their energy assets. This trend for countries to nationalize their energy assets has largely coincided with the increasingly lower amounts of production flowing from the privately owned profit-driven developed-market producers. Put another way, just as the world has been finding it more difficult to locate and produce additional oil, the large majority of existing reserves are now held by entities that, in a head-to-head comparison with Western operators, forfeit innovation and reinvestment in favor of exploiting current reserves (the bird in the hand).

This trend of nationalization and declining production from Western players has culminated in a market paradigm in which national oil companies now control 77% of the world's proven oil reserves. Not surprisingly, the Western "big oil" companies most often vilified by the press during periods of excess profits control less than approximately 10% of reserves. In effect, Western big oil is increasingly taking a backseat on the world stage from a reserve standpoint. But to counter this paradigm, Western big oil companies also tend to corner the market on human capital, because the competition for new resources has intensified to the point of causing them to seek an intellectual edge whenever possible. The fact that national oil companies control 77% of the world's proven reserves does not necessarily mean that these resources are left in incapable hands. However, it is fundamentally certain that the national oil companies are beholden to fulfilling social promises in their respective homelands in lieu of pursuing more profits. The by-products of this social policy lead to excessive employment and selling product at subsidized prices to the consumer. The end result is a business that addresses political objectives first, and invests less in its future reserves, and favors current exploitation. To be sure, gifted engineers and technically minded innovators are working in these nationalized outfits. But their expertise is smothered by serving political objectives first and running a good business second. Based on a revealing study[1] conducted by the Baker Institute at Rice University, we can see the empirical effects of the national oil companies' market paradigm versus the Western companies that are privately held and driven by consideration of shareholder profits (see Tables 8.6 and 8.7). Table 8.6 shows that, by and large, the national oil companies are remarkably inefficient when examined on a revenue-per-head and revenue-per-reserve basis.

TABLE 8.6 National Oil Companies' Revenues Per Employee and Reserves

	Revenue Per Employee	Revenue Per Reserves	Government Ownership	Country
Adnoc	$205	$0.20	100%	UAE
CNOOC	$2,656	$2.97	71%	China
EcoPetrol	$824	$2.26	100%	Colombia
Eni	$1,056	$10.50	30%	Italy
Gazprom	$103	$0.16	51%	Russia
INA	$187	$11.70	75%	Croatia
KMG	NA	NA	100%	Kazakhstan
KPC	$1,650	$0.34	100%	Kuwait
MOL	$635	$42.37	25%	Hungary
NIOC	$283	$0.11	100%	Iran
NNPC	$1,460	$0.56	100%	Nigeria
Norsk Hydro	$673	$11.37	44%	Norway
OMV	$2,214	$8.90	32%	Austria
ONGC	$298	$2.11	84%	India
PDO	$1,591	$0.98	60%	Oman
PDVSA	$1,985	$0.66	100%	Venezuela
Pemex	$506	$4.01	100%	Mexico
Pertamina	$453	$0.73	100%	Indonesia
Petrobras	$773	$3.39	32%	Brazil
Petro-China	$111	$2.52	90%	China
Petroecuador	$1,026	$1.25	100%	Ecuador
Petronas	$1,202	$1.45	100%	Malaysia
PTT	$2,896	$16.68	100%	Thailand
QP	$1,800	$0.10	100%	Qatar
Rosneft	$86	$0.19	100%	Russia
SaudiAramco	$2,261	$0.40	100%	Saudi Arabia
Sinopec	$192	$19.76	57%	China
Socar	NA	NA	100%	Azerbaijan
Sonangal	$755	$1.37	100%	Angola
Sonatrach	$688	$0.93	100%	Algeria

TABLE 8.6 National Oil Companies' Revenues Per Employee and Reserves (continued)

	Revenue Per Employee	Revenue Per Reserves	Government Ownership	Country
SPC	$375	$1.71	100%	Syriac
Statoil	$1,910	$10.85	71%	Norway
TPAO	$154	$1.53	100%	Turkey
Average	**$1,000**	**$5.23**		

Source: Baker Institute, Rice University

TABLE 8.7 Private Oil Companies' Revenues Per Employee and Reserves

	Revenue Per Employee	Revenue Per Reserves	Government Ownership	Country
BP	$2,788	$15.68	0%	UK
Chevron	$2,606	$12.78	0%	US
ConocoPhillips	$3,368	$14.03	0%	US
ExxonMobil	$3,148	$12.26	0%	US
Shell	$2,418	$21.67	0%	Netherlands
Amerada Hess	$1,532	$16.07	0%	US
Anadarko	$1,838	$2.52	0%	US
Apache	$2,019	$2.71	0%	US
BG	$1,547	$3.64	0%	US
Burlington	$2,537	$2.74	0%	US
Chesapeake Energy	$1,577	$3.22	0%	US
CNR	$4,606	$3.85	0%	Canada
Devon	$2,356	$4.33	0%	US
Dominion	$847	$13.81	0%	US
EnCana	$2,915	$4.48	0%	Canada
EOG	$1,844	$2.38	0%	US
ForestOil	$1,841	$4.02	0%	US
HuskyEnergy	$2,149	$9.53	0%	Canada
Imperial	$2,838	$35.72	0%	Canada
Kerr-McGee	$1,263	$4.15	0%	US

TABLE 8.7 Private Oil Companies' Revenues Per Employee and Reserves (continued)

	Revenue Per Employee	Revenue Per Reserves	Government Ownership	Country
Lukoil	$233	$1.68	0%	Russia
Maersk	$60	$2.90	0%	Denmark
Marathon	$1,757	$39.14	0%	US
Murphy	$1,436	$21.60	0%	US
Newfield	$2,114	$4.45	0%	US
Nexen	$1,048	$4.25	0%	Canada
NipponOil	$2,690	$131.74	0%	Japan
Noble	$2,433	$2.54	0%	US
Novatek	$220	$0.21	0%	Russia
Occidental	$1,577	$4.46	0%	US
PennWest	$1,577	$2.53	0%	Canada
Petro-Canada	$2,370	$9.24	0%	Canada
PetroKazakhstan	$546	$4.12	0%	Kazakhstan
Pioneer	$1,183	$1.76	0%	US
Pogo	$5,088	$4.38	0%	US
RepsoIYPF	$1,561	$10.79	0%	Spain
Santos	$789	$1.92	0%	Australia
Sibneft	$189	$1.81	0%	Russia
Suncor	$1,447	$78.50	0%	Canada
Surgutneftegas	$121	$1.01	0%	Russia
Talisman	$2,207	$3.26	0%	Canada
TNK	$63	$1.66	0%	Russia
Total	$1,406	$14.33	0%	France
Unocal	$1,259	$4.63	0%	US
Vintage	$1,136	$1.76	0%	US
Woodside	$758	$2.11	0%	Australia
XTO	$1,437	$1.94	0%	US
Average	**$1,760**	**$11.67**		

Source: Baker Institute, Rice University

In sum, it is easy to discern that the privately owned companies generate considerably higher revenues per employee and revenues per reserve. In fact, revenues per employee are, on average, 76% higher, and revenues per reserve are 123% higher, among the private companies versus the national oil companies. These observations lend empirical support to our earlier assertions that the national oil companies' adherence to social policies lead to wasteful head counts and inefficient production. Moreover, the national oil companies often face a squeeze on the amount of top line they can generate, because subsidies tend to dominate the pricing landscape for nationalized oil markets. This is yet another by-product of managing a business in which the government prioritizes social benefits ahead of profitability.

As shown in Figure 8.5, the large majority of countries with gasoline prices below the U.S. level possess high levels of government ownership and low levels of operating efficiency. Taking all this into consideration, a clearer picture begins to emerge. Seventy-seven percent of the world's proven reserves lie in the hands of operators who cannot obtain market prices, who are coerced into carrying too many employees, and who cannot produce nearly the amount of revenue their reserves would suggest. In other words, the overwhelming majority of the world's oil and gas reserves are being mismanaged. When an operator in the commodity business is said to be "mismanaged," this usually has one clear interpretation: It is a high-cost operator. In free markets, these operators normally face a swift, judicious exit from the marketplace if they cannot right their ship. In this case, however, with so much of production lying in the hands of these operators and dwindling supplies available to the world's most efficient operators, a perverse reality is emerging. The low-cost producers are fighting for survival, and the high-cost producers are crowding out the market. Irrespective of this strange distortion in the marketplace, the simple fact remains that unless the world's dominant suppliers shift their models away from generating positive social externalities in favor of sheer profitability, the price of oil is set to rise. And this sliding scale of inefficiency embedded in the cost structures of the world's dominant producers will continue. In sum, as long as this market paradigm holds, the price of oil will not decline due to the search for productivity gains through better technology and innovation (the search for lower breakevens).

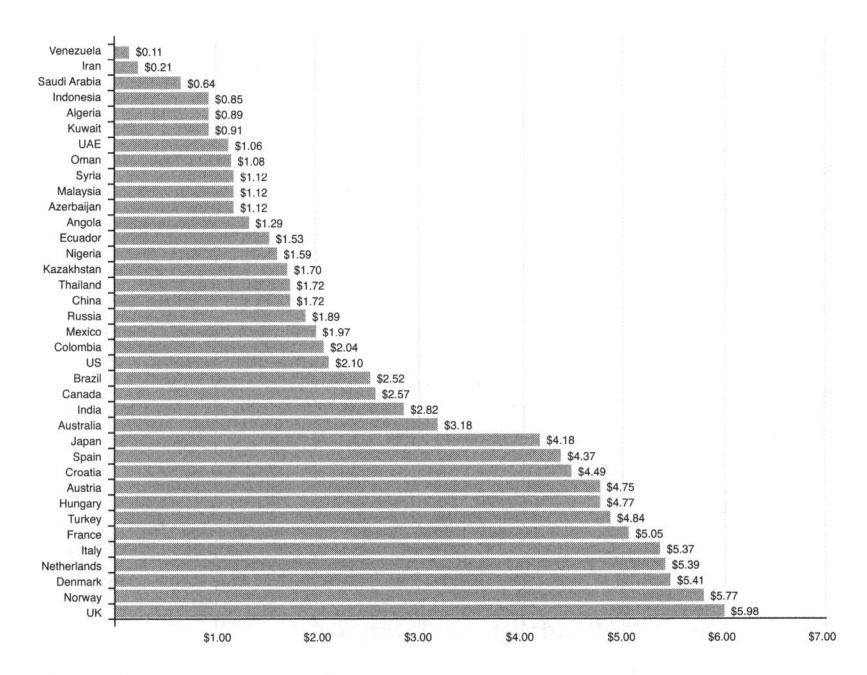

Country	Price
Venezuela	$0.11
Iran	$0.21
Saudi Arabia	$0.64
Indonesia	$0.85
Algeria	$0.89
Kuwait	$0.91
UAE	$1.06
Oman	$1.08
Syria	$1.12
Malaysia	$1.12
Azerbaijan	$1.12
Angola	$1.29
Ecuador	$1.53
Nigeria	$1.59
Kazakhstan	$1.70
Thailand	$1.72
China	$1.72
Russia	$1.89
Mexico	$1.97
Colombia	$2.04
US	$2.10
Brazil	$2.52
Canada	$2.57
India	$2.82
Australia	$3.18
Japan	$4.18
Spain	$4.37
Croatia	$4.49
Austria	$4.75
Hungary	$4.77
Turkey	$4.84
France	$5.05
Italy	$5.37
Netherlands	$5.39
Denmark	$5.41
Norway	$5.77
UK	$5.98

Figure 8.5 Average gasoline price survey

Source: Baker Institute, Rice University

Market Distortions from the Fed's Loose Credit and Easy Money

In addition to the geopolitical backdrop for oil production, many producers at large have effectively clipped their own wings through a mix of easy access to capital, response to higher energy prices, and too much competition over limited resources. Put another way, the latest up cycle may have produced some casualties as a large number of firms leveraged their balance sheets in the chase for future reserves. Measured on a barrel of oil equivalent (BOE) basis, firms across the industry increased their debt slightly more than 100% from the beginning of the bull market in oil in 2001 through 2008, as shown in Figure 8.6.

Also, the most dramatic increases in debt occurred in the past three years, just as the amount paid for acquiring new assets also surged. Although each transaction could vary by firm, this suggests that many firms were borrowing money to fund purchases at exorbitant prices. This behavior is no different from buying stocks on margin just prior to a stock market crash or taking out loans to speculate in home prices before the real estate meltdown.

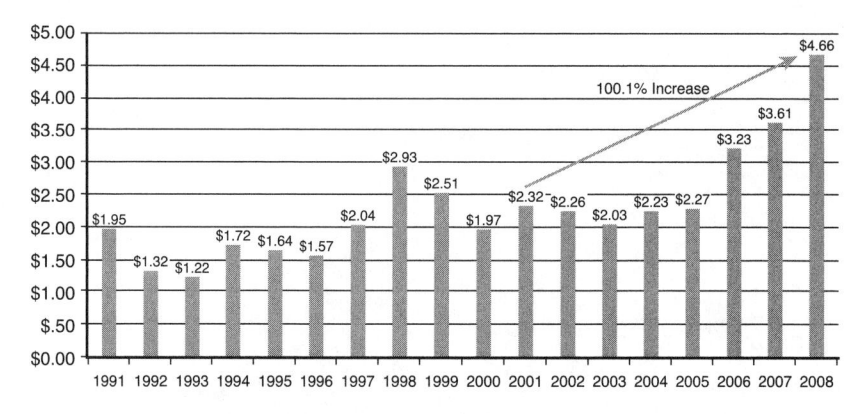

Figure 8.6 Debt per BOE (dollars per BOE)

Source: Company reports, CSFB

This behavior during the run-up and subsequent collapse in energy prices beginning in late 2008 suggests that many marginal producers, using debt to chase the rising acquisition costs in 2008, have been hanging on at best following the financial crisis. On the other hand, early or longtime players that behaved prudently and maintained healthy balance sheets may in time become the consolidators of distressed assets. The key take-away from this discussion, though, is the simple observation that with many players too leveraged, combined with volatile credit markets, it could take some time before production sees another surge in investment. No different from the situation with the national oil companies, with worldwide players possessing less capital to be deployed into future projects, supply faces yet another headwind from lack of investment. With these additional fundamental impediments to supply in place among many Western operators, this suggests that once demand recovers in the developing nations, and more normalized activity resumes in the developed-world economies, prices will again be set to rise for years to come.

As we put everything together in the supply and demand equation, the simple truth is that the key determinants for both demand and supply have shifted away from the old twentieth century model of the United States and friends buying oil from the Middle East. Even so, this new picture of supply and demand does not extricate the United States and the Western establishment from an active role in the oil equation. Instead, the United States and its economic allies will still remain a driving force behind the future price of oil, but perhaps more so from a financial standpoint than from any other perspective. More specifically, aggressive U.S. monetary policy following the financial crisis and any resultant monetary inflation could also come into focus in its relationship to oil prices during the coming years.

Since the United States dissolved the Bretton Woods system of exchange convertibility in 1971 and formally removed itself from the gold standard by doing so, the influence of monetary policy and the effects of inflation have become familiar to most Americans. To be fair, this policy change has had further-reaching implications because it also encompasses countries that possess a managed float or some form of structured convertibility with the U.S. dollar. Despite the overarching importance of oil in the world economy and, in particular, the U.S. economy, the price of oil in and of itself made a particularly lackluster investment in the period stretching from 1928 to 1971 (see Table 8.8). In fact, an investor who had decided to purchase a barrel of oil in 1928 and keep it in the garage for those 43 years would have been disappointed to generate an annualized return of only 1.5%. He probably would have dumped the oil in his yard and used the barrel for something more useful after seeing that his stocks from the Standard & Poor's (S&P) 500 returned an annualized 8.1% in comparison. Even government bills and bonds had better performance than the price of a barrel of crude oil.

TABLE 8.8 Annualized Returns 1928–1971

Oil	S&P 500	T-bills	T-bonds
1.52%	8.05%	2.04%	2.93%

Source: BP Statistical Review, Lauren Templeton Capital Management, LLC

The dissolution of Bretton Woods changed these relationships from 1971 through the present, though (see Table 8.9). Generally speaking, all commodities received a nominal lift in their returns thanks to their ability to create a store of value when placed in the context of a loosely printed fiat currency. The role of a fiat currency doubling as the world reserve, combined with the shifting dynamics in supply and demand discussed earlier, likely changed the role of oil in the financial marketplace, as its return profile began to reflect these factors.

TABLE 8.9 Annualized Returns 1971–2007

Oil	S&P 500	T-bills	T-bonds
10.1%	11.1%	5.9%	7.7%

Source: BP Statistical Review, Templeton Capital Management, LLC

In a dramatic shift from the preceding 43 years, the 26 years following 1971 marked a substantial change in the price return from a barrel of oil (see Table 8.10). Far from being a laggard, oil's compounded price return of 10.1% was nearly on par with the S&P 500 and outpaced assets that generally suffer in inflationary environments, such as T-bills and T-bonds. For better clarity on the role that inflation may have played in the acceleration of oil prices, we can see that in the period from 1971 to 2007, the Consumer Price Index (CPI) run rate increased nearly 3 percentage points annually. Furthermore, in some ways, the CPI is a massaged data point that can portray a watered-down reality for U.S. consumers and the impact of inflation on their day-to-day purchasing power.

TABLE 8.10 Annualized Inflation Measured by CPI

1928–1971	1971–2007
1.3%	4.1%

Source: Bureau of Labor Statistics

Given the ubiquitous nature of oil in the world's economy, oil is well positioned as a store of value during a period of monetary expansion and any resulting inflation. For that matter, oil has, at least in the past, demonstrated its ability to outpace equity returns during periods of stagflation, such as the 1970s. It has been well documented since the 1970s that the decade was a truly difficult stretch of time for equity investors. However, this was not the case for oil prices, because a barrel of crude enjoyed a significant bull market. Even if we toss out the price spike from the 1979 Iranian hostage crisis and embargo (but unavoidably include the 1974 crisis) and measure returns from 1970 to 1978, it is worth noting that the price of oil compounded at 29.3% versus the 4.7% in the S&P 500.

Aside from the simple compounded returns of oil since the dissolution of Bretton Woods, sometimes a picture is worth a thousand words. You have seen Figure 8.7 before, in Chapter 4, "Quis Custodiet Ipsos Custodes?" but here we offer another brief illustration of the tremendous expansion in the monetary base.

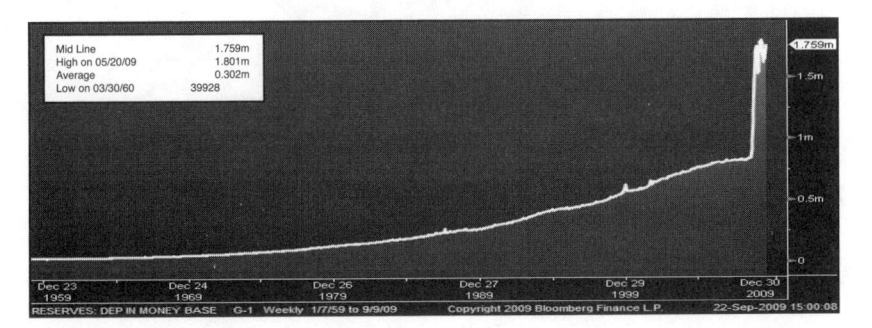

Figure 8.7 U.S. monetary base

Source: Federal Reserve

From Figure 8.7, it is relatively clear that since the early 1970s the expansion of the monetary base has continued unabated, and then of course it was punctuated by the binge printing of late 2008 and early 2009. The implications of a loose money policy are straightforward. It causes higher inflation and the likelihood of drifting from one asset bubble to another over time as the preceding easy access to capital leads individuals into risk taking or speculative ventures.

Now that we have highlighted and discussed the central arguments for higher future oil prices, the question remains as to what to examine regarding investments in this space. In this regard, the job of the investment manager becomes more familiar. First, in light of our previous discussion, one of the primary focus points for an investment would be firms that possess the balance sheet and proven expertise to expand production over time. One simple test is to review the firm's ability to replace its reserves over time, as well as its average growth in reserves over time. Over the past 17 years, reserve replacement has averaged 242% across the industry, as shown in Figure 8.8. Firms with above-average records and/or a perceived ability to maintain or generate this continued above-average performance should be considered.

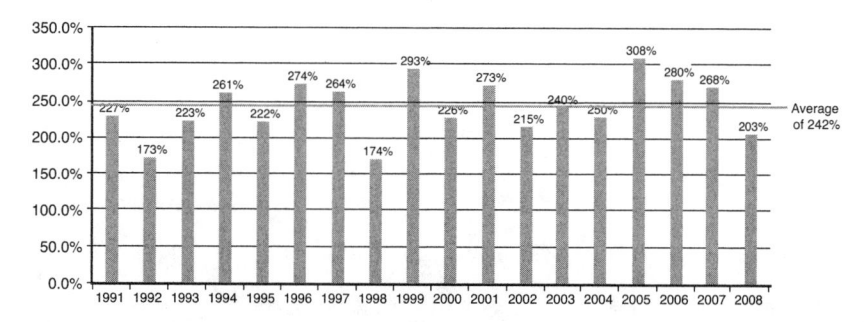

Figure 8.8 Worldwide median reserve replacement

Source: Company reports, CSFB

Historically, firms that have been able to create a strong mix of reserve replacement, growth in production, and a low cost of production, combined with a conservative balance sheet, have performed well in the stock market. Tables 8.11 through 8.13 show the market's preference for these factors in a correlation study between the variables of reserve growth, production growth, and low cost structures. In each study the correlation coefficients between the variables and stock market returns are statistically significant at 0.6 for reserve growth, 0.6 for production growth, and −0.6 for cost structures. (This means that higher dollar-per-barrel costs coincide with lower market returns.)

8 • Formula for Success: Rise Early, Work Hard, Strike Oil

TABLE 8.11 Correlation Between Annualized Reserve Growth and Stock Market Returns

	Company Name	Annualized Reserve Growth	Five-Year Total Return
CRZO	Carrizo Oil & Gas Inc	35%	17.4%
SWN	Southwestern Energy Co	30%	66.1%
BBG	Bill Barrett Corp	28%	NA
UPL	Ultra Petroleum Corp	23%	24.5%
PVA	Penn Virginia Corp	23%	3.5%
BRY	Berry Petroleum Co	22%	6.9%
GDP	Goodrich Petroleum Corp	21%	24.2%
KWK	Quicksilver Resources Inc	20%	3.2%
ATPG	ATP Oil L& Gas Corp	18%	6.0%
XTO	XTO Energy Inc	15%	23.3%
RRC	Range Resources Corp	15%	40.4%
DNR	Denbury Resources Inc	15%	29.6%
ECA	EnCana Corp	15%	22.7%
PQ	Petroquest Energy Inc	13%	8.0%
UNT	Unit Corp	12%	1.8%
NFX	New Field Exploration Co	11%	7.2%
COG	Cabot Oil & Gas Corp	11%	20.5%
XEC	Cimarex Energy Co	10%	2.1%
ARD	Arena Resources Inc	10%	49.8%
EOG	EOG Resources Inc	9%	21.8%
NXY	Nexen Inc	8%	19.1%
EQT	EQT Corp	6%	11.0%
CNQ	Canadian Natural Resources Ltd	6%	31.6%
DVN	Devon Energy Corp	5%	15.6%
FST	Forest Oil Corp	5%	1.4%
APA	Apache Corp	5%	15.4%
SM	St Mary Land & Exploration Co	5%	5.0%
PXD	Pioneer Natural Resources Co	4%	-3.5%

TABLE 8.11 Correlation Between Annualized Reserve Growth and Stock Market Returns (continued)

	Company Name	Annualized Reserve Growth	Five-Year Total Return
WLL	Whiting Petroleum Corp	4%	13.5%
CHK	Chesapeake Energy Corp	3%	10.3%
NBL	Noble Energy Inc	3%	20.8%
TLM	Talisman Energy Inc	3%	19.0%
OXY	Occidental Petroleum Corp	1%	24.3%
HK	PetroHawk Energy Corp	0%	23.4%
EAC	Encore Acquisition Co	0%	11.9%
MUR	Murphy Oil Corp	0%	12.8%
APC	Anadarko Petroleum Corp	0%	11.0%
PLLL	Parallel Petroleum Corp	-2%	-13.2%
SFY	Swift Energy Co	-3%	-7.2%
WRES	Warren Resources Inc	-8%	NA
WTI	W&T Offshore Inc	-8%	NA
CRK	Comstock Resources Inc	-9%	14.9%
CWEI	Clayton Williams Energy Inc	-9%	-0.8%
SGY	Site Energy Corp	-15%	-31.4%
PXP	Plains Exploration & Production Co	-16%	5.5%
CPE	Callon Petroleum Co	-30%	-28.3%
	Correlation Coefficient		**0.6**

Source: Lauren Templeton Capital Management, LLC

TABLE 8.12 Correlation Between Annualized Production Growth and Stock Market Returns

	Company Name	Annualized Production Growth	Five-Year Return
ARD	Arena Resource Inc	46%	49.8%
SWN	Southwestern Energy Co	32%	66.0%
UPL	Ultra Petroleum Corp	31%	24.6%
WRES	Warren Resources Inc	26%	NA
PQ	Petroquest Energy Inc.	21%	7.9%

TABLE 8.12 Correlation Between Annualized Production Growth and Stock Market Returns   (continued)

	Company Name	Annualized Production Growth	Five-Year Return
CRZO	Carrizo Oil & Gas Inc	20%	17.4%
KWK	Quicksilver Resources Inc	19%	3.1%
UNT	Unit Corp	17%	1.8%
GDP	Goodrich Petroleum Corp	16%	24.2%
ATPG	ATP Oil & Gas Corp	16%	5.9%
XTO	XTO Energy Inc	16%	23.3%
PVA	Penn Virginia Corp	14%	3.3%
BRY	Berry Petroleum Co	11%	6.8%
EOG	EOG Resources Inc	11%	21.8%
PLLL	Parallel Petroleum Corp	10%	-13.1%
EAC	Encore Acquisition Co	10%	11.9%
SM	St Mary Land & Exploration Co	9%	4.9%
NBL	Noble Energy Inc	8%	20.7%
DNR	Denbury Resources Inc	6%	29.6%
RRC	Range Resources Corp	5%	40.4%
NXY	Nexen Inc	5%	19.1%
ECA	EnCana Corp	5%	22.6%
EQT	EQT Corp	5%	11.0%
APA	Apache Corp	4%	15.4%
APC	Anadarko Petroleum Corp	4%	10.9%
XEC	Cimarex Energy Co	4%	2.1%
TLM	Talisman Energy Inc	3%	19.0%
WLL	Whiting Petroleum Corp	3%	13.5%
HK	PetroHawk Energy Corp	2%	23.4%
CNQ	Canadian Natural Resources Ltd	2%	31.5%
COG	Cabot Oil & Gas Corp	2%	20.6%
CRK	Comstock Resources Inc	2%	14.8%
CHK	Chesapeake Energy Corp	2%	10.3%

TABLE 8.12 Correlation Between Annualized Production Growth and Stock Market Returns (continued)

	Company Name	Annualized Production Growth	Five-Year Return
MUR	Murphy Oil Corp	1%	12.7%
OXY	Occidental Petroleum Corp	1%	24.3%
DVN	Devon Energy Corp	1%	15.5%
CWEI	Clayton Williams Energy Inc	0%	-0.8%
SFY	Swift Energy Co	-2%	-7.2%
NFX	New Field Exploration Co	-3%	7.2%
PXP	Plains Exploration & Production Co	-4%	5.5%
WTI	W&T Offshore Inc	-5%	NA
FST	Forest Oil Corp	-9%	1.4%
PXD	Pioneer Natural Resources Co	-9%	-3.5%
SGY	Stone Energy Corp	-12%	-31.5%
CPE	Callon Petroleum Co	-21%	-28.4%
	Correlation Coefficient		**0.6**

Source: Lauren Templeton Capital Management, LLC

TABLE 8.13 Correlation Between Total Cost Structure and Stock Market Returns

	Company Name	Total Cost Structure $ per BOE	Five-Year Return
UPL	Ultra Petroleum Corp	15.89	24.6%
NBL	Noble Energy Inc	20.03	20.7%
EOG	EOG Resources Inc	20.53	21.8%
EQT	EQT Corp	20.9	11.0%
SWN	Southwestern Energy Co	21.5	66.0%
ECA	EnCana Corp	25.55	22.6%
APA	Apache Corp	26.41	15.4%
CLR	Continental Resources Inc/OK	26.44	NA

TABLE 8.13 Correlation Between Total Cost Structure and Stock Market Returns (continued)

	Company Name	Total Cost Structure $ per BOE	Five-Year Return
CHK	Chesapeake Energy Corp	26.6	10.3%
CXG	CNX Gas Corp	27.03	NA
DVN	Devon Energy Corp	27.46	15.5%
PXD	Pioneer Natural Resources Co	27.59	-3.5%
XTO	XTO Energy Inc	28.19	23.3%
CNQ	Canadian Natural Resources Ltd	28.22	31.5%
UNT	Unit Corp	28.29	1.8%
RRC	Range Resources Corp	28.62	40.4%
COG	Cabot Oil & Gas Corp	29.45	20.6%
ARD	Arena Resources Inc	29.99	49.8%
APC	Anadarko Petroleum Corp	30.59	10.9%
XEC	Cimarex Energy Co	31.56	2.1%
FST	Forest Oil Corp	32.28	1.4%
BBG	Bill Barrett Corp	32.31	NA
CRK	Comstock Resources Inc	32.6	14.8%
NFX	New field Exploration Co	32.7	7.2%
KWK	Quicksilver Resources Inc	32.73	3.1%
OXY	Occidental Petroleum Corp	32.78	24.3%
CRZO	Carrizo Oil & Gas Inc	33.11	17.4%
MUR	Murphy Oil Corp	33.36	12.7%
SM	St Mary Land & Exploration Co	33.86	4.9%
DNR	Denbury Resources Inc	34.42	29.6%
BRY	Berry Petroleum Co	34.94	6.8%
PQ	Petroquest Energy Inc	37.23	7.9%
XCO	EXCO Resources Inc	37.88	NA
NXY	Nexen Inc	38.06	19.1%

TABLE 8.13 Correlation Between Total Cost Structure and Stock Market Returns (continued)

	Company Name	Total Cost Structure $ per BOE	Five-Year Return
CXO	Concho Resources Inc/Midland TX	38.16	NA
PLLL	Parallel Petroleum Corp	39.78	−13.1%
CWEI	Clayton Williams Energy Inc	40.09	−0.8%
EAC	Encore Acquisition Co	40.32	11.9%
WLL	Whiting Petroleum Corp	40.84	13.5%
TLM	Talisman Energy Inc	40.97	19.0%
ATPG	ATP Oil & Gas Corp	41.12	5.9%
PVA	Penn Virginia Corp	41.41	3.3%
ME	Mariner Energy Inc	41.5	NA
HK	PetroHawk Energy Corp	41.94	23.4%
SFY	Swift Energy Co	42.50	−7.2%
SD	SandRidge Energy Inc	43.09	NA
SGY	Stone Energy Corp	44.14	−31.5%
PXP	Plains Exploration & Production Co	44.54	5.5%
VQ	Venoco Inc	46.12	NA
WTI	W&T Offshore Inc	46.74	NA
GDP	Goodrich Petroleum Corp	27.25	24.2%
WRES	Warren Resources Inc	49.99	NA
CPE	Callon Petroleum Co	61.28	−28.4%
REXX	Rex Energy Corp	81.64	NA
	Correlation Coefficient		**−0.6**

Source: Lauren Templeton Capital Management, LLC

Among the E&P names illustrated in these tables, an investor might focus on those with the best mix of reserve growth, production growth, and low cost structures. Similarly, an investor might consider eliminating from consideration firms with poor track records in these variables, as well as firms with above-average financial leverage on their balance sheets. From a fundamental perspective, an investor should also focus on the geopolitical risks described in the earlier discussions as a possible limiting factor insofar as safeguarding against the company assuming too much risk toward the possible nationalization or even expropriation of shareholders' assets.

Seeking Alternatives in the Hydrocarbon Space

The problem of geopolitical risk in the sense of nationalization, and even expropriation in some cases, has forced the publicly traded energy companies to increasingly think outside the box in their pursuit of future reserves and growing profits on behalf of their shareholders. In other words, these firms are pushing considerably harder into the alternative energy space. The key attraction in the alternative space for the publicly traded companies is that they provide a growth area. But they also circumvent the geopolitical risks to a larger extent, because production can be located in shareholder-friendly developed markets that protect property rights. For the purposes of our discussion, we will contain our thoughts to the alternative energy sources that are tied to hydrocarbons, rather than solar and wind power. Basically we are referring to oil production that will over time come more and more from the conversion of oil sands, natural gas to liquids, and perhaps even coal to liquids. We should make a few points before we get ahead of ourselves. First and foremost, currently no forms of alternative energy can simply step in and totally supplant our need for oil. Second, although the circumstances can vary by asset, these alternative forms of energy also require relatively high prices of oil over some period of time to maintain their commercial feasibility and expand production in a meaningful way. Since we have made the case for higher future oil prices, this is a worthwhile exercise to define and illustrate the potential opportunities. Simply put, these areas possess outstanding potential for growth in the coming years, particularly since the existing capacity in place is beginning from a relatively small base. Based on the most recent data, the unconventional oil in the market was just under 4% of supply in 2006. But based on projections provided by the Energy Information Administration (EIA), this level of supply could reach 13% in the coming 20 years (see Figure 8.9). In other words, based on these projections, this segment of the industry is projected to grow at 8.9% compounded over the next two decades.

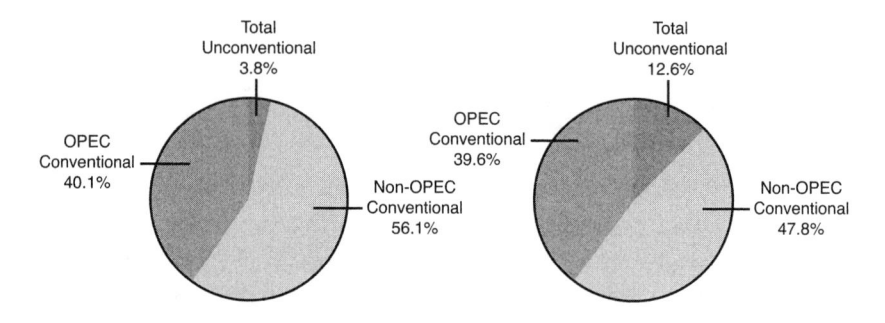

Figure 8.9 World supply of liquids in 2006 and 2030

Source: EIA

2006:
- Total Unconventional 3.8%
- OPEC Conventional 40.1%
- Non-OPEC Conventional 56.1%

2030:
- Total Unconventional 12.6%
- OPEC Conventional 39.6%
- Non-OPEC Conventional 47.8%

Clearly, this is an industry projection. We should expect that some producers will grow at rates above this trend line, and others will grow below it. In any event, let us now discuss the unconventional or alternative sources of hydrocarbons that we can reasonably expect to constitute this quickly growing portion of the energy market. We will begin with the Canadian oil sands, because this asset base may present the best opportunity over the coming five to ten years from a growth standpoint. Measured on a reserve basis, the Alberta Energy Resources Conservation Board estimates that based on current technology, 170 billion barrels of recoverable reserves are in the Canadian oil sands. This puts Canada second in the world behind Saudi Arabia. Naturally, this is still a developing industry. As technology advances through continued commercialization and competition, these reserves could actually increase from this number over time. Again, before we get carried away, we should emphasize that the industry is still developing (it only began in the late 1960s). Realizing anything close to this full potential could take a good while. With ostensibly all the major oil sands contained within three locations in Alberta, the North American industry is relatively geographically concentrated. Within Alberta are three deposit locations—in the Athabasca, Peace River, and Cold Lake regions. One reason why the industry will take time to develop is that there are two ways to extract the oil sands. One is close to the surface, where the oil sands are mined in an open pit. The second occurs when the oil sand deposits lie much farther below the surface. Not surprisingly, the open-pit-close-to-surface process is more economical, but only 20% of the total deposits sit close to the surface. The remaining 80% are extracted through an in-situ process at levels too deep for open pits (much greater than 200 feet). The in-situ process involves introducing heat into the mine through the use of steam, which raises the viscosity of the bitumen. This process involves far more energy usage and lower recovery rates, both of which conspire to raise costs. In time, however, the cost of production involved with the deeper deposits should fall, because the burden lies on technology that should be improved over time. This contrasts with the open-pit process, which is more labor-intensive, thereby making the cost of production more difficult to drive down from current levels. No matter where the deposits lie, the process to obtain a barrel of a refined product is rather burdensome. When we use the term oil sands, we mean that within this collection of sand, clay, shale, sandstone, and other surface materials is the presence of bitumen. This bitumen is what matters. The bitumen is what gives the oil sands their tarlike qualities. Obviously this material is not particularly viscous relative to other oil deposits, which are far more liquid. When the oil sands are mined from the ground, all these tagalong materials must be separated to obtain the bitumen. To bring this process into perspective, it takes roughly two tons of this mined material to make one barrel of oil. If that sounds like a lot of work to get one barrel of oil, you are right. If that also sounds like an expensive undertaking to obtain one barrel of oil, right again. There is no way around this at the moment. To bring these cost relationships into perspective, an oil sands operation may require a capital expenditure of $100,000 per daily barrel, which is about four to six times higher than the cost of deepwater drilling. Another complicating factor is the recovery rate from the mined material. Near the surface it is very high at 75% to 95%, but when mined through the in-situ process, the rate becomes far less certain and can range from 25% to 75%. So if we put all this together, it is hard to get a one-size-fits-all picture of the underlying economics-to-oil-sands production because, just as in oil, the rate of return can vary by site. Nevertheless, if we consider what is currently known about the current cost of production, it is believed that the price of oil needed in the market ranges anywhere from $35 to $85. It goes without saying that the low-cost producers making this product at less than $35 per barrel feel relatively comfortable. But the projects on the other side of the cost spectrum at $85 have much to consider before the producers sink billions of dollars into a site that takes years to construct. For that matter, new projects during the last several years became particularly prone to cost overruns due to the wild run in steel prices, which comprise approximately 50% of the capital outlay. Reports of costs rising fourfold on these projects were not uncommon. Despite the risks and complexities involved, a plethora of energy companies currently are involved or getting involved in the oil sands, so clearly these experts recognize the potential of this unconventional product. With that said, at the margin these businesses require a relatively consistently high oil price approaching $90 for many of them to make sense. In time, the breakeven price for a barrel of oil may fall as these professionals become more proficient in the space and begin to innovate. In the meantime, investors with a long-term horizon should examine these companies. In particular, they should do so when they have concerns about the price of oil due to weakening cyclical variables that can fluctuate over the course of a business cycle. In other words, this is an area for secular growth in the energy industry where investors may have opportunities to take advantage of market volatility.

The oil sands are a compelling growth story within the energy industry. But this is still just one of many possible solutions to get more production to the market to counter the stagnating production in the traditional sources. Another solution lies in a technology that was first developed in the 1920s by German scientists Franz Fischer and Hans Tropsch. The Fischer-Tropsch process involves converting a mixture of hydrogen and carbon monoxide into syngas (see Figure 8.10). It is then reacted with a catalyst such as iron or cobalt, leaving a waxy substance that can easily be converted into synthetic liquid fuels. Most important, the mixture of hydrogen and carbon monoxide can be obtained from natural gas, coal, and biomass, thereby creating liquid fuels from these raw materials. One of the key advantages of the coal-to-liquids and gas-to-liquids production through the Fischer-Tropsch process is that the end product is readily useable in the current energy consumption infrastructure. Just like creating refined product from oil sands, filling stations and various transportation vehicles are ready to consume the Fischer-Tropsch end product.

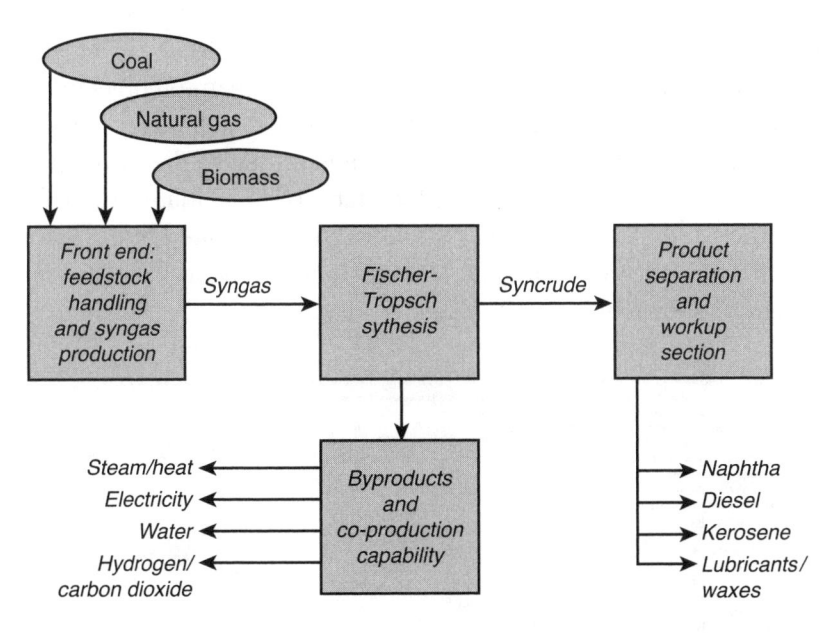

Figure 8.10 **Synthetic fuel production in the Fischer-Tropsch process**
Source: EIA

Although this process has been around since the 1920s, and the Germans used it during World War II to create fuel, it has only been commercially adopted in the past 50 years. Most notably, the South African firm Sasol has been creating coal-to-liquid synthetic crude since the 1950s. During the past 50 years, the world's economies have received plenty of proof that this process can be done, but this method of fuel production has not proliferated by any measure. Without question, this technology has been met with heavy resistance from the green parties and their views on what constitutes an appropriate form of alternative energy. In this respect, the use of coal as a feedstock for synthetic crude production faces an uphill climb in developed nations, such as the United States. The major objections include coal's mostly indefensible reputation as a dirty form of energy. This is well known and creates a barrier to the expansion of Fischer-Tropsch technology producing crude with coal as its feedstock. On the other hand, technology on carbon sequestration is advancing and could potentially weaken these objections. Despite green objections, it will be tough to eliminate the possibility of this technology's entering the fray sometime in the years to come as one of the developed market's energy solutions. The United States is appropriately referred to as the Saudi Arabia of coal. Not only does the United States have coal, it has more coal than any other nation in the world by a wide margin, as shown in Figure 8.11.

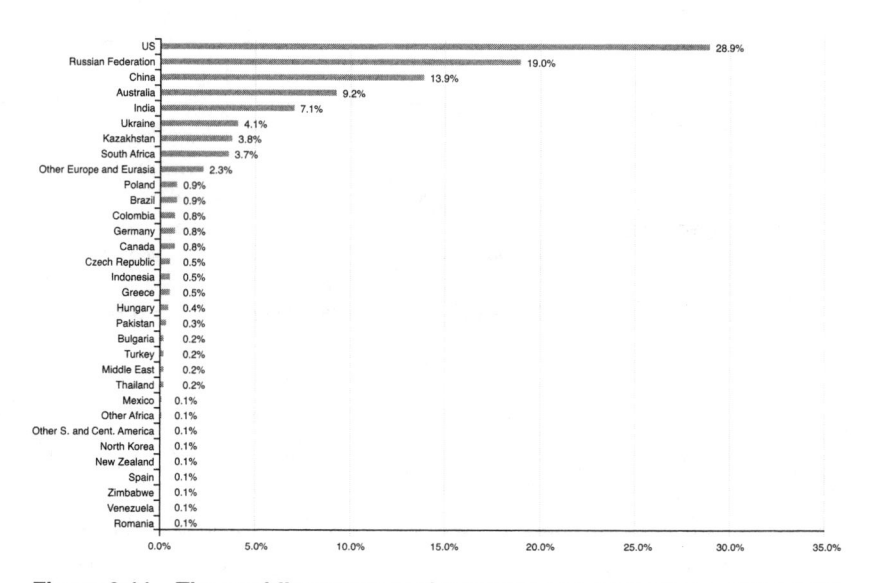

Country	%
US	28.9%
Russian Federation	19.0%
China	13.9%
Australia	9.2%
India	7.1%
Ukraine	4.1%
Kazakhstan	3.8%
South Africa	3.7%
Other Europe and Eurasia	2.3%
Poland	0.9%
Brazil	0.9%
Colombia	0.8%
Germany	0.8%
Canada	0.8%
Czech Republic	0.5%
Indonesia	0.5%
Greece	0.5%
Hungary	0.4%
Pakistan	0.3%
Bulgaria	0.2%
Turkey	0.2%
Middle East	0.2%
Thailand	0.2%
Mexico	0.1%
Other Africa	0.1%
Other S. and Cent. America	0.1%
North Korea	0.1%
New Zealand	0.1%
Spain	0.1%
Zimbabwe	0.1%
Venezuela	0.1%
Romania	0.1%

Figure 8.11 The world's proven coal reserves as a percentage of the total

Source: BP Statistical Review

Along with the institutional resistance to coal-to-liquid fuels due to environmental factions, we must consider the economics of production. On this front, the cost of production is actually not much of a serious deterrent within the market paradigm of consistently higher oil prices. Most estimates suggest that an oil price of only $45 to $50 is needed in the market. On the other hand, the issue of carbon sequestration has come under debate, because it has never been tried on the scale necessary to bring parties together on the environmental impacts of this technology. There is little question that a great deal of the carbon dioxide created during the production process needs to be removed from the air through sequestration and hypothetically stored in mass containment centers thousands of feet underground. This process in and of itself would raise the breakeven cost per barrel of oil in the market by $5 per barrel. All this assumes that the sequestration process goes according to script. Last, this entire process could face significant cost headwinds if a cap-and-trade policy on carbon emissions goes into effect, since the production process involves heavy emission of carbon dioxide. In the event of the passage of a cap-and-trade policy in the U.S. legislature, the effect would be a blow not only to the prospects for coal-to-liquid technology, but also to the coal industry in general, since it is also a heavier emitter of carbon dioxide relative to other industries in the United States. Basically, a cap-and-trade policy would force the cost of production higher in the coal industry (which must purchase the carbon allowances). The cost of purchasing these credits would then be passed on to end users in electric generation (as elsewhere). Eventually, these costs would arrive monthly in the mailboxes of U.S. consumers, printed on their utility bills. Conversely, in the absence of such legislation and the eventual emergence of coal-to-liquid technology, there would be opportunities for investors, as well as the coal companies themselves, to invest directly in existing technology providers for coal-to-liquid applications. A new layer of consistent demand would emerge for coal that would in turn make the reserves more valuable in the market. Furthermore, although we couched much of our coal-to-liquids discussion around the market in the United States, the coal-to-liquids market also has potential outside of the country and may expand faster in the international markets. One instance lies in China, where coal-to-liquids technology was recently put in place through the construction of a coal-to-liquids plant by the Shenhua Group. China, like the United States, has a relatively large coal resource and is searching for ways to power the growth of industrialization since it too has limited oil resources. Coal can be controversial in some corners, primarily among developed nations' green parties.

On the other hand, natural gas, the other significant feedstock for the Fischer-Tropsch process of synthetic crude production, is somewhat less of a hot-button natural resource. Gas to liquids (GTL) represents another future growth mechanism in the energy field that investors need to eye for long-term potential. GTL is a synthetic crude product that undergoes the same basic process as coal-to-liquids production in the Fischer-Tropsch process but obviously substitutes natural gas for coal as the feedstock. The South African firm Sasol is a leader in this production process, along with Shell, which both separately constructed GTL plants through joint ventures in Qatar. One of the interesting dynamics at play for the GTL market is its potentially multifaceted application. In the GTL plants in Qatar, we are talking about massive engineering feats that are situated close to large, long-lasting supplies of natural gas. However, the GTL process is also being innovated to monetize unique situations, including remotely located supplies of natural gas, as well as the natural gas supplies that often accompany oil fields and are most often flared. For quick background, it has been common practice for oil producers to install a flaring device that burns off the accompanying natural gas from an oil field. This can be seen as wasteful and polluting. In fact, many producers have reduced or eliminated this practice. Historically, there has been little opportunity to economically produce the accompanying natural gas due to the location of the oil field and the generally cost-prohibitive methods of transporting gas versus a liquid. The market potential for this application is recognizable. Estimates provided by the World Bank suggest that the equivalent of 700 million barrels worth of oil is wasted through flaring in a given year. Through the GTL application, however, oil producers may in the future be able to use the converted natural gas by-product as a readily marketable product for sale. Likewise, a similar approach to using smaller-scale GTL plants or conversion processes may open the market for one-off localized applications in a number of previously inconceivable market circumstances. Despite the market potential in a number of scenarios, GTL faces the same economic impediments as the previous unconventional liquids, such as oil sands and coal-to-liquids products. The necessary cost per barrel in oil prices can range from around $38 all the way to more than $100 per barrel. In other words, the early projects, such as those in Qatar, may represent the lowest cost of production, and the ones on the horizon likely will require higher oil prices. However, given our backdrop of higher oil prices over the coming years, investors need to be opportunistic and look for investments before oil prices make it abundantly clear that these technologies have growth potential and projects are announced left and right. Summarily speaking, our introduction of these unconventional liquid technologies and their promise for growth are meant to provide investors with energy themes possessing growth potential. Unfortunately, it is difficult to establish the static, end-all breakeven price per barrel of oil for these technologies since the circumstances can change quickly. For example, as we mentioned earlier, steel comprises approximately 50% of the cost in the capital outlay, and the price of this commodity has been and likely will remain volatile. Also, the cost of production can vary by the natural resources itself. Producing oil at a relatively low depth in the middle of a wide-open space in Saudi Arabia costs less than putting together an operation in the icy waters of the inhospitable arctic regions. With that said, we can still gain some perspective from estimates compiled by the International Energy Agency (IEA) regarding what it believes to be a range of the cost of production across various oil-producing regions and technologies. Table 8.14 should provide investors with some perspective on how distant the advent of our described technologies (among others) may be in relation to oil prices quoted in the market.

TABLE 8.14 Breakeven Costs Measured in Oil Prices Per Barrel by Source of Supply (2008)

Oilfield/Source	USD per Barrel
Mideast/North Africa oilfields	$6–$28
Other conventional oilfields	$6–$39
CO2-enhanced oil recovery	$30–$80
Deep/ultra-deep-water oilfields	$32–$65
Enhanced oil recovery	$32–$82
Arctic oilfields	$32–$100
Heavy oil/bitumen (oil sands)	$32–$68
Oil shales	$52–$113
Gas to liquids	$38–$113
Coal to liquids	$60–$113

This chapter tried to highlight the importance of the oil and energy markets and provide a framework for how to approach them over the coming years by identifying the most important drivers surrounding supply and demand. These factors will no doubt be tested over time, because they quickly fade into the background during periods of cyclical weakness, just as they did during the financial crisis and the subsequent collapse in oil prices. However, with a good knowledge of the long-term secular trends in this market, investors should be well-positioned with the psychological fortitude to step into the void and buy, should the market experience further corrections, pessimism, and disruptions—which it always does over time.

Endnote

[1] Stacy L. Eller, Peter Hartley, and Kenneth B. Medlock III. "Empirical Evidence on the Operational Efficiency of National Oil Companies." Prepared in conjunction with an energy study sponsored by the James A. Baker III Institute for Public Policy and Japan Petroleum Center. Rice University, March 2007.

9

An All-Too-Common Tragedy

In his 1968 essay "The Tragedy of the Commons," published in *Science* magazine, biology professor Garrett Hardin reintroduced an economic phenomenon that has prevailed among mankind probably since the first herders roamed the land with their flocks. In 1832, the topic was formally introduced by Oxford economist William Forster Lloyd. In *Two Lectures on the Checks to Population*, he discussed an economic paradigm that has puzzled centuries of observers: how to solve the problem of eventual destruction that nearly always confronts commonly held resources. This dilemma still exists today and can present potential opportunities for investors who identify their solutions.

The tragedy of the commons comes from a nineteenth century inquiry from William Forster Lloyd. It concerned lands held in common in England, and the relative state of cattle and grounds compared to cattle and grounds that were privately owned. Lloyd observed that the relatively "puny and stunted" cattle and "bareworn" land of the commons contrasted with the healthy, thriving cattle and grasses of the adjoining privately controlled enclosures of land. Lloyd theorized (and his theory was expounded on by Hardin in the twentieth century) that the herdsmen of the commons would continue to add cattle to the point of overcapacity. Behaving in their own self-interest, they had ample incentive to seize as much reward as possible from the public resource and to force the consequences on the remaining herdsmen. In other words, when a natural resource is held in common and shared by many, each individual has outsized incentive to exploit the resource and little or no incentive to assume the responsibility to conserve. A herdsman who does not take as much as he can will lose out to another herdsman who will. Once this process ignites through the self-interested behavior of one participant, other participants observe the prior's behavior and, in their own self-interest, compete for as much as possible of the commonly held resource. This cascading behavior continues until the public resource becomes exploited to the point of exhaustion. Contrast this with the privately owned model of herdsmen and their land, where the herdsmen have tremendous incentive to protect the finite allocation of the resource. In the privately held model, the herdsmen recognize that in order to maximize their interest, they must conserve portions of land by rotating the herd so that the land's nutrition can be efficiently allocated both now and in the future. The contrast in human behavior in these two settings has proven timeless rather than a novelty of centuries past. As Professor Hardin pointed out in later work, satellite images taken of Africa in 1974 revealed a peculiar 390-square-mile dark patch of land surrounded by light-colored, barren land. An investigation revealed that the dark patch was lush with foliage, surrounded by a fence, and privately owned. So whether we are discussing the commons of England in the 1800s or the expanse of Africa in the twentieth century, this thread of human behavior prevails and is timeless.

Human Behavior Is Timeless

Not only is this behavior timeless, but also the contrasting results from the exploitation of public versus private resources can manifest themselves across a number of media. One modern example can be seen in the use of earmark spending or tax exemptions that are common in legislation created in the United States Congress. In this case, rather than land, the primary resource is publicly provided tax revenue that is held in common and exploited by members of Congress. If a Congressman were asked if he supported earmarks slipped into bills, he would likely denounce the practice. On the other hand, these same politicians enthusiastically participate in creating these earmarks, because they understand that the practice will occur either way. If they do not participate, their constituents may lose the benefits of these resources. If that happens, the politicians may not be reelected. In other words, members of Congress believe they must compete to obtain as much as possible of the common resource, lest the other politicians wrest away more of the funds for *their own* constituents in other states. For taxpayers who feel that their hard-earned money is exploited or wasted, this is an all-too-common tragedy. Since politicians seek the favor of their voters, it is easy to see why this universally deplorable behavior occurs in a competitive, unbridled fashion. One specific example of this behavior hard at work can be seen in the use of public taxpayer money to rescue failed financial institutions in 2008 and 2009. In the case of the financial crisis, lenders including Fannie and Freddie (and probably others that thought they were too big to fail) knew they were backed by public resources. Therefore, they pursued their own course of greed, risk, and profits to the point of nearly exhausting the entire financial system. Whether the investment banks were wagering behind closed doors that they were too big to fail remains conjecture. However, in the end, the consequences of their reckless exploitation fell on the general public and their provision of financial resources held in common. As we can see, this behavior and this paradigm of the selfish exploitation of public goods have transcended both time and a multitude of resources. The bottom line is that this is simply a matter of human behavior that occurs repeatedly.

For our purposes, we will return to the world of natural resources. We will identify another clear modern-day example of this paradigm and seek to profit from its rather predictable outcome. In this case, we turn to the most obvious present-day example of the tragedy of the commons: the world's oceans.

The declining state of the world's fisheries has been a long time in the making and is becoming less of a secret in this age of instant global communication. Still, thanks to the human condition and the predictable outcome of profiteers vigorously exploiting a commonly held resource—in this case, the ocean—we can anticipate the world's fish stock being exploited in a relentless effort toward, but hopefully stopped well short of, exhaustion.

To be sure, this process is well under way. The world's oceans are, for all intents and purposes, vast and shared by all in spite of countries' wishes to gain increased private control of these frontiers. With that said, fishermen have openly exploited the world's fisheries with reckless abandon for centuries. Clearly, advances in technology and the industrialization of societies during the twentieth century accelerated the rate at which fishermen could haul in their next catch. In time, the effects of these advances have revealed the full extent of this exploitation. Figure 9.1 shows that fish production from capture out of the world's oceans grew at a steady rate of 4.4% from 1950 through 1989. This period represents the heyday of exploitation, when fishermen around the world could increase their hauls over time. Growing consumer demand due to rising standards of living in the U.S. and other developed markets was met with little problem through this practice. In the wake of this bonanza, however, from 1989 through 2007 the rate of exploitation began to take its toll. The rate of fish capture in these 18 years collapsed annually to a yearly decline of –0.5%. Basically, in predictable fashion, the world's fisheries became overexploited. The situation has worsened over the past several years, with actual production 8% below its peak in 1989.

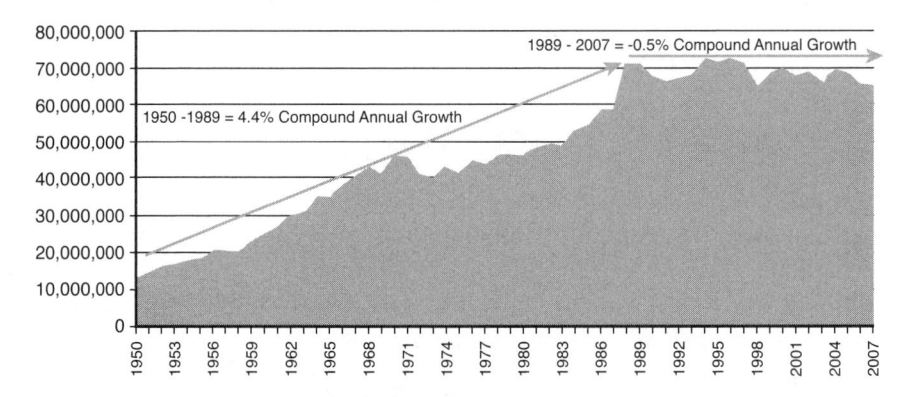

Figure 9.1 World fish production by capture

Source: FAO

The problem of overexploitation is punctuated by a not-so-coincidental sharp 46% increase in the number of fishers in the world, starting with the peak of production in 1989 and going through recent years. The problem, as expected, has been a large rise in the competition to obtain fish from the commonly shared world's oceans. Simply put, after decades of expansion, beginning in the 1990s too many fishers were chasing too few fish (see Figure 9.2).

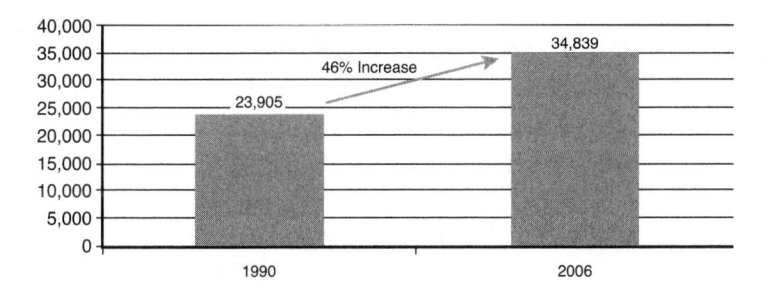

Figure 9.2 World fishers

Source: State of the World Fisheries and Aquaculture 2008

(1990: 23,905; 2006: 34,839; 46% Increase)

During the past several years, this decades-long activity has finally reached a point where the world's fisheries by and large cannot produce anything material beyond their current output. Figure 9.3 shows the FAO's assessment of the world's fishery resources in the 2009 publication "State of the World Fisheries and Aquaculture 2008." This report stated that only 20% of the world's fisheries could "perhaps produce more." This 20% includes the designations of underexploited (2%) and moderately exploited (18%). This leaves the remaining 80% of the world's fisheries as effectively tapped out and unable to produce anything more.

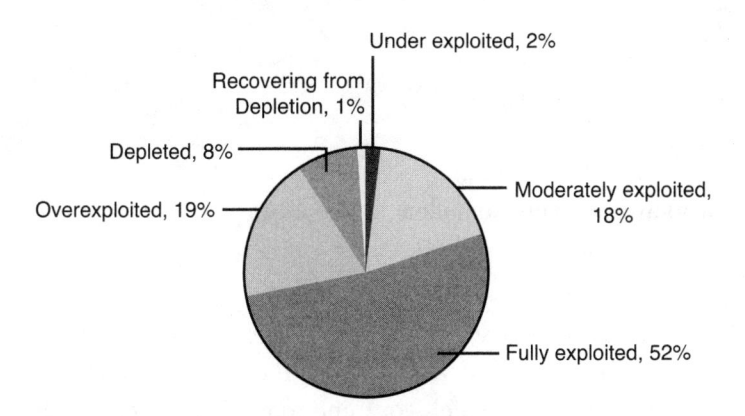

Figure 9.3 Status of fishery resources

Source: State of the World Fisheries and Aquaculture 2008

Strong Demand Underscores the Overexploitation

Importantly, this overexploitation of the world's oceans is not occurring based solely on the paradigm of sharing common waters. Rather, we must be careful to acknowledge that a sound demand driver is prompting this exploitation as the world continues to consume increasing amounts of fish. For instance, from the short period of 1980 through 2003, world fish consumption doubled, based on a steady 4.1% compound annual growth spanning the decades from 1961 through the early 2000s (see Figure 9.4). The presence of strong demand set against this economic paradigm is what paves the way for an investment opportunity. But before we explore the opportunity, let us review these demand drivers.

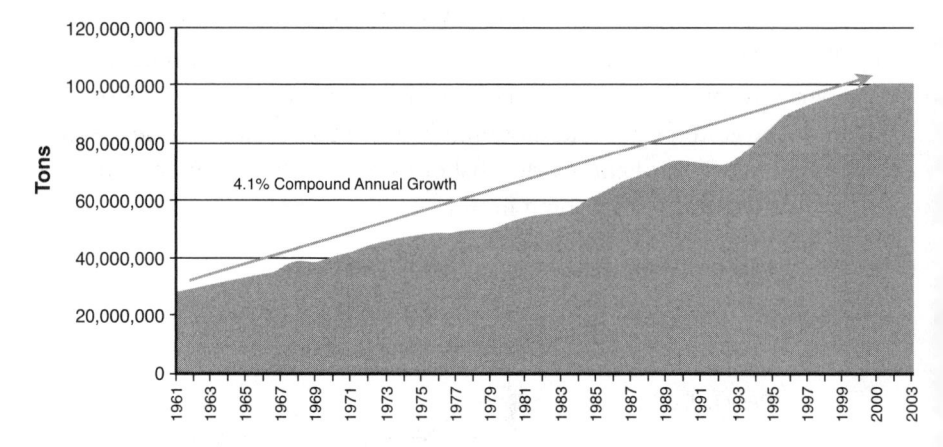

Figure 9.4 Worldwide fish consumption

Source: FAOSTAT (data available only through 2003)

Two significant modern-day trends have propelled this meaningful growth in demand. The first comes from the growing demand from the developing markets, which continue to consume increasing amounts of fish based on their rising standards of living. Given that fish is a source of protein, the relationship at play is no different from our related discussions of protein consumption, such as poultry, in the emerging markets being driven by growing affluence. As an example, Figure 9.5 shows the exponential rise in the per capita consumption levels of seafood in China, developing Asia, and the overall developing world. The rise in per capita consumption in China that followed the opening of its economy after decades of stagnation has proven dramatic.

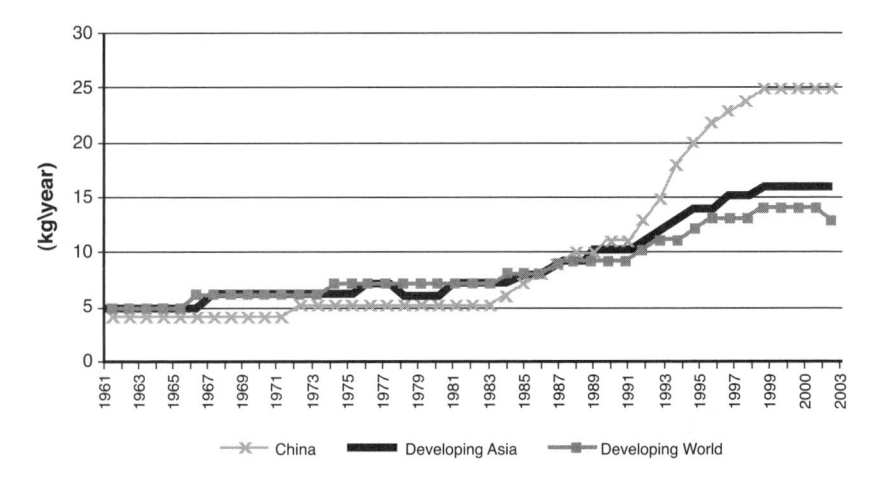

Figure 9.5 Seafood fish per capita consumption (kilograms per year)
Source: FAOSTAT

In similar form, if we examine the overall growth in tons of seafood consumption in the developing world, we can see that the rate of growth in these economies was 5.9% from 1961 to 2003 and lay well above the 4.1% world average (see Figure 9.6).

In addition to the developing markets in general, the growth rates in developing Asia have been even higher at 6.2%, compounded over a four-decade span (see Figure 9.7). This higher growth rate is likely driven by the traditional role of fish as a staple in Asian diets; its consumption often varies across Western diets.

The growth in the developing markets is impressive but not totally unprecedented, because fish consumption has been more prevalent over time in the Asian region. On the other hand, some might be surprised to discover that the developed markets too have been eating more seafood. If we examine per capita consumption trends in the U.S. from the early 1970s through the early 2000s, Americans have clearly been adding more seafood to their diets (see Figure 9.8). The reason for this behavior in the United States is that people have turned to seafood as a healthy alternative. Specifically, research has shown that incorporating seafood into a diet significantly helps reduce the risk of heart disease. For instance, a 2006 study from the Harvard School of Public Health found that consuming one or two servings of fish per week reduced the risk of a heart attack by 36%.[1] So in both the developing-market and developed-market economies, increasing fish consumption appears to coincide with growing affluence. Higher standards of living prompt larger discretionary incomes in the developing markets and healthier choices in the comparatively wealthy developed markets.

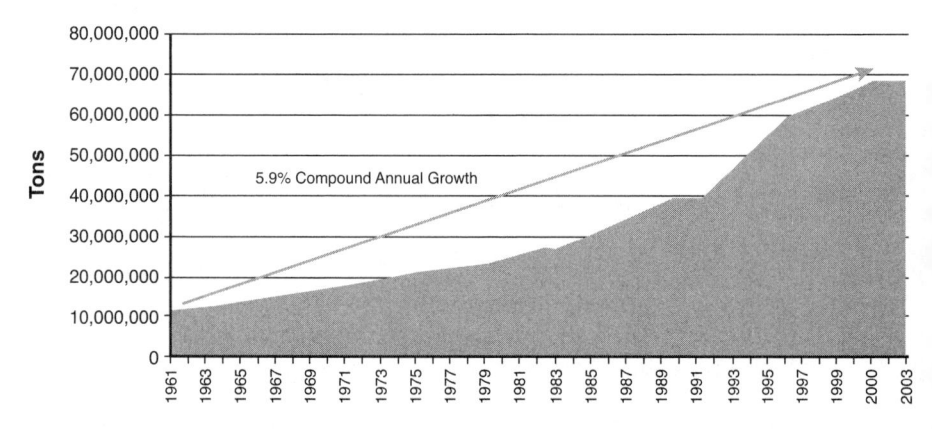

Figure 9.6   Fish consumption in developing countries
Source: FAOSTAT

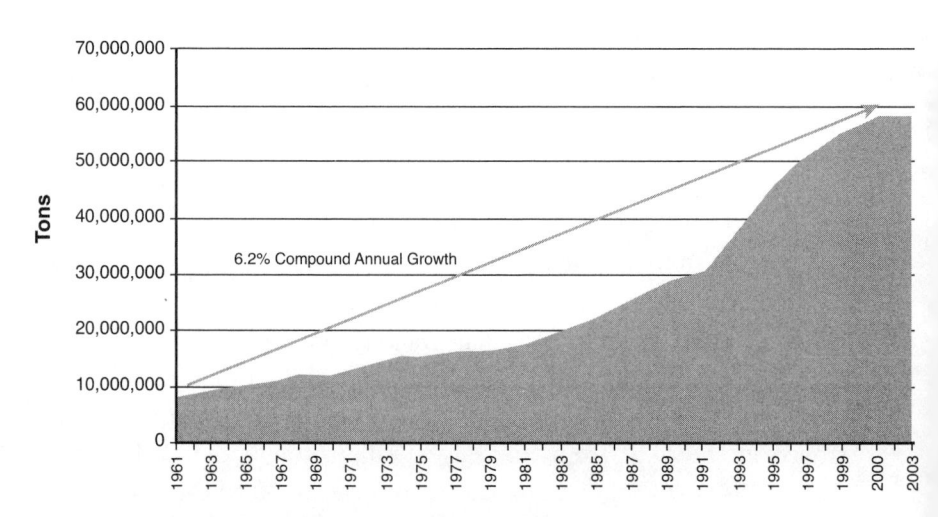

(Chart shows 5.9% Compound Annual Growth, Tons from 0 to 80,000,000, years 1961–2003)

Figure 9.7   Fish consumption in developing Asia
Source: FAOSTAT

(Chart shows 6.2% Compound Annual Growth, Tons from 0 to 70,000,000, years 1961–2003)

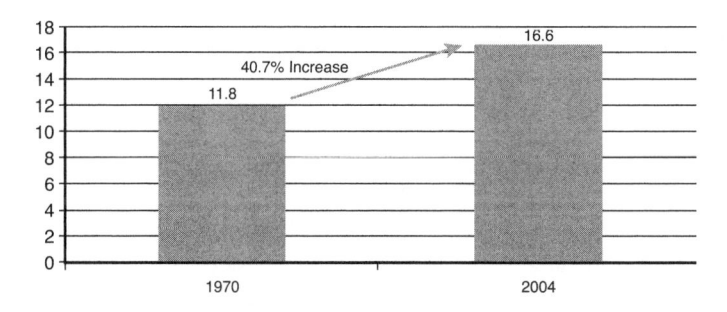

Figure 9.8 Per capita fish consumption in the U.S. (in pounds)
Source: NOAA

So far, we have described an overexploited resource of wild fish in the world's oceans, driven by the existence of a shared resource, as well as strong underlying demand drivers from both the developing and developed markets. The first conclusion we can reach is to acknowledge that the world's fisheries have been thoroughly prospected for product, and supply will remain relatively fixed going forward. The second conclusion is that demand will remain strong over the next five to ten years thanks to the consumption drivers of rising standards of living in the developing markets and increased health consciousness in the developed markets. Despite the dire picture for the world's fisheries, it seems unlikely that the darkest scenario of an eventual total collapse will ever be realized. At a minimum, the world's fisheries that lie within the general jurisdictions of the developed world are receiving some relief through the issuance of quotas for fishers. This form of regulation was tried with general success in New Zealand and is now being replicated in various forms by other nations. The reason this form of regulation provides a better alternative than the free-for-all approach is that the quotas represent an allocation of the resource in the form of property. When the fishers treat their quotas as a form of property ownership, they in turn alter their behavior toward a more efficient form of exploitation, including acts of conservation. The change in behavior represents a shift from exploitation at all costs for near-term gain to one of responsible exploitation. This shift is accompanied by stewardship, because the fisher now has added incentive to ensure the longevity of the resource. However positive this outcome may be, we are still confronted with a basic question: Where will the consumers of tomorrow obtain their seafood fish if the production of the world's oceans has peaked?

A Tragedy Leads to an Opportunity

Luckily, the world has found an answer in the business of aquaculture, or fish farming. Aquaculture is really no different from livestock production in the beef, poultry, and swine industries, except that in this case the farming occurs in captive areas of the sea. The industry has existed for several decades and has enjoyed years of growth, registering an 8.6% compounded growth rate from 1950 to 2007 (see Figure 9.9). During the past several years, this industry has come increasingly to the fore thanks to the poor state of the world's fisheries.

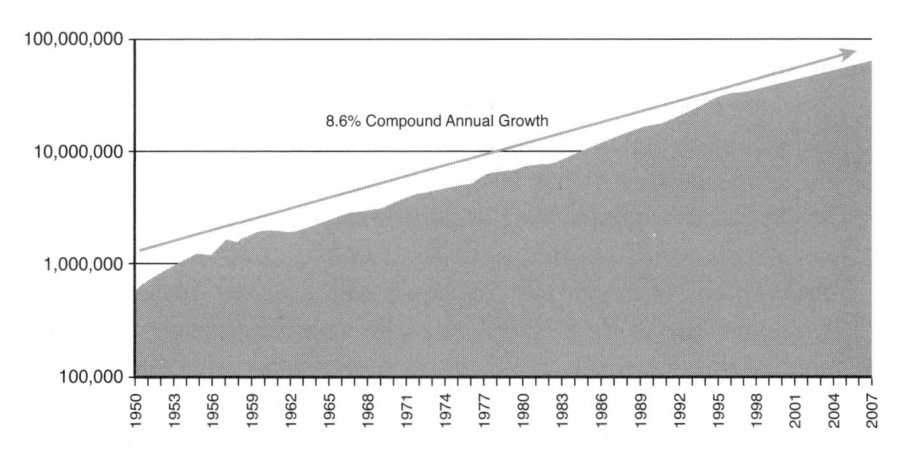

Figure 9.9 Total aquaculture production
Source: FAOSTAT

Despite the steady growth seen over the past 60 years, the industry has only recently become a significant player in the role of human food consumption. Despite the latecomer status, supply from this source has stormed onto the scene as FAO estimates suggest that in 2007 the aquaculture industry supplied 47% of the fish consumed globally compared to just 3.9% in 1970. Most importantly, though, because of the factors of growing demand and overexploitation in the supply, which we discussed earlier, nearly all future growth in fish supply for consumption will also come from aquaculture, rather than the world's oceans. In fact, this trend has already begun in the wake of the stagnation in wild capture during the early 1990s. At the same time, we must be careful to recognize that the term aquaculture is a (no pun intended) catchall for many different species of aquatic animals. Figure 9.10 shows that the aquaculture market is diverse, encompassing fish products ranging from freshwater fish to mollusks and crustaceans.

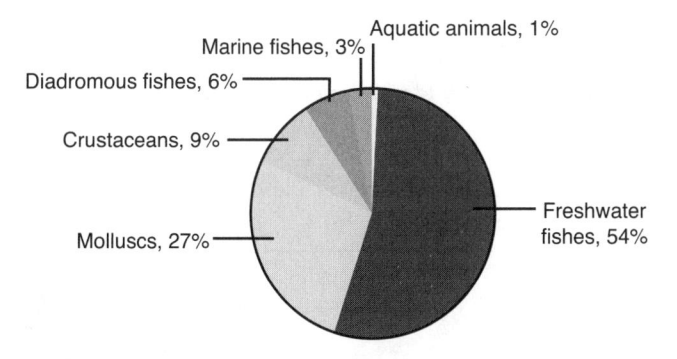

Figure 9.10 Aquaculture production by species

Source: State of the World Fisheries and Aquaculture 2008

Although the entire category should enjoy growth in the coming years, the subcategories of diadromous fishes and marine fishes are particularly relevant from a growth perspective and likely will receive investors' attention. Diadromous fish, or fish that travel between salt water and freshwater, such as salmon and trout, have strong commercial value, as do the marine fishes. The higher value of these products relative to the overall market is easy to see if we compare quantity in tons versus value in U.S. dollars (see Figure 9.11). Put another way, diadromous and marine fishes comprise considerably more of the market in U.S. dollars versus their representation in volume.

With that said, commercialization of these aquaculture categories has responded well to the overexploitation of the world's fisheries, and production has posted strong growth rates since the early 1990s, as shown in Figure 9.12. In short, the business has risen from near obscurity to becoming a considerable portion of overall production in these fish proteins over the past several decades.

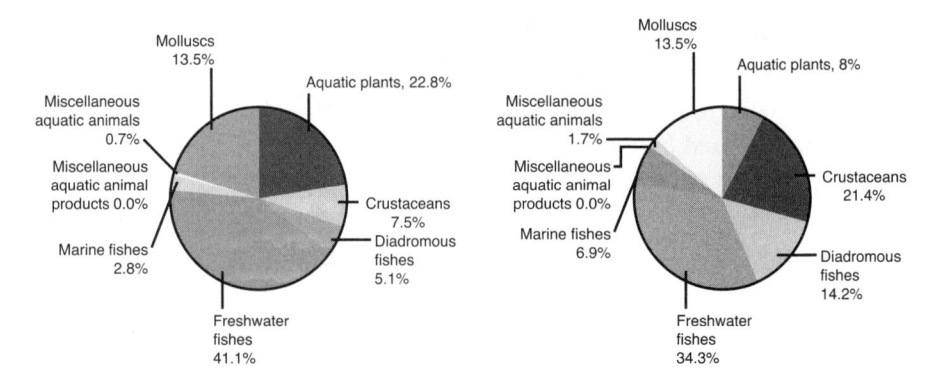

Figure 9.11 Aquaculture market by tonnage and U.S. dollar

Source: FAOSTAT

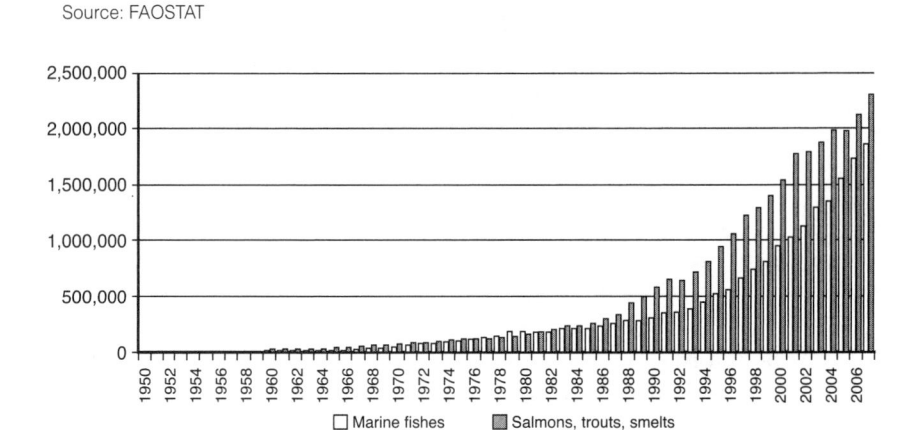

Figure 9.12 Aquaculture production of diadromous and marine fishes

Source: FAOSTAT

From 1990 through 2007, the marine fish category has grown in volume by 11.1% per year, and the diadromous category has grown at 8.3% per year. This growth in the industry has been enabled by continued advances in aquaculture farming techniques that have persistently driven the cost of production lower. For example, if we look at the cost of production since the early 1990s (see Figure 9.13), the cost of production in salmon farming has dropped by approximately 50%, meaning that the price of salmon has also dropped. One important takeaway from this trend is that salmon has become incrementally less expensive over the past 15 to 20 years thanks to these lower costs. Therefore, salmon is more competitive with the remaining proteins in the market, such as beef, poultry, and swine.

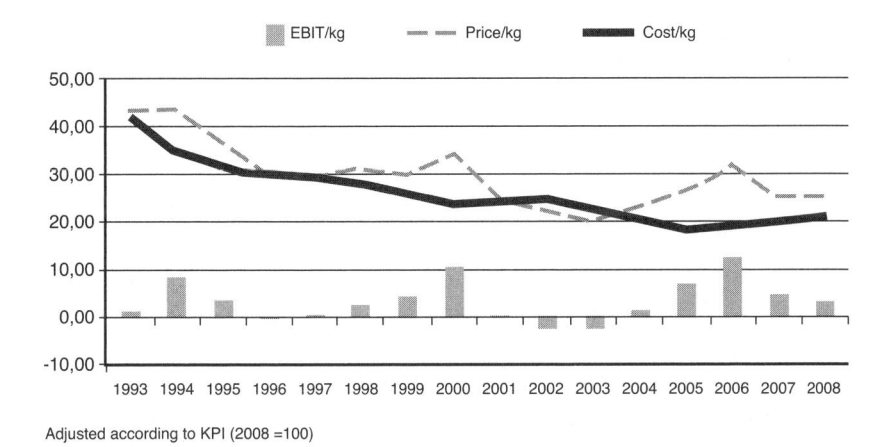

Figure 9.13 Inflation-adjusted price and production cost in the Norwegian market

Reprinted with permission from Marine Harvest, Salmon Farming Industry Handbook 2009.

The other important observation from an investment standpoint is the cyclical nature of prices in the market. As shown in Figure 9.13, prices tend to rise above the cost of production for approximately three years and then approach breakeven or even loss-making levels. This is likely due to the three-year production plans and the recurring collapse in prices. Producers will add capacity as long as prices exceed the cost of production, until prices eventually decline from oversupply. The bargain hunter for investments in this space and many other commodity markets typically reaps the highest benefits from investing ahead of the cycle while the firms are at breakeven or are suffering losses due to supply-led price collapse. Despite this built-in timing device, many investors instead do the opposite and invest when the market looks prosperous, just prior to a collapse.

Irrespective of investor folly, the salmon farming industry is largely relegated to a handful of countries and regions, including Norway, Scotland, Chile, and Canada. All these major markets have experienced significant harvest growth rates during the past few decades, but Chile stands out with a 21% compounded annual growth rate, as shown in Figure 9.14.

The historic growth rate of the Chilean market registering twice the level of Norway and Scotland did not occur by chance. The Chilean market for aquaculture and salmon farming in particular has specific

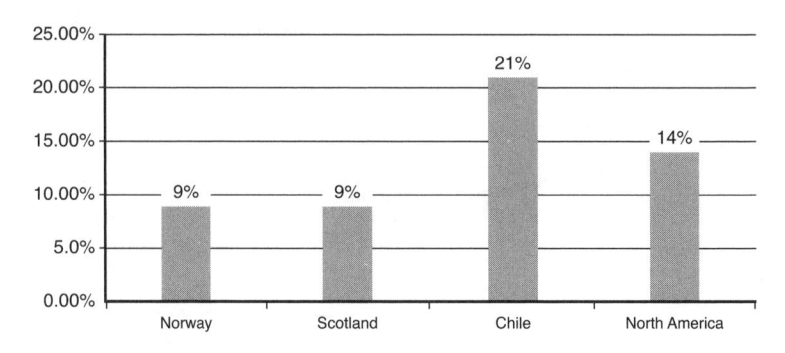

Figure 9.14 Salmon farming compound annual growth from 1990 to 2008
Source: Marine Harvest, Kontali Analyse

competitive advantages. One deep competitive advantage of the Chilean market is its relatively stable water temperature. It varies annually by approximately 4 degrees Celsius, versus the other competing regions, where the water temperature may vary by as much as 10 degrees. Since Chile's average temperature is more stable and, on average, a few degrees higher than the remaining major producing regions, its fish tend to grow faster by approximately three months. Likewise, in the Chilean market, the farmers can release smolt (young fish) throughout the year. The other regions, such as Norway, must adhere to a seasonal pattern when the water becomes warmer. The bottom line is that producers in Chile can grow fish faster and also produce more fish in any given year thanks to these competitive advantages.

Despite these advantages, Chile's rapid growth and emergence as a significant industry player came at a tremendous cost. In the typical "commodity style, grow at all costs, and add capacity while it is profitable" fashion that is found across all farming businesses, the Chilean producers ignored industry best practices. Ignoring best practices led to unbridled growth and capacity additions. Across the Chilean industry, farmers adopted rather weak industry practices, which led to a massive outbreak of a biological disease called Infectious Salmon Anemia (ISA). The ISA outbreak in Chile during mid 2007 devastated the industry and resulted in substantial layoffs, culled harvests, and financial losses for producers in that market. Perhaps this situation will be remedied in time. But there is no easy fix to a disease outbreak of ISA—which incidentally highlights an important risk factor to consider.

On the other hand, this phenomenon actually may have provided the industry with a meaningful boost to its broader supply-and-demand cycle. Given the scope of the problem in Chile, the removal of supply among these producers due to culling has actually helped offset the ill effects of the global recession and the resulting declines in demand. So although the Chilean situation has been a disaster, and most producers have been losing money in these operations, it has actually been somewhat of a mixed blessing. Profits in other regions have picked up in response to declining supplies in Chile. To bring the Chilean supply shock into perspective, the overall supply of salmon is expected to fall 75% from 2008 to 2010 by some estimates. The reduction in supply volumes has already begun to affect pricing in salmon, because production declines have outpaced any decline in demand due to a softer economic backdrop. While projections and estimates vary by source, there is a fairly wide consensus that the problems in Chile will affect supply volumes in the years to come. Based on most expectations, supply volumes are expected to decline during 2009 and 2010 as farmers in Chile continue to sort out these biological issues with their supply (see Figure 9.15).

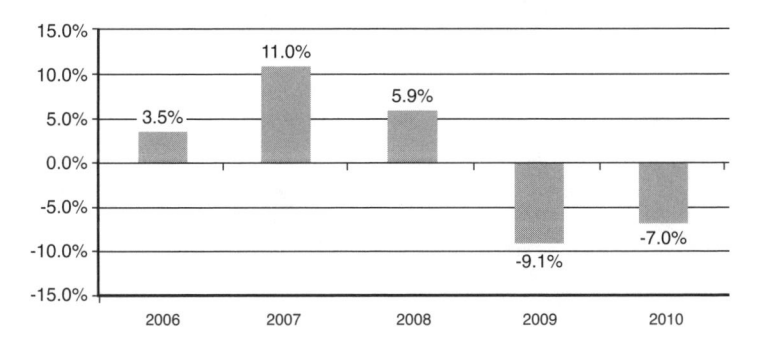

Figure 9.15 Farmed salmon, coho, and sea trout supply estimates
Source: Fondsfinans

In the meantime, estimates from industry executives highlight the severity of the Chilean issue. Aulie Michelet, the CEO of Marine Harvest, a large Norwegian producer with operations in Chile, has stated in interviews with Bloomberg[2] that it could take until 2014 or 2015 for production volumes in Chile to resume their prior levels. Until then, the demand for salmon and seafood of all varieties should continue marching on in step with the demand drivers present in both the developing and developed markets. Set against this demand backdrop, it seems probable that the market could become and remain undersupplied, creating a bullish environment for aquaculture producers with operations in other locations such as Norway. Because many of the publicly traded large producers have operations across the major markets, they too could benefit from this market paradigm, notwithstanding continued weakness in their Chilean operations. In any event, thanks to the unique set of circumstances surrounding the world's fisheries and demand drivers across all markets and economies, we can have some confidence that growth will continue in this industry over the coming years. This growth represents an opportunity for investors who can look beyond the near-term problems in the Chilean supply.

Endnotes

[1] Christy Feig. "Seafood benefits outweigh risks, government says." CNN.com, November 2, 2006.

[2] Meera Bhatia. "Marine Harvest Chief Says Salmon Supply Squeeze Will Persist." Bloomberg, August 20, 2009.

10

What Happens When 700 Million Students Want Extra Help?

"If I am walking with two other men, each of them will serve as my teacher. I will pick out the good points of the one and imitate them, and the bad points of the other and correct them in myself." Confucius spoke these words more than 2,000 years ago, yet their wisdom still holds true. Moreover, this sage advice captures the approach to globalization from the most successful emerging markets. Simply put, countries across Asia, along with a few in Latin America, have borrowed what works (open trade, freer markets, competition) from the wealthy nations and have discarded what has not worked (profligacy) from their own economic models. This approach has proven successful to date, because fewer emerging markets became ensnared by the consequences from the latest episode (there was the Asian Financial Crisis of the late 1990s though) of debt-riddled financial speculation that nearly dismantled their developed-market counterparts.

This method of learning by example may also prove successful in tackling the remaining problems that create medium-to-long-term obstacles in the continued progress of the emerging-market economies as they reach for higher standards of living. For starters, many of the key emerging markets are confronting the divide between the competitiveness of their higher-education system versus levels that were long ago achieved in the developed markets. To be sure, the global landscape for schooling and education has long been dominated by the higher-learning institutions of the West, including all the famous Ivy League schools of the United States. American colleges and universities have afforded the country a longstanding and nearly unparalleled competitive advantage relative to approximately

90% of the remaining world. This advantage has played a notable role in creating the economic miracle of the United States, and its high standard of living that evolved over the course of the twentieth century. In contrast, much of the developing world lacks this bedrock of higher education. For generations, these developing countries have sent their best and brightest to study in the United States. In this respect, for developing markets such as China, Brazil, and India to continue their forward march toward an increasing standard of living and higher levels of prosperity, they must find ways to narrow the gap between their workforces and those of the developed world. One mission-critical element of this strategy is strengthening the educational resources of their own nations. If this is not achieved, these markets will eventually encounter capacity constraints on the level of value-added components and processes that can be added to their economies. These constraints in turn could stall the countries' ability to create greater per capita wealth and increase their future standards of living. Table 10.1 shows the divide that separates key emerging markets from the top decile of countries as they are ranked by their competitiveness in higher education.

TABLE 10.1 Higher Education Competitiveness Ranking

	Rank	Decile
Finland	1	10
Denmark	2	10
Sweden	3	10
Iceland	4	10
Singapore	5	10
Switzerland	6	10
United States	7	10
Belgium	8	10
Canada	9	10
Netherlands	10	10
Brazil	58	40
China	61	40
India	66	40

Source: The Global Competitiveness Index, 2009 to 2010

There is some good news for these nations. Thanks to a confluence of technology and globalization during the past ten years, these markets have a unique opportunity to close the gap at a faster pace than could have been imagined a few decades ago. The technology available today has provided a profound push that favors these markets. Rather than adding to physical infrastructure through costly investments, and undergoing years of construction to catch up with the developed markets, the emerging markets can connect their people and share valuable information at a fraction of the cost compared to a few decades ago. Through this evolution of rapid communication, it is unnecessary to construct bricks-and-mortar learning centers, or house students in a university, if the only goal is for them to learn and advance their minds and skill sets. In regards to education, many of these countries have made strides since the 1990s. They have been dedicated to improving educational resources well in advance of developments in technology that now make the process even cheaper and easier.

The simplest example comes from China, where the value of education is deeply embedded in the culture. This is true of many other Asian countries as well, thanks to the lasting and shared influence of Confucian doctrine that has spread across the region during the past 2,000 years. In the Confucian realm of influence, education is prized and translates prominently into various perceptions of success, self-worth, and achievement in society. In fact, from around the Sui dynasty of the seventh century through the Qing dynasty of the twentieth century, the only surefire way for the Chinese to advance in society was to take and pass an academic-based civil service examination called the Keju. Passing this test could elevate Chinese without any form of socioeconomic discrimination into the various ranks of the state bureaucracy. This was a surprisingly meritocratic practice in a time of human history dominated by kings, emperors, dynasties, and bloodlines. The exam had three levels: local, provincial, and palace. Passing these hierarchical exams could bring not only power through government appointments to rule, but also wealth, and titling that could be passed to offspring. As they say, membership has its privileges—and the privileges of achieving these ranks were material. Because of the high societal value given to individuals who passed the tests, the country in time became obsessed with studying for and hopefully passing the civil service exam. The exam was administered annually for 1,299 years. Suffice it to say that the concept of studying to get ahead is ingrained in Chinese culture. In the twentieth century, however, this system of studying to get ahead became sidetracked by foreign invasions as well as the social and political upheavals that resulted from the initial communist rule. China's embrace of education was pried critically loose by the devastating effects of the Cultural Revolution during the late 1960s. This led to school closure and the persecution of intellectuals for several years. When Deng Xiaoping reinstitutionalized the Chinese obsession with education through a new set of college entrance exams in the late 1970s, the Chinese in particular had much catching up to do following the temporary dismantling of all formal education. From a broader perspective, since the 1990s, when China, India, Brazil, and many other emerging markets began initiating more open trade policies, these policy changes stimulated competition among the people in their economies. This led to accelerating enrollment in higher education, through attending college or other postsecondary institutions. The rise in enrollment in China has been particularly robust. The percentage of students enrolled jumped exponentially from 3% in the early 1990s to 23% by 2007, as shown in Table 10.2.

TABLE 10.2 Tertiary School Enrollment Rate as a Percentage of the Total

	1990	2007
Brazil	11%	30%
China	3%	23%
India	6%	12%
United States	72%	82%

Source: World Bank

Spending on Education Takes Precedence in Many Emerging-Market Households

The strong growth in postsecondary school enrollment underscores a tangible desire in the emerging-market countries just mentioned to become more competitive in the global economy supported by the pursuit of learning and education. This phenomenon is also revealed in various other indicators, such as the amount of money spent on education taken as a proportion of household income. Specifically, Chinese parents spend a considerable amount of their household budget on the competitive positioning of their "Little Emperor," as the only child in the family has come to be known. From the Chinese viewpoint there is no better way to ensure their child's success than to focus on his or her education. Backed by thousands of years of practice in Confucian principles, it is not surprising to find that the Chinese spend more of their household income on education than their American counterparts (see Figure 10.1).

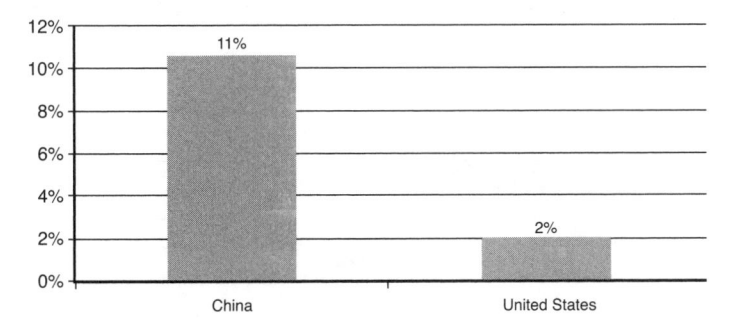

Figure 10.1 Education as a percentage of household consumption

Source: China Statistical Yearbook, United States Department of Labor

Figure 10.1 shows that as a percentage of the household budget, the Chinese have a remarkable dedication to spending on education. Even outside of China, though, basic household surveys among the people of developing nations across Asia reveal a shared, intense commitment to education. Based on the recently initiated Global Purchasing Priorities Survey by MasterCard, citizens of both China and India list spending on education as one of their top three priorities. For instance, in the survey for India, an overwhelming 86% of married people polled placed their children's education as the number one purchasing priority. This priority ranked well ahead of buying, renovating, and upgrading their property. Back in China, this dedication to spending on education is yet another important driver behind the high personal savings rate found among the Chinese. While the U.S. lavishes more money on public education than any other country, about 6% of GDP, China's public expenditure is actually much smaller, approximately 3% of GDP. This has important ramifications. For starters, because of the Chinese people's cultural preference for education and the outsized demand borne from this preference, the public services provided by the state represent a supply deficit versus the level of demand in the market. The Chinese have a large and widely unmet appetite for educational resources, compared to what is available from public-funded schooling provided by the government. To bring this relationship into perspective, Figure 10.2 compares supply and demand for higher learning in China, as measured by the growth in the number of enrolled students relative to the growth in the number of higher-learning institutions. Furthermore, we can draw a comparison to the same relationship historically found in the United States.

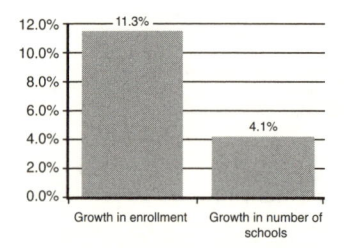

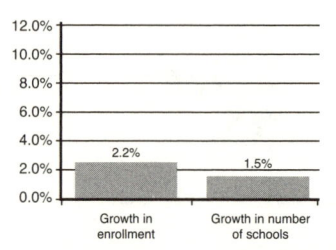

Figure 10.2 Growth in enrollment and institutions of higher learning in China, 1978 to 2007 (left) and the U.S., 1975 to 2005 (right)

Source: China Statistical Yearbook, U.S. Census Bureau Statistical Abstracts, 2008, 1978

Without question, the growth in college enrollment is sharply outpacing the growth in the number of colleges in China during the past 30 years. Comparatively speaking, in the United States the number of institutions has largely kept pace with the growth in enrollment. The difference likely is because of expanding student bodies within the existing schools. In China, however, where the education market has not kept pace with demand, the number of students studying abroad has exploded. It has grown at a compounded rate of 19.3% during the comparable time periods described earlier. Because of this top-level shortfall of resources relative to other nations, and the intense competition for coveted educational institutions and services, the Chinese have been saving more of their income to dedicate spending to the hopeful success of their Little Emperors. In fact, the parents have a vested interest in seeing their children succeed, because it is also a Chinese custom for children to care for their parents as they age. With that said, these parents have incentives to see their children become financially successful, ranging from altruistic love to retirement planning. For many economists who puzzle over what may help unlock higher domestic spending in the future, the ensuing growth in the education sector and parents' willingness to spend in this category may be one of the keys. Because of the intense competition in the system, the Chinese look for effective ways to distinguish their child in the race for excellence and standing in the classroom. This has led to a demand for goods and services that are not provided by the state, but instead have been provided by the private market or, as we mentioned earlier with the studying abroad, in markets outside China, depending on people's age and circumstances. More important than the trend toward studying abroad has been the continuing advance of market-based solutions within China. Entrepreneurs have a significant opportunity to step into the supply void and create useful goods and services that aid these students' success rates. The solutions that have come forth have not necessarily followed traditional models of education known and practiced for centuries in the West. Instead, technology has been embraced as an innovative solution that can also be proliferated with relative ease.

The Role of Technology and Innovation

The Chinese have been quick to use the Internet as a conduit for education. From 2004 to 2007 the number of students enrolled in Internet-based courses increased by 31%, from 2.4 million students to 3.1 million. The utilization of Internet-based education is in keeping with the broader surge in Internet usage across the country. China actually became the world's largest country of Internet users in 2008 with 298 million users, a 42% jump from the 2007 level (see Figure 10.3).

Despite the impressive record of Internet usage growth in China, it is estimated that still only one out of every four Chinese has Internet access, leaving much room for future growth. The growth in Internet usage, combined with the intense competition for educational resources among Chinese students, has led to a vibrant market for online-based education. By some estimates, the market is expected to reach nearly $6 billion in U.S. dollars by 2011, from just $1.5 billion in 2004 (see Figure 10.4). The use of online education is a natural fit for the Chinese for a few different reasons. First, given the general paucity of physical school resources, capacity can be added to the learning system at a low cost, and with relatively instant lead times compared to adding capacity in the real estate format. Additionally, distance learning through television was already commonly practiced in China before the Cultural Revolution upended the entire educational system for several years, so this is not an unfamiliar format.

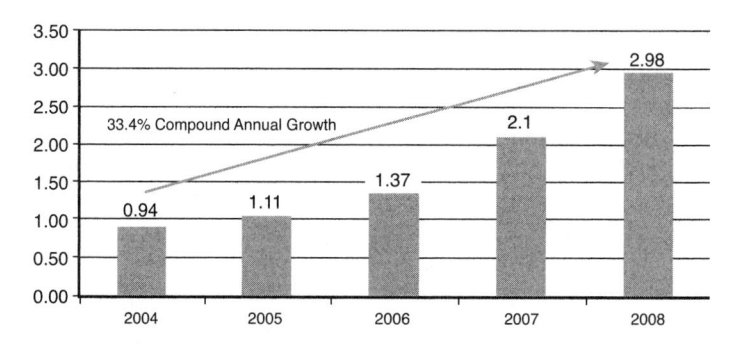

Figure 10.3   Internet users in China (in hundreds of millions)

Source: CNNIC

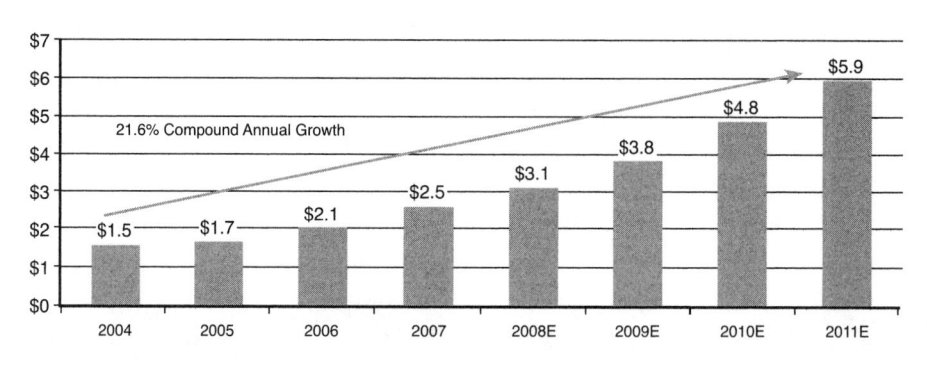

Figure 10.4   China's market for online education (in billions of U.S. dollars)

Source: China Distance Education Holdings

10 Million Students Applying for 6 Million Spots in College—No Pressure

The growth in online education has been impressive and tends to capture the market for courses in a number of subjects, as well as the audience for tutoring and test preparation. The drive toward academic competitiveness begins at an early age in the Chinese system and often starts with learning English, which is seen as the language of business in China. Many parents believe that if their children learn English at an early age, they will gain a competitive edge and increase their future marketability as a student beyond the secondary level (see Figure 10.5).

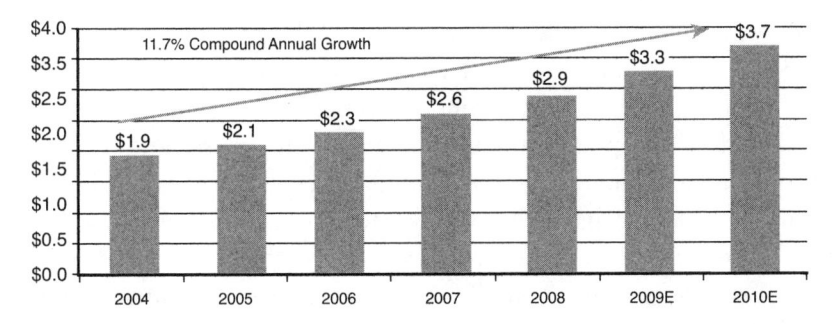

Year	Value
2004	$1.9
2005	$2.1
2006	$2.3
2007	$2.6
2008	$2.9
2009E	$3.3
2010E	$3.7

11.7% Compound Annual Growth

Figure 10.5 China's market for English language training (in billions of U.S. dollars)

Source: China Education and Training Industry Report

In addition to English classes, the market for tutoring is important as parents attempt to bolster their children's classroom performance. Tutoring is seen as advantageous because the curriculum in the public school system is highly regimented and rigidly prescribed. On the other hand, tutoring in the private market can be highly customized to the student's skill level and learning style. Because of these advantages, the market for tutoring services in China has also grown at an accelerated pace, as shown in Figure 10.6.

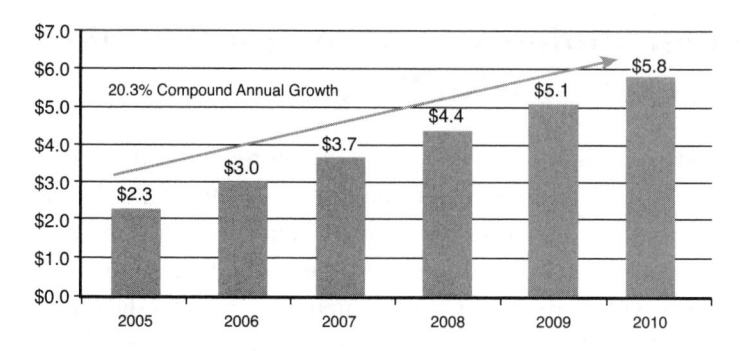

Figure 10.6 China's market for tutoring (in billions of U.S. dollars)

Source: Morgan Stanley

Year	Value
2005	$2.3
2006	$3.0
2007	$3.7
2008	$4.4
2009	$5.1
2010	$5.8

20.3% Compound Annual Growth

After the parents have invested in English classes and after-school tutoring, hopefully the child is in a solid position to enter an institution of higher learning. Even if that is the case, the student must pass the hand-wringing, nine-hour-long sole determinant of his or her college acceptance, the Gaokao test. Although somewhat similar in concept to the SAT in the United States, this one test is for all the marbles, rather than another factor to be weighed alongside GPA. This three-day-long annual exam tests an average of 10 million students for approximately 6 million spots in college. Not surprisingly, the Gaokao seems like a modern reenactment of the Keju, and its importance cannot be overstated. This test can reasonably be seen as a cause of collective nationwide anxiety, and sleeplessness among the participating students and their parents. Preparation for this test is paramount to any prior effort in the classroom and can incorporate some relatively expensive measures, according to a June 2009 article in the *New York Times*, "China's College Entry Test Is an Obsession."[1] Parents have gone so far as to pay to have their children study in hospitals while hooked up to oxygen machines in the hopes of improving their memory retention. One unfortunate child profiled in the article failed the exam. "My mother was very angry. She said, 'All these years of raising you and washing your clothes and cooking for you, and you earn such a bad score.' I cried for half a month." Given the pressure to succeed on this exam, it is no wonder that the market for Gaokao preparation has been thriving. Figure 10.7 shows the steady growth in the market for Gaokao retakers—students who use test preparation services before their next sitting for the exam.

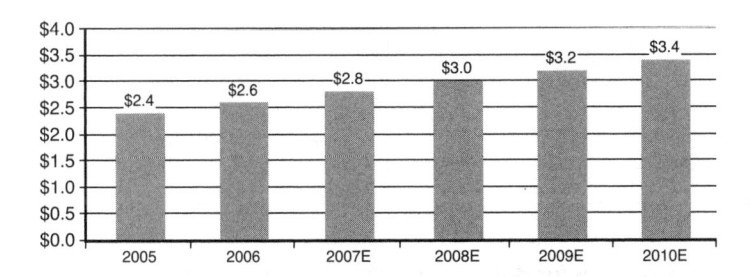

Figure 10.7 China's market for Gaokao retakers (in billions of U.S. dollars)

Source: New Oriental Education

Continuing Education

For students who are fortunate enough to advance past the Gaokao exam and attend college, the bar has been increasingly raised toward obtaining degrees beyond the undergraduate level. This pressure to advance is heavily stimulated by the empirical translation of higher education into higher salaries (see Figure 10.8).

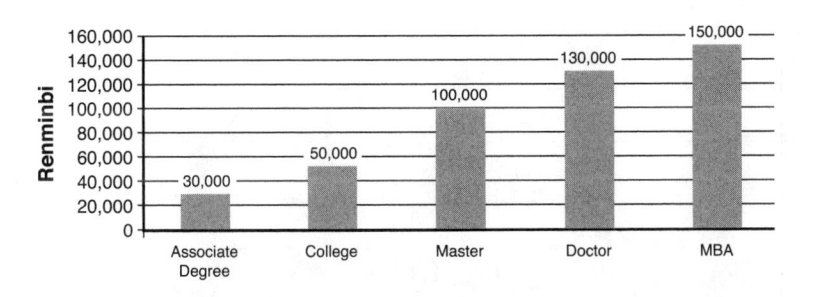

Figure 10.8 Pretax income by degree in renminbi (RMB 000)

Source: ChinaHR

Recognition of this market driver has helped propel a spike in the number of enrollments for both master's degrees and doctorates, as shown in Figure 10.9. Obviously, obtaining these degrees requires more study, outside-of-the-classroom preparation, and test taking. In other words, advanced degrees provide yet another market opportunity for private study guide providers and tutoring services.

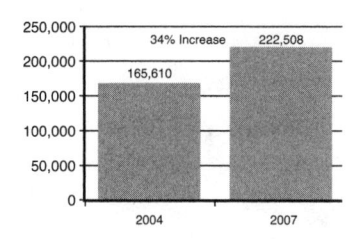

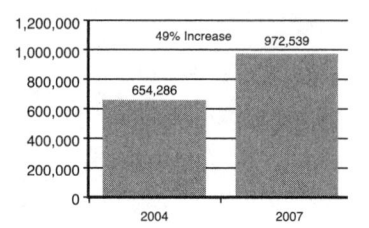

Figure 10.9 Enrollment for doctorates (left) and master's degrees (right)
Source: China Statistical Yearbook 2008

In addition to the sharp rise in enrollments for these degrees, the steady growth in undergraduate enrollment over the past several years bodes well for future demand for advanced degrees. However compelling the market for degree-based educational services may be, we should also appreciate the scope for continuing education in the job market as it relates to vocational skills. In keeping with the trend, a large and growing market related to professional licensing and certification also is riding this secular wave of self-improvement. The market for professional certifications and licenses, ranging from CPAs to healthcare professionals, is large and rapidly expanding, as shown in Figure 10.10.

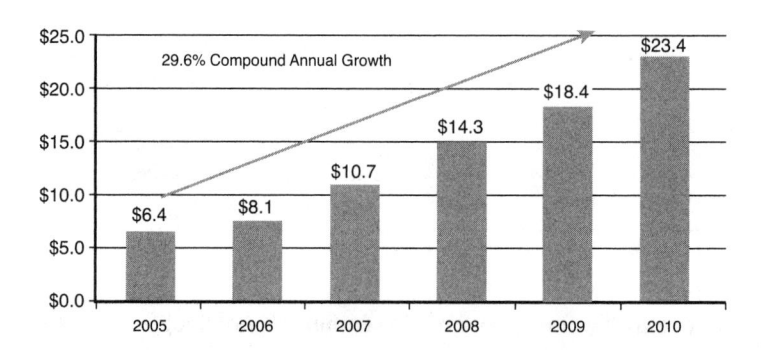

Figure 10.10 China's market for professional education and test preparation (in billions of U.S. dollars)
Source: China Distance Education Holdings

The growth in professional testing and, for that matter, the number of professionals in a developing economy may be one of the clearest indicators of a progressing society. The number of lawyers and accountants in China is set to continue rising as the economy marches toward higher standards of property rights and universal accounting standards. Remarkably, in 1985 there were only 5,000 lawyers in China to service a population of over 1 billion. As pleasant as this sounds, it was actually endemic to a society where few property rights were conveyed to individuals. Since the market has adjusted to allow greater protection of property, the number of lawyers has risen to 150,000. Likewise, in the accounting profession it is expected that by 2013 about 90% of the world's GDP will have adopted the International Financial Reporting Standard (IFRS). This will create a greater need for uniformly trained CPAs, who naturally must go about passing their host of exams. Effectively, as China and other key emerging markets continue to globalize, the composition of their workforce will require more professionals, who in turn take their fair share of tests.

The demand for professional education and advanced degrees is also creating stronger local markets for MBAs and other business curricula. This development will also play a critical role in the creation of domestic economies in the emerging markets as workers with increasingly sophisticated skill sets integrate into the economy. Within China, we can already see signs of progress on this front. In a recent global ranking of MBA programs by the *Financial Times*, a business school in Shanghai, China Europe International Business School (CEIBS), cracked the top 10 of programs worldwide for 2009, as shown in Table 10.3.

TABLE 10.3   FT.com Global MBA Rankings, 2009

1	University of Pennsylvania: Wharton	USA
2	London Business School	UK
3	Harvard Business School	USA
4	Columbia Business School	USA
5	Insead	France/Singapore
6	Stanford University Graduate School of Business (GSB)	USA
7	Instituto de Empresa (IE) Business School	Spain
8	China Europe International Business School (CEIBS)	China
9	Massachusetts Institute of Technology (MIT) Sloan School of Management	USA
10	New York University: Stern	USA

Source: FT.com

Financial Crisis Portends Continued Growth in the Emerging-Market Education Services

In the coming years, we can expect to see an even greater representation of Chinese and emerging-market business schools joining what had otherwise been an elite club of schools reserved for Western institutions. To be sure, however, Wharton will be Wharton, and Harvard will be Harvard, and attending schools of this caliber will remain in high demand for the foreseeable future. If we take a comprehensive view of the global higher education market, though, it is easy to see that the underlying fundamentals portend high growth rates for years to come in the consumption of advanced degrees among emerging-market students. Where they obtain those degrees, however, may be changing for a number of reasons. In the past, high demand fed a constant pipeline of bright students from the emerging markets into Western institutions. In the present day, however, with the growing presence of outstanding institutions in their home markets, some demand from the emerging markets for higher education may stay home. To begin, these students already face the inertia of obtaining visas, and now borrowing from reluctant lenders post-financial crisis creates yet another obstacle toward attending these big-sticker-price schools. In any event, the Western schools would have a hard time matching the capacity growth of their emerging-market counterparts. The reason for this is simple. In no uncertain terms, the Western schools from top to bottom took it on the chin from the financial crisis and are actually *contracting* their resources. This creates an additional market opportunity for the local providers in the emerging market to expand their operations alongside the rising demand.

The easiest way to describe the current turmoil in the Western institutions is to start with their endowments. During the 2000s, many college endowments entered a phase of annualized returns that in retrospect was euphoric. These returns were courtesy of broader financial markets such as the stock market and the fixed-income market and its derivatives, as well as gains derived from hedge funds and private equity funds. The returns obtained during this stretch were a heady departure from the 6% to 9% annualized returns that most institutions had sought in prior decades. In January 2008 an article in *USA Today* titled "College Wealth Soaring"[2] captured the height of this feel-good era by reporting that the average college endowment earned 17.2% in the prior year. As if the stellar investment returns were not enough to fuel feel-good vibes among university administrators, they also had routine tuition increases, which most estimate at around 7% annualized. As much as Western students and their parents bemoaned this steady tuition inflation, they had easy access to credit, which so defined the first decade of the twenty-first century. It is estimated that about 50% of all U.S. students in institutions of higher learning fund their enrollment through borrowed money. They are no more immune to this steady inflow of tuition and endowment returns than their counterparts in the consumer realm. A wealth effect set into the university system that began to influence spending behavior. Universities expanded their current curricula or added new ones on the basis of this increasing wealth. These capacity additions in many cases added fixed costs to the school's budgets. But the run of double-digit endowment returns and any spending excesses they may have caused relative to periods of more normal investment returns would not last. Only one year after the *USA Today* article, in January 2009 the *Wall Street Journal* ran an article titled "College Endowments Plunge"[3] that described the relative carnage that the financial crisis had unleashed on these portfolios. The article illustrates the fallout of the financial crisis and shows how, in less than six months, the fortunes of these institutions were drastically altered. From July 1, 2008 through November 31 of the same year, college endowments across the board lost well over 20% of their nest eggs, as shown in Figure 10.11.

The effects of this almost overnight decline in the worth of these institutions cannot be understated. For instance, as much as 40% to 50% of the annual budget can come from the endowment at universities such as Harvard and Princeton. An article titled "Cutbacks on Campus"[4] published by Kaplan College Guide in August 2009 revealed that many of these schools had to quickly shift their budgets and planned capital expenditures. Harvard reacted quickly by canceling the planned construction of a $1 billion science complex. It also has cut the number of entering doctoral students, eliminated hot breakfasts from weekday menus, and curtailed student bus schedules.

Princeton cut 5% of its head count and enacted caps on salaries above $75,000. Yale mandated a 7.5% salary cut and is also suspending construction on dormitories. The losses felt among schools have been compounded by at least a temporary absence from their big donors. In the past these people were looser with their own coffers, but now they have clammed up a bit after absorbing their own losses in the markets. As it turns out, the managers of these endowments committed the same errors as the mortgage borrowers and investment banks. They tied up too much wealth in illiquid assets while having short-term obligations, like keeping the school running. Even a year after the crisis, the *Wall Street Journal* continues to report on university endowments trying to unwind illiquid stakes in various financial instruments.

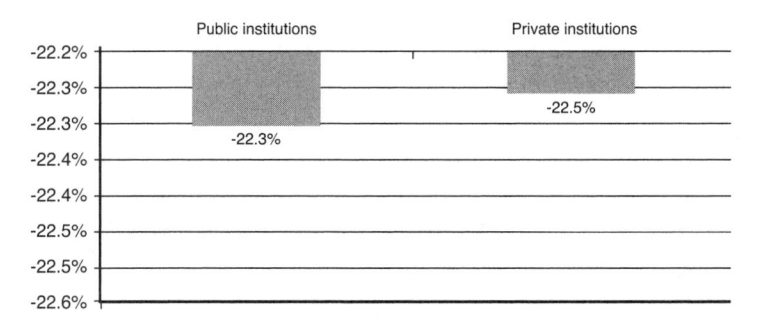

	Public institutions	Private institutions
-22.2%		
-22.3%		
-22.3%		-22.5%
	-22.3%	
-22.4%		
-22.4%		
-22.5%		
-22.5%		
-22.6%		

Figure 10.11 Average endowment investment returns, July 1 through November 30, 2008

Source: *Wall Street Journal*, National Association of College and University Business Offices, Common Fund, TIAA-CREF

The situation is really no better on the public side of the college endowment spectrum. Not only did these schools get hammered in their endowments, but in many cases they are also being penalized by the weak finances prevalent among the state governments from which they also receive funding. One example comes from Florida State University. In Florida an estimated $5.7 billion budget deficit has prompted the university to propose cutting 21 degree programs, as well as closing campuses and laying off faculty. Not surprisingly, the situation is at least as bad in California, the poster child of weak government finances, where student enrollment for freshmen has been capped.

The discussion thus far has ignored yet another critical source of funding that is under stress—the financial state of the student population. Students are grappling with diminished access to funding tuition through borrowing, not to mention the generally high outlays for college education present under any funding scenario. In short, college is expensive, and borrowing the money for it has become more difficult. The borrowing behavior of students who attend U.S. colleges has mirrored the broader phenomenon of the credit cycle during the past decade or so. In 1993, only about 32% of students borrowed money to attend their university, compared to roughly 50% in 2008. The balance sheet weakness and consequential risk aversion among U.S. financial institutions has not spared this market for borrowers and reveals yet another unhealthy exposure of U.S. colleges to the financial crisis. Naturally, this says nothing of recent graduates. If they borrowed their tuition money, they are now saddled with, on average, $40,000 in debt while confronting a domestic job market that is not exactly teeming with opportunity. These most recent graduates quite possibly are facing the worst mismatch between their large investment and their probable payback period. The rate of tuition inflation has been 7%, while job market salaries and the general rate of inflation have been considerably lower. This combination has saddled these young adults with a disproportionate amount of fixed debt and interest payments relative to their near-to-medium-term earning power in the job market. The translation is that it may take recent graduates longer to pay down debt loads that are, on average, 70% higher than graduates accumulated in the early 1990s. So just as the U.S. consumer absorbed higher oil and gasoline prices through additional borrowing, college students offset rising tuition fees through borrowing.

The availability of funding to students as a variable in school selection should not be overlooked. In particular, this point might affect business schools in the U.S. that hope to continue attracting international students. Specifically, many U.S. financial institutions have backed away from lending programs that circumvent having an American cosigner on the loan. This would make it more difficult for international students to borrow for tuition. Regulation has also created impediments as the job market in the U.S. for these international students has been artificially shrunken by financial regulation connected to rescue funds. Financial institutions that have received bailout money and have laid off employees find it more difficult to hire H1B visa workers. This peculiar form of protectionism clearly limits the marketability of U.S. business schools to international candidates hoping to earn lucrative developed-market-level salaries in U.S. financial institutions. In sum, the strings attached to receiving bailout money have been bad news for universities that promote themselves to international students on the basis of their high-profile finance-related job placement for alumni.

So for many of the reasons just described, we can expect that the international markets creating the largest growth in demand for higher education are accelerating the process of developing their own resources to a level where they can attract their best and brightest to stay at home for their education. Over the longer term, as these schools attract increasing amounts of homegrown talent who in turn become successful in the global market, these same alumni will eventually endow their alma maters to levels more competitive with the developed markets. In other words, once this growth process takes hold in these local institutions, it becomes a self-reinforcing phenomenon. Finally, the point is that the market for education in emerging markets is entering an exciting growth phase. This will create a wide array of opportunities, including private-market solutions extending to students, societies, and investors alike. The competition for students in this growth phase will always include the premier Western schools. But in the absence of major expansion, the largest benefits should accrue to the local institutions and the service providers that surround them in the private market.

Education Plays and Their Fundamental Dynamics

As we turn to the actual market for securities in the education sector, we should highlight a few different attributes. First and foremost, the market for stocks in the education services industry can command higher valuation multiples than the broader market. The reasons for this phenomenon vary, but one of the clear advantages that these business models possess relative to the broader economy is their countercyclical nature. When this aspect is combined with a growing market, investors take notice and become more comfortable holding the names, and occasionally even bidding up their valuations in the market. Despite this backdrop, this phenomenon is not bulletproof. Investors in the market still routinely sell stocks for shortsighted reasons, no matter the group, and this group of stocks is no different. As a matter of background, historically postsecondary education receives a boost in revenue and enrollment during recessionary periods. Many unemployed individuals seek to improve their skill set and marketability or simply wait out a weak job market by attending school. Investors in the stock market have come to recognize the defensive attributes to the business model and often reward these stocks with higher valuation multiples.

The other attributes that help support steady valuations in the stock market lie in the high earning power of these businesses. This attribute can be clearly seen in the conventional methods of measurement, including operating margins and returns on capital. We can look at Standard and Poor's 1500 Education Services Subgroup Index as an example. If we compare it to the S&P 500, the profitable nature of these education services companies versus the broader market is easily identifiable (see Table 10.4).

TABLE 10.4 Profitability Comparison Between Educational Services and the Broader Economy

	EBIT Margin	Return on Capital	3-Year Average Return on Capital
S&P 500	13.7%	11.4%	13.4%
S&P 1500 Education Services	16.7%	28.3%	17.8%

Source: Bloomberg

In light of these characteristics, investors should take an opportunistic approach to purchasing shares in the education services stocks. On occasion these stocks become depressed from their historical valuations due to broader market declines, or possibly even sector rotation by some investors who are seeking to shift capital into procyclical names as they attempt to time a turn in the economy. Whatever the reason, an opportunity can present itself when least expected. Because of these dynamics, education stocks are prime candidates for a purchasing technique utilized by Sir John Templeton. His idea was to create and maintain a wish list of stocks in his desk drawer that he turned to during periods of market corrections or turmoil. The benefit of this approach to purchasing education stocks—in particular, names from the emerging markets across Asia—is that they are backed by a long-term secular growth trend that should remain in place for many years. Up to this point we have highlighted the strong growth and relative underpenetration of the emerging economies into education. But we have not estimated how long this demand could persist. Figure 10.12 illustrates the backlog for demand in these emerging economies. We can see in data compiled by the UN that nearly 40% of the world's population between the ages of 5 and 25 lives in China and India. In other words, there will be heavy demand for these educational services for years to come.

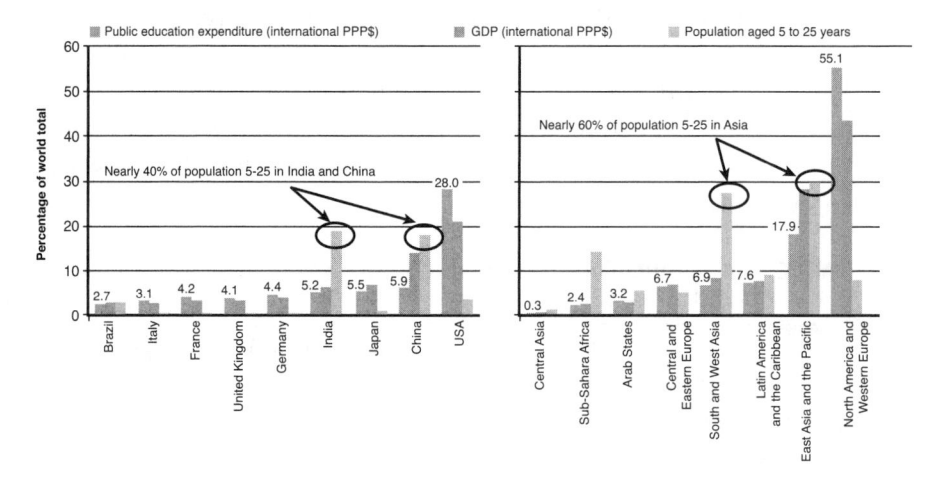

Figure 10.12 Global distribution of public expenditures on education, GDP, and population aged 5 to 25, by region and for selected countries, 2004

Reprinted with permission from UNESCO Institute for Statistics (UIS), Global Education Digest 2007

Identifying the scale of this fundamental growth backdrop is important because it gives investors confidence that, in the future, when the market and economy appear shaky, they can rely on the steady presence of a long-term secular growth trend in the for-profit education market that resists cyclical pressure. Fortunately, the stock market is considerably more volatile than this growth trend and should present opportunities over time. Additionally, because this area is poised for substantial growth over the coming years, we can expect more names to be added to the stock market over time. Table 10.5 lists companies that operate in the educational services space in the emerging markets, as well as other Asian markets.

TABLE 10.5 Emerging-Market and Asian Educational Services Companies

Bloomberg Ticker Code	Company Name	Country	Description
AEDU11 BZ	Anhanguera Educacional Participacoes SA	Brazil	A group of universities offering undergraduate and graduate studies in the state of Sao Paulo. It offers courses in business administration, law, engineering, psychology, physiotherapy, and other subjects.
ATAI	ATA, Inc./China	China	Provides computer-based testing services, along with career-oriented, test-based educational programs and test preparation solutions. Delivers tests from the China Banking Association and the China Securities Association.
DL	China Distance Education Holdings, Ltd.	China	Offers a range of online and test preparation courses and other related services and products. Courses are designed to help professionals and participants obtain and maintain skills, licenses, and certifications necessary to pursue careers in China in the areas of accounting, law, healthcare, engineering, and information technology, among others.

TABLE 10.5 Emerging-Market and Asian Educational Services Companies (continued)

Bloomberg Ticker Code	Company Name	Country	Description
EDU	New Oriental Education & Technology Group, Inc.	China	Offers educational services including foreign language training; test preparation courses for admissions and assessment tests in the U.S., the PRC, and Commonwealth countries; primary and secondary school education; development and distribution of educational content, software, and other technology; and online classes.
APTR IN	Aptech, Ltd.	India	Provides computer training and multimedia services. Owns and franchises IT training centers in India and abroad.
EDSL	Educomp Solutions, Ltd.	India	Sets up and runs computer education programs in schools. Also trains teachers, students, and parents; sets up Internet campuses for educational institutions; and markets educational CDs and toys.
RLS SP	Raffles Education Corp., Ltd.	Singapore	Provides training programs and courses in various areas of design and management. Education services include fashion design, visual communication, multimedia design, interior design, design management, fashion marketing, and business administration.
072870 KS	MegaStudy Co., Ltd.	South Korea	Offers online and offline educational programs to high school students. Provides college entrance test prep courses, e-learning, and college admission advisory services.
095720 KS	Woongjin Thinkbig Co., Ltd.	South Korea	Specializes in publishing tutoring books, as well as tutoring programs incorporated into after-school tutoring sessions held at the school.

Endnotes

[1] Sharon LaFranier. "China's College Entry Test Is an Obsession." *New York Times*, June 12, 2009.

[2] Mary Beth Marklein. "College Wealth Soaring." *USA Today*, January 24, 2008.

[3] John Hechinger. "College Endowments Plunge." *Wall Street Journal*, January 27, 2009.

[4] Matthew Phillips. "Cutbacks on Campus." Kaplan College Guide, August 12, 2009.

11

A Rare Opportunity

In 1992, Deng Xiaoping, the man who led China into its free-market reforms, made a rather arcane statement: "There is oil in the Middle East; there are rare earths in China." While only some observers might have understood the implications of this proclamation a few decades ago, chances are that nearly everyone will come to view Deng's words as prophecy in time.

To begin, a reasonable question may be, What is rare earth? Depending on your perspective, rare earth could refer to a rock band that had a few Top 40 hits for Motown in the early 1970s, or a set of elements clustered on the periodic table that you probably studied in high school chemistry. Not to take anything away from the band, but this chapter focuses on the rare earths from the science classroom. In practical terms, rare earths are actually nothing more than some ore materials that are mined from the ground. Rare earths, or rare earth metals as they are also called, are found in the third column of the periodic table. Typically, they are identified by their silvery to gray color, luster, and high electrical conductivity.

What makes them so relevant to the world we inhabit is that in spite of their "rare" name, they in fact are highly ubiquitous to the daily experience of most humans. Incidentally, rare earth applications comprise some of the basic raw materials of technology and have done so for decades. In a trivial sense, people may have marveled back in May 1953 at how scientists at RCA came up with the first color television. However, the answer is simple: a new application of the rare earth europium was used to form the red phosphors of the TV. Likewise, many people have seen video footage or photos of the early computers, which appeared to be the size of 18-wheelers, consuming an entire room, weighing many tons versus pounds, and containing thousands of vacuum tubes, flashing lights, and controls. Today, people have computers that are exponentially more powerful that sit discreetly on their desks, thanks in part to advances in rare earth applications such as neodymium, which drove the miniaturization of the magnetic disk drive. Far from even recognizing the critical role these metals play in their lives, people might be surprised to discover that without the rare earth europium creating the red phosphor in the cathode ray tube and the LCD display, there could be no color televisions or computer screens. In a similar vein, without the rare earth erbium, there could be no fiber-optic cables connecting the world in a dazzling web of efficient, high-speed communication. Most developed-market consumers take for granted their cell phones, TVs, and iPods, even as these devices become increasingly miniaturized. Miniaturization in consumer technology devices is often the result of a new rare earth application such as neodymium magnets in the iPod. The medical field uses rare earth applications in its MRIs and CT scans, and sophisticated defense departments use rare earth applications in their guided missiles, lasers, and smart bombs. With that said, it should be apparent that people come into contact with rare earth materials daily whether they realize it or not. Much of our modern economies and societies would be crippled without their applications. We have all heard someone proclaim that he does not know what he would do without his cell phone, or he could not live without his computer. We can see that a critical rare earth application lies behind many of the technological advances and devices that citizens of the twenty-first century now take for granted.

Demand for Global Technology Remains Strong

To be sure, we can expect demand for technology, and therefore its raw materials, to continue to grow at a steady pace. This will be particularly true as we look to emerging-market consumers as a source of future growth. Consider a simple proxy for technology demand, such as cell phone handsets. We can see that in large developing markets such as China and India, cell phone penetration rates remain well below developed-market standards and still have much room for future growth as their economies continue to advance. For example, cell phone penetration rates in China and India are approximately half those of the developed-market levels found in North America and Western Europe, as shown in Table 11.1.

TABLE 11.1   Selected Global Cell Phone Penetration Rates

	2005	2006	2007	2008	2009	2010	2011
India	6%	11%	17%	24%	31%	39%	44%
China	28%	32%	37%	43%	50%	56%	59%
Northern America	68%	76%	82%	86%	89%	91%	95%
Western Europe	85%	89%	95%	98%	97%	99%	99%

Source: IDC, ITU, Bank of America—Merrill Lynch

If we turn to other major consumer-driven technology categories such as LCD panels, we discover a similarly low base of penetration. Based on research from Morgan Stanley,[1] the rate of LCD panel penetration is currently about 10% in China, and the installed penetration base of other televisions is closer to 80%. This suggests that there will be much additional room for growth in this industry as consumers over time replace their CRT TVs with LCD TVs.

Irrespective of the compelling data that suggests continued technology demand growth in the emerging markets, these are just two simple proxies for future growth in consumer technology devices. In the cases we just discussed, we highlighted the demand for technology among emerging-market consumers who are still entering the modern economy through the process of globalization. Still though, even within the broader confines of technology across all profiles of economies, whether developed or developing, there is scope for continuous new demand thanks to the critical role of innovation in the field. So although the developed markets may possess cell phone penetration rates of around 100%, we would be remiss to think that product demand does not ebb and flow on the basis of innovation in these markets. One fine example comes from the emergence of the smartphone within the mobile device space, since these products are continuing to redefine the capabilities of handheld technology productivity. Technology producers continue to bring new value propositions to end users by offering them increased computing power, messaging capabilities, video and audio capabilities, and mobile Internet. As long as this happens, it is probable that even within a mature market such as the United States, demand can be created anew for rare earth applications on the basis of these devices. So in this sense, technology is a unique industry because of its constant upheaval and obsolescence. This reality poses challenges and risks to investors who are unable to detect or anticipate these technological advances. At the same time, the constant drive toward product innovation generates a steady demand for the rare earth materials that drive innovation or that remain essential to the device's construction. So in other words, no matter what device comes into the fore of industry demand, there will likely be a continued new source of demand for rare earths, since these materials are often essential to the device. In the case of the smartphone, Figure 11.1 shows that, based on a collection of industry sources, this product is projected to represent 24% of global handset volume, or more than twice its 2007 level. From the perspective of a rare earth supplier or fabricator, even demand in the mature markets will continue to grow thanks to the role of innovation alone.

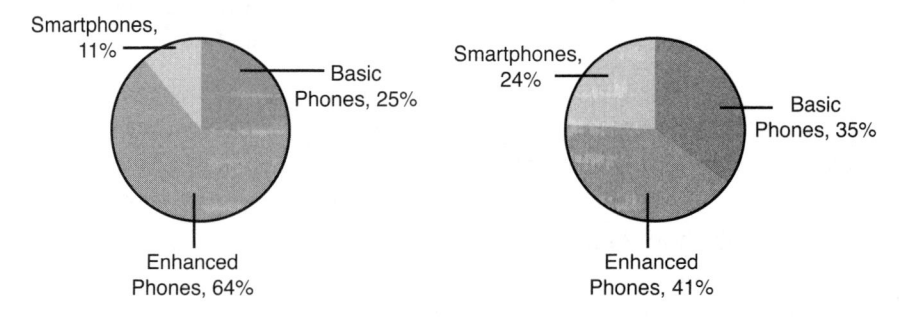

Figure 11.1 Global handset volume mix in 2007 and 2015, estimated

Source: Gartner, CSFB

Based on our discussion of demand drivers, we can now appreciate that technology demand can occur from two principal backdrops: increased access from new users, and upgrades from existing users as new technologies unfold in the market. Thus far, we have discussed rare earths and their end products only from the standpoint of consumer handheld devices and TVs, which is, incidentally, a narrow focus. This does the materials a disservice, because they are critical components of yet another developed-market demand driver that has taken on greater social significance. With that said, these raw materials are also significant because of growing demand from a trend that is under way in the developed markets relating to energy conservation, eco-friendly practices, and, generally speaking, all the manifestations of environmentalism in the form of technology application.

It's Not Easy Being Green

As you will recall from our earlier discussion of the growing scope of government regulation and its general intrusion into the private sector, one of the major socioeconomic objectives propelling this activity is the advancement of a green economy. One of the largest conduits for this industrial policy that has been pushed by the Obama administration is the U.S. government's 60% ownership of General Motors. GM recently announced its plans to, in the words of its North American president, "become the greenest car company in the world." As it turns out, a good bit of rare earth material is required to manufacture many green energy technologies, including hybrid automobiles and wind turbines. For example, the electric motor of the most popular hybrid vehicle, the Toyota Prius, requires between 2 and 4 pounds of the rare earth metals neodymium and dysprosium. Its battery uses 20 to 30 pounds of the rare earth lanthanum. The same will likely apply to the much-ballyhooed Chevy Volt when it hits the streets with its reported 230-miles-per-gallon fuel economy, because it too will require a considerable amount of rare earth material. Table 11.2 shows how prevalent rare earths are in the construction of the Prius, along with its broad assortment of applications.

TABLE 11.2 The Toyota Prius and Its Many Applications of Rare Earths

Rare Earth	Application
Cerium	Glass and mirrors polishing powder, UV cut glass, diesel fuel additive, hybrid NIMH battery, catalytic converter, LCD screen
Europium	LCD screen
Lanthanum	Diesel fuel additive, hybrid NIMH battery, catalytic converter
Neodymium	Hybrid electric motor and generator, magnets for more than 25 motors throughout the vehicle

TABLE 11.2 The Toyota Prius and Its Many Applications of Rare Earths

Rare Earth	Application
Praseodymium	Hybrid electric motor and generator
Terbium	Hybrid electric motor and generator
Yttrium	LCD screen
Zirconium	Catalytic converter

Source: Arafura Resources, IMCOA

Just as important as the Prius's overall consumption of rare earth is the growing consumption of the Prius by drivers around the world. Figure 11.2 shows the Prius's growing popularity; its U.S. sales grew 52% from 2000 to 2008. As we just said, the green movement has become a significant secular trend in the United States and other high-income nations, and many consumers participate by purchasing goods that contribute to the movement or at least announce their support for a green lifestyle.

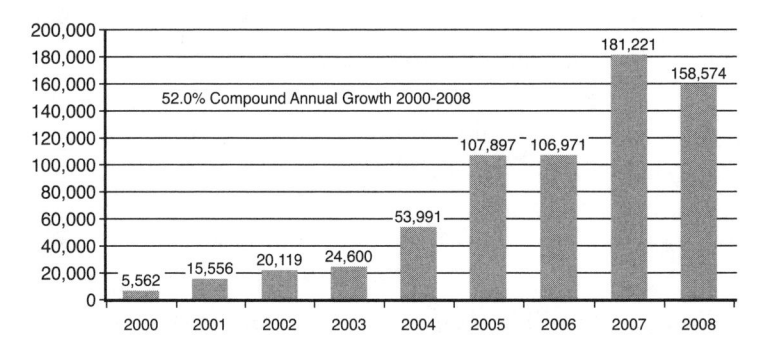

Figure 11.2 U.S. sales of the Toyota Prius (unit volume)

Source: U.S. Department of Energy

Because of the popularity of the Prius, and the copycat nature of the auto industry, nearly all the manufacturers are following suit with their own hybrid vehicles. This spells even further future demand for rare earth materials. Based on projections by Goldman Sachs[2] (and shared by others), the market for hybrid vehicles is expected to reach ten million units by the year 2020 (see Figure 11.3). This represents a compound annual growth of 27%. Although this growth may seem robust, industry forecasters are largely taking their cue from the auto manufacturers themselves, because they are making capital investments that could support this level of volume in 2020. Based on Toyota's success in the market, they plan to produce over one million hybrids per year after 2010. The underlying logic of reaching ten million hybrid vehicles in 2020 is that hybrids will compose 10% of global auto sales at that point. Viewed in this light, the projection does not appear unreasonable. If this does not come to fruition, it will not be from a lack of trying on the part of developed-market governments through regulation and developed-market consumers further embracing green lifestyles. In May 2009, President Obama announced that the preexisting Corporate Average Fuel Economy (CAFE) standards that were in place for 2020 would be pulled forward to 2016. This means that fuel efficiency standards will need to improve by 40%, to 35 miles per gallon from the current 25 miles per gallon. Given that this standard is too onerous for conventional engines, these new regulations should push manufacturers to sell a higher percentage of hybrid vehicles. In fact, even meeting the previous CAFE standards was too hard and led to lighter, less-safe cars rather than the desired innovations in fuel efficiency. Unfortunately, several studies have demonstrated that the first CAFE standards increased annual traffic fatalities by 2,000 people per year. In any event, in keeping with the manufacture of additional hybrid vehicles, we can anticipate an accompanying relative surge in demand for rare earth materials.

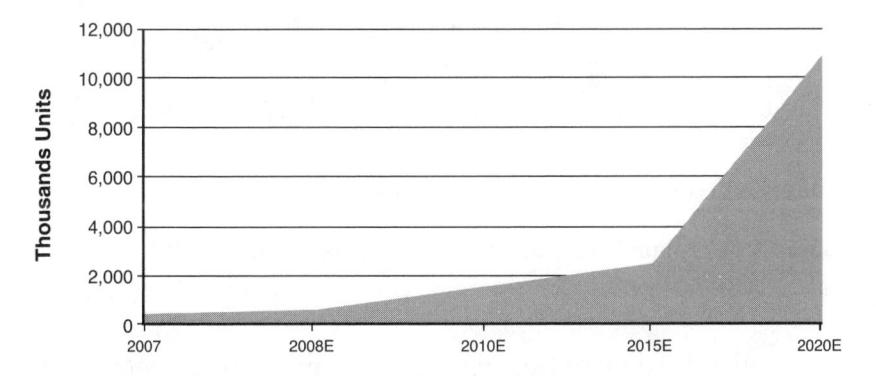

Figure 11.3   Hybrid vehicle market forecast through 2020

Source: Goldman Sachs

Meanwhile, the Prius and other hybrid vehicles are not the only green technologies starving for rare earth applications. A utility-scale wind turbine reportedly uses over 700 pounds of neodymium. In line with its green makeover for the economy, the U.S. government is also pushing hard and fast toward a substantial build-out of wind turbine-generated energy for electricity (see Figure 11.4). The U.S. Department of Energy published a report titled "20% Wind Energy by 2030" that details this ambition. Naturally, it parades a host of economic benefits, ranging from the number of newly created green jobs to new tax revenues on the properties occupied by the turbines. Although they are well and good, these plans will help push rare earth demand into overdrive, especially when combined with the natural growth in the technology devices and hybrid vehicles mentioned earlier. According to an estimate by rare earth industry consultant Jack Lifton, an efficient wind turbine requires one ton of neodymium per megawatt of generating capacity. This implies that the government's wind turbine construction plans alone would soak up approximately 60% of the annual production of neodymium based on the current level of production. The program will hit its stride in 2017 to 2018. Although this is unlikely to happen, for a number of reasons, it just provides another view of how hungry the world is for rare earths.

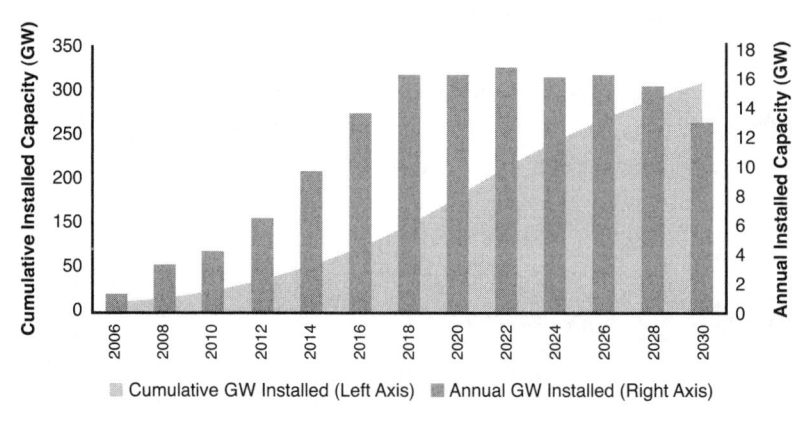

Figure 11.4 Annual and cumulative wind installations by 2030

Source: Department of Energy

Another bright idea from the regulators was to phase out the use of incandescent light bulbs in the United States by 2012. Based on regulations set forth in the Energy Independence and Security Act of

2007, the good old trusty light bulbs invented by Edison will no longer be available. Instead, consumers must turn to the more efficient (and expensive) compact fluorescent light (CFL), along with its neurotoxic levels of mercury and its necessary rare earth materials of yttrium/europium and lanthanum/cerium/terbium. The good news is that this too will help propel demand for rare earths, because tungsten bulbs will also be phased out in Europe, Australia, and some developing countries in Asia. The bad news is that consumers might also become irritated by having to double-bag burned-out CFL bulbs in Ziploc bags before putting them in the trash, or having to take them to a recycling center. Perhaps Kermit the Frog had it right when he said, "It's not easy being green."

There Is Oil in the Middle East; There Are Rare Earths in China

So far, we have discussed the demand for technology and the easily discernible accelerating demand for green technologies, ranging from hybrid vehicles, to wind turbines, to fluorescent bulbs. The world has a substantial appetite for the rare earth materials that are absolutely essential to the production of these products. The acknowledgment of this surging demand prompts the question, Who supplies rare earth?

The answer returns us to our opening mention of Deng Xiaoping, and a somewhat unsettling reality for technology companies around the world: One country ostensibly controls the entire world's current supply of rare earth—China.

For much of the first decade of the twenty-first century, China was often noted for its relative paucity of vital commodities needed for the construction of its growing economy, including copper, cement, and forest products. These supply-and-demand relationships have been real, but as it turns out, the country controls the supply of commodities that is the bedrock for all current and future innovation in technology. As obscure as his statement was in 1992, Deng had it right—China has rare earth. In fact, by most recent estimates, the country controls from 95% to 97% of the world's current supply of rare earth raw materials. iPods, cell phones, LCD TVs, hybrid vehicles, wind turbines, computers, and, yes, even fluorescent light bulbs are drawing on the production of rare earth materials that are supplied almost entirely by this one country. Concern is growing over this supply-and-demand dynamic, because some observers are worried that China will hold the world hostage. This outcome is very unlikely, barring any unprompted and totally ill-advised trade war coming from elsewhere. China's goal is to find the best way to monetize its asset. If China were to pursue this course of action, and prices rose too high, there would be a supply response in time from other countries such as Australia, Canada, Brazil, and the United States. All these countries possess these assets in some way, shape, or form, but in lower concentrations and at higher costs of production. Actually, rare earth materials are found all over the globe in the crust of the Earth. Conversely, finding a heavy concentration of these materials in one place, and extracting them in an economical way, is a totally different story. For this reason, China sits on the world's most abundant localized supply of rare earth. In a fit of irony, it is also an inconvenient truth that the key ingredients of all these important green technologies are extracted through a highly ungreen and polluting process. Most often, the crude form of the process has involved applying acid directly to the ore source in the ground that in turn leaches the ore from the other soil materials but leaves the acid behind. For that reason, the United States' own source of rare earth raw materials in Mountain Pass, Calif., which saw its production heyday during the initial boom in color TVs, was mothballed years ago. Not surprisingly, China—as always, stereotyped by its notoriety for exploiting natural resources for profit (just like the United States 100 years earlier)—was left as one of the few producers. Other governments killed the industry with regulation for its potentially contaminative processes. In the past few years, though, a consortium of private equity investors have backed a firm named Molycorp to begin production at Mountain Pass. Numerous other announcements in the past few years have come from mining companies in Canada and Australia. However, optimistically speaking, it will take years for these projects to come online, and then a few more years to reach full production, while technology demand continues to pace ahead. The announced projects to date represent only a fraction of the output from China, which still holds about 80% of the market. For that matter, these are optimistic scenarios for production responses from outside China. Mining rare earths is far from simple, and refining them into something useable is a whole other ball of wax. One good example comes from Lynas Corp. of Australia, which is working on rare earth extraction from the Mount Weld project in that country. After decades of commercial interest, the project has yet to produce the materials. The capital it needs to subsist has been choked off—at least intermittently thanks to the financial crisis. Here again, we find strong evidence of another headwind facing the production of rare earth from locations outside China. Ever since the financial crisis, capital has become much scarcer. More importantly, capital-seeking risky ventures such as getting in on the ground floor of a start-up mining project are becoming scarce, notwithstanding the attractiveness of the opportunity, thanks to good old-fashioned risk aversion. Taking these factors into consideration, it is reasonable to conclude that the supply response from outside China will be years in the making. With all that said, let's take a closer look at the supply-and-demand relationship for rare earth materials as it is currently understood. Figure 11.5 shows four relationships using data from the Industrial Minerals Company of Australia. To begin, we have rare-earth supply from China, rest of world (ROW) supply, global demand for rare earth on the top line, and finally Chinese demand on the bottom line. This figure points out two significant facts. The first is that the rate of change in global demand has been outpacing the rate of change in supply from China. The second is that the rate of change in Chinese demand has also been outpacing the growth in supply from China.

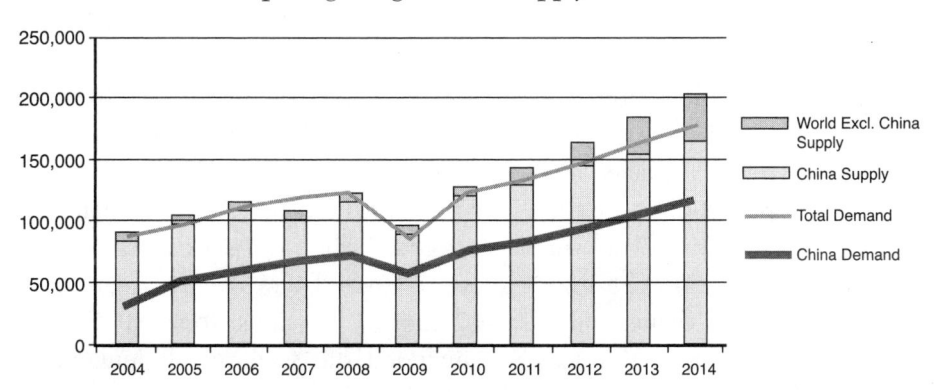

Figure 11.5 Rare-earth market supply and demand, both recent and projected

Source: Dudley Kingsnorth, IMCOA

These relationships, insofar as they persist, have important implications for the price of rare earth materials in the coming years. Global demand for rare earth materials has consistently ranged in the high single digits to low double digits since the early 2000s. Despite the approximate matching of Chinese supply to worldwide demand, with intermittent deficits and surpluses thus far, the industry will need to raise production levels in light of the increasing demand owed to the secular trend of consumption derived from green technology. As we look at expected demand levels over the next five years, meeting the world's production requirement will increasingly fall on producers from outside China. To bring these specific relationships into better focus, let us take a closer look at the expected growth dynamics in the coming years. In particular, the fastest demand growth is occurring in the metal alloys and magnets. Here consumption is expected to continue growing over the next several years in the range of 10% to 20% per year, depending on the specific product. So where does this leave potential supply and demand in the coming years? Based on what is known and available to outsiders, China's recent annual production of rare earth has been approximately 115,000 metric tons, and total global supply was 124,000 metric tons in 2008. Therefore, outside sources need to start bringing new supply onto the market to meet projected demand during the next several years or risk supply deficits. There are many potential, but unproven, sources, including a host of sites such as Mountain Pass, Calif.; Mount Weld, Australia; Dubbo, Australia; Nolans, Australia; Hoidas Lake, Canada; and India. In order for these projects and other outside sources to close the possible deficit that may appear in the coming years absent their supply, production will need to almost double from 2008 levels. This feat would meet the projected deficit and keep the market roughly balanced. Whether producers outside China can raise world production more than twofold over the coming years remains to be seen. Historically, miners often struggle bringing capacity on line as soon and as easily as expected. Even if they can, the market will still only balance out based on these projections from IMCOA. Finally, this discussion has not included the scenario of demand growth above the mid-single digit growth projections offered in the data which, based on historical levels, is closer to 8% per year in the several years leading up to 2008. If the market for rare earths entered a supply deficit in the coming years, this would not be without precedent. During 2007, as evidenced in Figure 11.5, global demand far outstripped all the combined supply sources. As the market tightened in the procession to this event, prices in key rare earths such as neodymium skyrocketed, as shown in Figure 11.6. Technology producers had to continue buying these materials either way to continue selling their product.

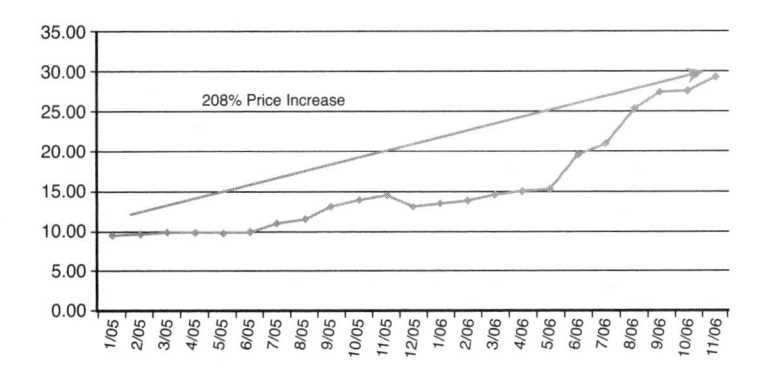

Figure 11.6 Neodymium prices in USD/KG

Source: Feller Magnets

The future always remains unknown. However, the supply-and-demand relationships we have discussed create a bullish scenario for rare earth prices, as well as for producers lying in the upstream to midstream portions of the value chain that can pass along price increases. Moreover, in accompaniment with the rising demand dynamic, China is progressing in ways that will limit the future amount of rare earth available on the world market for foreign technology companies. The United States eventually recoiled at the environmental consequences of the commercial production of rare earth. And now China is clamping down on the weaker operators in the industry and driving out the most polluting producers in an effort to better care for its environment. Indeed, the sign of a prospering country is its increasing attention to environmental matters at the expense of unchecked commercial interests. Also, as China continues to develop its economy, it is increasingly moving its own technology industry up the value chain and into higher, more sophisticated technology products. The easiest detectable by-products of this shift, and a direct manifestation of these developments, are China's export and production quotas that have continuously restricted the availability of rare earths for export to entities outside China. This paradigm has been misconstrued by outside observers as an aggressive move to limit availability. On the other hand, it is more likely that the quotas simply underscore the changing attitudes of a progressing nation that wants to develop a key natural resource in the most economic and efficient way possible. In the coming years, China will continue to consume more of these goods internally due to its own development, which may lead to a few side effects. First, this will prompt foreign companies to move their own production to China to gain secure access to rare earths. Second, it should help advance the technology industry within China, because the country has relatively unfettered, low-cost access to these critical raw materials. In both respects, this helps China monetize the natural resource in a more constructive manner. In the first case, when foreign manufacturers bring their operations into China, this will create much-needed employment in higher-wage, value-added segments. In the second case it will provide Chinese technology firms with a competitive advantage in the sourcing of raw materials. Both cases create an enterprise-based solution to China's constant need to gainfully employ its citizens, particularly in the absence of the long-ago discarded "iron bowl" of social safety nets. Finally, since these raw materials are at the epicenter of technology innovation, in the years and decades to come China can eventually position itself at the headwaters of innovation in technology. This represents a significant opportunity for progress in China's economy and standard of living. The bottom line is that in the twenty-first century, China has a deep competitive advantage in the race toward advanced technology. Careful observers have seen some evidence of the competitive advantage the Chinese possess thanks to their cheap access to rare earths and their relentless drive to compete and innovate. For instance, a battery producer called BYD (Build Your Dreams) used its expertise to build a sedan called the E6 that reportedly gets 249 miles per charge. The Chevy Volt reportedly travels only 40 miles on one charge. This says as much as anything about what China really wants to accomplish through its control of rare earths—creating products that can compete and win in the global marketplace.

In sum, the rare-earth industry presents a growing opportunity for investors to participate in the rapid growth of technology. For starters, investors can sidestep the most glaring pitfall and risk of technology investment—the constant threat of obsolescence. No investor wants to load up on shares of the manufacturer of the Betamax VCR when the VHS VCR will be introduced a year later. Likewise, the Walkman gave way to the CD player, which gave way to the iPod. Technology is about innovation, and innovation leads to upheaval. If an investor knows, however, that many key technologies spring from the application of a few raw materials, that investor can focus on these upstream products; therefore, risks are tied less to obsolescence as he or she seeks to capitalize on the constant demand in this industry. Finally, it is difficult to overlook the potential role the Chinese will play in technology in the years to come, blessed with these competitive advantages.

Endnotes

[1] Frank A.Y. Wang. "Taiwan TFT LCD." Morgan Stanley Research Asia Pacific, January 16, 2009.

[2] Koto Yuzawa. "We expect the coming hybrid era to bring earnings growth." Goldman Sachs, May 28, 2008.

INDEX

A

adjustable-rate mortgages (ARMs), 29-31, 53-54
agribusiness, 161-163
  Brazil, 152-160
agriculture
  arable land
    Brazil, 152
    China, 147-148
  farm equipment market, 162
  production and consumption, China, 147-151
  water, China, 148-151
AIG, 63-67, 75
AIGFP (AIG Financial Products), 64
Alt-A mortgages, 29
alternative energy, 191-192, 195
  carbon sequestration, 197
  coal, 196
  GTL (gas to liquid), 198
  natural gas, 198
  syngas, 194
American Recovery and Reinvestment Act of 2009, 76
Americas, water, 148
animal spirits, 84
aquaculture, 210-215
arable land
  Brazil, 152
  China, 147-148

Argentina, tractors, 162
ARMs (adjustable-rate mortgages), 29-31, 53-54
Asia
  educational services companies, 237-238
  fish consumption, 207
  oil demand, 166
Asian tiger model, 119
asset-backed securities, 22
automobiles
  in China and India, 171
  fuel efficiency standards, 247
  hybrids, 246
average gasoline price survey, 178

B

bailouts, people's confidence in, 75
Bank of America, 98
  Lehman Brothers, 63
  Merrill Lynch, 65
banks, U.S. government and, 97
Barclays, 63
bargain hunters, 2
barrel of oil equivalent (BOE), 179
bear markets, 77
Bear Stearns, 36-39
  Enhanced Fund, 36-39
  fall of, 58-60
  High Grade Structured Credit Fund, 36-39

beef
  Brazil, 154
  China's consumption of, 143-146
Bernanke, Ben, 72, 83
bitumen, 193
Blankfein, Lloyd, 45
BOE (barrel of oil equivalent), debt, 179
Brands, China, 134
Brazil, 111-113
  agribusiness, 152-160
  arable land, 152
  corn, 157
  feed grain, 159
  fertilizer application, 160
  grains, 156
  International Monetary Fund (IMF), 112
  poultry exports, 153
  tractors, 162
breaking the buck, 66
Bretton Woods system, 182
budgets of regulatory agencies, 95
BYD (Build Your Dreams), 254

C

CAFE (Corporate Average Fuel Economy), 247
Canada, oil sands, 192-193
cap-and-trade policies, alternative energy, 197
capitalism, 102
  China and, 119
carbon sequestration, 196-197
cars in China and India, 171
Case-Shiller home price index, 49
Cayne, James, 58
CDOs (collateralized debt obligations), 27, 36, 48, 57
CDS (credit default swap), 64
cell phones
  China, 136
  penetration rates, 242
CFL (compact fluorescent light), 248

changing landscape, 114
character, credit, 19
Chevy Volt, 245, 254
Chile, aquaculture, 213-215
China, 119
  agriculture, production and consumption, 147-151
  arable land, 147-148
  automobiles, 171
  beef and poultry consumption, 143-146
  brands, 134
  capitalism, 119
  cell phones, 136
  cities, growth of, 131
  commodities, 126
  construction, 126
  consumerism, 128-134
  domestic economy, 128-134
  earthquakes, 120
  education, 219-220
    English language training, 225
    Gaokao test, 226
    higher education, 227-229
    online courses, 223-224
    spending on, 220-223
    tutoring, 225
  entrepreneurialism, 105-109
  financial crisis of 2008 and 2009, 117
  fish consumption, 206
  floods, 120
  GDP since 1980, 142
  generational divides, 129-131
  growth, 103
  innovation, 108
  insurance industry, 129
  Internet, 130, 223
  natural resources, 122-123
  online shopping, 136
  products, popular, 135-139
  professional testing, 228
  rare earths, 249-255
  savings, 119-122
  second-tier cities, 131

taste preferences, 132-134
technology, 136
third-tier cities, 131
Treasury holdings, 91
urbanization, 126-128
water, 148-151
women in the workforce, 145
China's sorrow, 120
Cioffi, Ralph, 37
cities in China, growth of, 131
Citigroup, 98
coal, 196
coal-to-liquids market, 197
collateralized debt obligations (CDOs), 27
college endowments, Western institutions, 230-231
commercial paper, 74
Commercial Paper Funding Facility (CPFF), 74
commodities
 China, 126
 future prices, 165
 oil. *See* oil
common owned versus privately owned, 201-202
Community Reinvestment Act of 1977, 21
compact fluorescent light (CFL), 248
compensation expenses, 45
competition, 101-105. *See also* entrepreneurialism, 105-109
confidence, velocity, 85
Confucian doctrine, 219
Confucian principle, 117
construction, China, 126
consumer credit, 24
Consumer Price Index (CPI), 12
consumer spending, GDP 2003, 10
consumerism, China, 128-134
consumers, 88
corn, Brazil, 157
corn consumption, 158

Corporate Average Fuel Economy (CAFE), 247
Countrywide Financial, 55
CPFF (Commercial Paper Funding Facility), 74
CPI (Consumer Price Index), 12, 182
Cramer, Jim, 62
CRB commodity index, 123
credit, 19-21, 24-25
 consumer credit, 24
 home equity line of credit, 14
 stop of, 67
credit bubble, 46-50
credit default swap (CDS), 64
credit rating agencies, 41
currency, debasement of, 82

D

debasement of currency, 82
debt. *See also* household debt, 8, 17, 49, 68
 per BOE (barrel of oil equivalent), 179
 U.S. government, 90-92
  financing, 86
debtor nations, 114
defaults, subprime mortgages, 55-57
deflation, 72
 quantitative easing, 80
deleveraging, 67
delinquency rates, 28
demand
 overexploitation, oceans, 206-209
 for rare earths, 252-255
demand for technology, 242-244
developing countries, fish consumption, 207
diadromous fish, 211
Dimon, James, 59
domestic economy, China 128-134

E

earthquakes, China, 120
economic recovery, built on borrowed money (2003), 8-13
economy, world economy, 67
education, 217
    China, 219-220
        English language training, 225
        Gaokao test, 226
        higher education, 227-229
        tutoring, 225
    emerging markets, 218-219
        household spending on, 220-223
    higher education, financial crisis portends continued growth in emerging, 230-234
    online courses, 223-224
    students, financial issues, 233
    technology and, 223-224
education services industry, stocks, 234-236
educational services companies, emerging markets and Asia, 237-238
Emergency Economic Stabilization Act, 73
emerging markets, 217
    education, spending on, 220-223
    educational services companies, 237-238
    financial crisis protends continued growth, 230-234
    higher education, 218-219
Emmanuel, Rahm, 76
endowments, Western institutions, 230-231
Energy Independence and Security Act of 2007, 157
English language training, China, 225
Enhanced Fund, 36-39
entrepreneurialism, 105-109
equation of exchange, 85
equity risk premium, 85
erbium, 242
ethanol consumption, 157
europium, 241
exploitation, oceans, 204-205
exploration and production (E&P), oil, 172-174, 178

F

Fannie Mae, 21
    subprime mortgages, 61
farm equipment, 162
farmers, U.S., 163
fat tailed, 64
FDIC (Federal Deposit Insurance Corporation), 45
Federal Housing Enterprises Financial Safety and Soundness Act of 1992, 21
Federal Register, 93-94
Federal Reserve
    chairman of, 83
    quantitative easing, 89
    timing markets, 13
feed grain, Brazil, 159
feed grain multiplier, 155
fertilizer application, Brazil, 160
"Financial Chaos," 50-52
financial crisis, continued growth in emerging market education services, 230-234
financial crisis of 2008 and 2009, China, 117
financing debt, U.S. government, 86
First Pacific Advisors, 41
Fischer, Franz, 194
Fischer-Tropsch process, 195
fish consumption, 206
    Asia, 207
    China, 206
    developing countries, 207
    U.S., 208

fisheries, 203-205
    aquaculture, 210-215
    salmon, 212
fishers, 209
Fitch, 41
flipping homes, 18-19
floods, China, 120
Florida State University, 232
foreclosure crisis (2008), 60
Frank, Barney, 98
Freddie Mac, 21, 61
Free to Choose, 95
Friedman, Milton, 81, 85, 95
fuel efficiency standards,
    automobiles, 247
Fuld, Richard, 45, 62

G

Gaokao test, 226
Garn–St. Germain Depository
    Institution Act, 47
gas to liquids (GTL), 198
gasoline, average price survey, 178
GDP (Gross Domestic Product)
    compared to protein
        consumption, 144
    growth (2003), 8
    per head since 1980, China and
        India, 142
Geithner, Timothy, 59, 63
General Motors (GM), 245
    GMAC, 48, 66
    Hummers, 16-17
    U.S. government's rescue of, 97
generational divides, China, 129-131
Getty, Paul, 165
Global Competitiveness Index,
    103-111
global economies, changing
    landscape of, 114
Global Purchasing Priorities
    Survey, 221
GM. *See* General Motors

GMAC, 48, 66
Goldilocks economy, 13-14
Goldman Sachs, 37
government regulation, 93-98
government take over of Fannie Mae
    and Freddie Mac, 61
grain prices, relationship to oil prices,
    161-162
grains, Brazil, 156
Great Britain, 92
Great Depression, household
    debt, 49
green economies, rare earths,
    245-249
Greenspan, Alan, 24
    inflation, 86
Greenwich Associates, 24
growth
    of cities in China, 131
    GDP 2003, 8
    government regulation, 94-98
    in monetary base of U.S., 80
    of prosperity China and India, 142
    regulation, 93
GTL (gas to liquid), 198-199

H

Hardin, Garrett, 201
hedge funds, 23-24
    Enhanced Fund, 36-39
    High Grade Structured Credit
        Fund, 36-39
**High Grade Structured Credit Fund,
    36-39**
higher education
    China, 219-220, 227-229
    emerging markets, 218-219
    financial crisis portends continued
        growth in emerging market,
        230-234
home equity line of credit, 14
home price index, 12

home prices, 11-12
   median house price versus median income, 39
home values, 11
homes, flipping, 18-19
household debt, 8, 17, 49
   divided by household net worth, 68
household net worth, divided by household debt, 68
household spending on education in emerging markets, 220-223
houses, vacant homes, 53
human behavior, 201-203
   oceans, 203-205
      overexploitation, 206-209
Hummer, 16-17
hybrid vehicles, 246
hydrocarbons, 192
hyperinflation, Brazil, 111

I

IFRS (International Financial Reporting Standard), 229
ILCs (Industrial Loan Companies), 47
in-situ process, oil sands, 193
India
   automobiles, 171
   education, spending on, 221
   GDP since 1980, 142
Industrial Loan Companies (ILCs), 47
IndyMac Corp., 60
Infectious Salmon Anemia (ISA), 214
Inflation, 81-86
   Brazil, 111
   risk, 3
initial public offering (IPO), 36
innovation, China, 108
insurance industry, China, 129
interest-only loans, 29
International Financial Reporting Standard (IFRS), 229

International Monetary Fund (IMF), Brazil, 112
Internet, China, 130
Internet usage, China, 223
IPO (initial public offering) 36
ISA (Infectious Salmon Anemia), 214

J

J.P. Morgan, 59
   Washington Mutual, 66
Jintao, President Hu, 127
June 25, 2003, 7

K

Keju, 219
Keynes, John Maynard, 84
Korea Development Bank, 62

L

LCD panels, 243
Lehman Brothers, 39-45, 63
   fall of, 62-64
lending money, criteria for, 19
Lewis, Ken, 65
liar loans, 30
LIBOR (London InterBank Offered Rate), 29
Lifton, Jack, 248
light bulbs, 248
Little Emperors, China, 129
Lloyd, William Forster, 201
loans, real estate loans as percentage of total loans, 46
London InterBank Offered Rate (LIBOR), 29
Lynas Corp. of Australia, 251

M

Mack, John, 45
Madoff, Bernie, 93
market distortions, oil, 179-184, 191
McMahon, Ed, 61

INDEX   263

McMansions, 16
Me Generation, China, 130
measures of volatility, 65
Merrill Lynch, 38, 65
Middle East, oil consumption, 167
miniaturization, rare earths, 242
Molycorp, 250
monetary base of U.S., growth of, 80
monetary expansion, 80-84
money, lending (criteria for), 19
money market funds, 66
Money Mischief, 85
money policy, oil, 183
Moody's, 41
Morgan, J. Pierpont, 19
mortgage brokers, 25, 28
mortgage-backed securities, 22
mortgages
    Alt-A, 29
    ARMs, 29-31, 53-54
    delinquency rates, 28
    subprime, 26-33
    U.S. chartered commercial banks'
        total mortgages, 45
Mount Weld project, 251
Mountain Pass, California, 250

N

The National Bureau of Economic
    Research, 76
nationally held oil companies versus
    privately held, 174, 178
natural disasters, China, 120-121
natural gas, 198
natural resources, China, 122-123
negative amortization loans, 30
neodymium, 242, 253
net worth of U.S. households, 15
New Zealand, quotas for fishers, 209
Norway, salmon fishing, 214

O

O'Neal, Stanley, 65
Obama, President Barack, 68
oceans
    human behavior, 203-205
    overexploitation, demand, 206-209
OECD (Organization for Economic
    Cooperation and Development), 17
oil, 17, 165
    breakeven costs measured in oil
        prices per barrel by source of
        supply, 199
    exploration and production,
        172-174, 178
    future prices, 165
    market distortions, 179-184, 191
    money policy, 183
    reserve growth, 184
    reserve replacement, 184
    supply and demand, 166-169
oil consumption, relation to
    prosperity, 170-172
oil prices, relationship to grain prices,
    161-162
oil sands, 194
    Canada, 192-193
online education, 223-224
online shopping, China, 136
Organization for Economic
    Cooperation and Development
    (OECD), 17
overexploitation
    fisheries, 204-205
    oceans, demand, 206-209

P

packaging home loans, 20
Pandit, Vikram, 98
Paulson, Henry, 59, 72
penetration rates
    cell phones, 242
    LCD panels, 243

petrocommodities, 161
Pickard, Lee, 43
Poole, William, 63
poultry, China's consumption of, 143-146
poultry exports, Brazil, 153
printing money, 80-82
privately held oil companies versus nationally held, 174, 178
privately owned versus common owned, 201-202
production, oil, 172-174, 178
productivity, U.S., 102
products, popular in China, 135-139
professional testing, China, 228
prosperity
    growth of, 142
    relationship to oil consumption, 170-172
protein consumption
    China 143-146
    compared to GDP, 144
public versus private resources, 201

Q

quantitative easing, 80, 89
quotas for fishers, 209

R

rare earths, 241-242
    China, 249-255
    demand for, 252-255
    green economies, 245-249
    neodymium, 253
real estate, flipping homes, 18-19
regulation, 93-98
regulators, SEC, 93
regulatory agencies, budgets, 95
reserve currency, 82
reserve growth, 184
reserve replacement, oil, 184

revenues, Lehman Brothers, 45
risk, inflation, 3
risk aversion, 85
Rodriguez, Robert, 41

S

salmon, 212-213
    Norway, 214
Sasol, 195, 198
Saturday Night Live, 117
savings, China, 119-122
savings rates, 8
Schumer, Charles, 98
Schwartz, Alan, 58
Schwarzenegger, Arnold, 16
SEC (Securities and Exchange Commission), 43
    Madoff, Bernie, 93
second-tier cities, China, 131
securities, 21
    asset-backed, 22
    mortgaged-backed, 22
securitization market, 20
shadow banking system, 74
Shell, 198
Shiller, Robert, 11
Singapore, 118
Singaporean model, 118
small business, regulation, 96
smartphones, 243
soybean oilseeds, 147
    Brazil, 154
spending on education in emerging markets, 220-223
    U.S. government, 86-89
spendulus package, 77
Standard and Poor's 1500 Education Services Subgroup Index, 235
stimulus package, 77
stock market valuations, 78
    fourth quarter 2008, 77
stocks, education services industry, 234-236

INDEX

students, financial issues, 233
subprime mortgages, 26-33
   defaults, 55-57
supply and demand, oil, 166-169
surveys, average gasoline price, 178
syngas, 194
synthetic fuel, 195

T

TALF (Term Asset-Backed Securities Loan Facility), 74
TaoBao, 136
TARP (Troubled Asset Relief Program), 73
taste preferences, China, 132-134
technology, 255
   China, 136
   demand for, 242-244
   education and, 223-224
Templeton, Sir John, 1-2, 11
   education stocks, 236
   "Financial Chaos," 50, 52
Term Asset-Backed Securities Loan Facility (TALF), 74
Thain, John, 65
third-tier cities, China, 131
thrift certificates, 47
Toyota, hybrids, 247
Toyota Prius, 245-246
tractors, 162
Treasuries, 89
Treasury bonds, 86
Treasury holdings, China, 91
Tropsch, Hans, 194
Troubled Asset Relief Program (TARP), 73
trust, break down in, 72
tutoring, China, 225

U

U.S.
   education, 218
      spending on, 221
   farmers, 163
   fish consumption, 208
   meat consumption, 143
   productivity, 102
   renewable fuels, 157
U.S. consumers, 88
U.S. dollar, 3
U.S. federal budget deficits, 87-89
U.S. government
   banks and, 97
   debt, 90-92
      financing, 86
   rescue of GM, 97
   spending, 86-89
urbanization, China, 126-128
utility-scale wind turbines, 247

V

vacant homes, 53
value investors, 2
velocity, confidence, 85
volatility index (VIX), 65

W

Wachovia, 66
Washington Mutual, 66
water, China, 148-151
wealth, 15
Wells Fargo, Wachovia, 67
Western big oil, 174
Western consumer goods, Chinese opinion of, 133-134
Western schools, financial crisis, 230
women in the workforce, China, 145
world economy, 67

X

Xiaoping, Deng, 103, 117-118, 241

Y-Z

Yale, loss of endowments, 232
Yangtze River, China, 120
Yellow River, China, 121
Yew, Lee Kuan, 118

FT Press
FINANCIAL TIMES

In an increasingly competitive world, it is quality of thinking that gives an edge—an idea that opens new doors, a technique that solves a problem, or an insight that simply helps make sense of it all.

We work with leading authors in the various arenas of business and finance to bring cutting-edge thinking and best-learning practices to a global market.

It is our goal to create world-class print publications and electronic products that give readers knowledge and understanding that can then be applied, whether studying or at work.

To find out more about our business products, you can visit us at www.ftpress.com.